THE NEW
ST. BERNARD

George & Maureen Gwilliam

RINGPRESS

Published by Ringpress Books Ltd,
PO Box 8, Lydney, Gloucestershire GL15 4YN

Designed by Rob Benson

First Published 2000
© 2000 RINGPRESS BOOKS

ISBN 1 86054 117 8

Printed and bound in Singapore
by Kyodo Printing Co

10 9 8 7 6 5 4 3 2 1

DEDICATION

Mrs Cecil Frances-Alexander writing in 1818 wrote these words:

'All thing bright and beautiful,
All creatures great and small,
All things wise and wonderful,
The Lord God made them all.'

This included children, as well as St. Bernards.

We would like to dedicate this book to our three wonderful children, whom we love dearly. The Coatham 'A' team, Andrew, Alison and Amanda, when teenagers, gave a lot of help with the supervision, care and management of our St. Bernards. This enabled us to attend Open and Championship Shows as exhibitors or officials pursuing this fascinating hobby.
Thank you and God Bless.

ACKNOWLEDGEMENTS

The St. Bernard world has altered vastly over the past few years – and will continue to do so if the UK Government does change its quarantine laws and introduce passports for pets, accompanied by appropriate vaccinations. Then more co-operation will take place between Britain and Europe. We shall be able to acknowledge merit where it exists, as, no doubt, some European Saints will qualify for Crufts in a few years time. It may also be possible for Saints from the UK to enter the famous WUSB Shows which are held in different countries.

We gratefully acknowledge the help and support given to us by the many St. Bernard enthusiasts throughout Britain, across Europe, in America and in the rest of the world, who have provided information and photographs for this book. These people are too numerous to mention individually.

However, there are some people we really do have to name. Andrew Brace and Eleanor Bothwell gave their permission for us to include information on Infertility Syndrome and some points on judging. Ann Robinson-Ruddock, our wonderful neighbour, has stoically taken on all the typing and provided technical expertise, as well as giving us encouragement to complete all the written work. Nick Cowie has given his continued help and support with some of the photographs.

We are most grateful to our daughter Alison and her husband Darren for sending so many e-mails around the world requesting information and following this through on our behalf.

Finally, we wish to thank Ringpress Books for inviting us to share our experience, knowledge and enthusiasm about the magnificent St. Bernard. If this book helps to promote the welfare of St. Bernards, and raises the awareness of potential breeders and judges, as well as pet owners, as to exactly what is entailed in nurturing and valuing St. Bernards, then the hard work has all been worthwhile.

CONTENTS

Acknowledgements   3

Chapter One: ORIGINS OF THE ST. BERNARD   6
Early development; Evolutionary influences; The Hospice of St. Bernard; The Hospice dogs; Saving the St. Bernard; Royal connections; The Hospice today.

Chapter Two: CHOOSING YOUR ST. BERNARD   13
Deciding on type; Male or female;Temperament; The dog's senses; Choosing a breeder; Pet or show dog? Price and terms; Long or short-haired?; Assessing your puppy; The potential show dog.

Chapter Three: CARING FOR YOUR ST. BERNARD PUPPY   22
Taking your puppy home; The first night; House-training; House rules; Lead training; Useful commands; Puppy parties; Puppy classes and adult classes; Exercise; Grooming (The smooth-coated St. Bernard; The rough-coated St. Bernard); Bathing;

Chapter Four: FEEDING AND HUSBANDRY   32
Protein; Fats; Carbohydrates; Minerals; Vitamins; Water; Digestible energy; Metabolisable energy; Determining growth; Feeding routine; Husbandry (The kennels; fencing; food preparation and storage; whelping area; hygiene; running a string of dogs).

Chapter Five: THE BREED STANDARD DISCUSSED   43

Chapter Six: BREEDING ST. BERNARDS   54
Appraising the bitch; Tracing pedigrees; A few words about genes (recessive, dominant, lethal and semi-lethal); The practicalities of breeding; Selecting the stud; The male organs; The brood bitch; Female anatomy; Oestrus; Metoestrus; Anoestrus; Types of breeding (outcrossing, line breeding, in-breeding); Timing the mating; The mating; Difficult matings; Stud fees; Artifical insemination; Sterility; (Infertility syndrome; Beta-haemolytic streptococcal (Lancefield type G and L) infection in the bitch and dog); Symptoms and diagnosis (abnormal seasons; sterility syndrome; absorption – abortion syndrome, fading puppy syndrome); Sources of infection; Treatment; Prevention.

Chapter Seven: WHELPING AND AFTERCARE   **70**
Feeding the pregnant bitch; Malnutrition; Worming; Signs of pregnancy; Preparation for the whelping; Pre-whelping behaviour; The whelping (parturition); Removing the puppies; Post-whelping; Dewclaws; A quick guide to normal whelping; Danger signs; Examining the puppies; Infectious diseases and puppies; Whelping complications; Fostering and hand-rearing; The foster mother; Bottle-feeding; Tube feeding.

Chapter Eight: WEANING AND SOCIALISING THE LITTER   **86**
Neonatal period; Transitional period; Coat type; Worming the litter; Weaning; The socialisation period; The importance of play; Dominant behaviour; Submissive behaviour; Group activities; The pack leader; Potential owners; Kennel Club registrations.

Chapter Nine: SHOWING YOUR ST. BERNARD   **96**
Basic show training; Teaching the stance; Emphasising the good points; Movement; Video help; How to show; Training for the showring; Disguising faults; Training and show leads; Grooming for the ring; The grooming table; Nails; Whiskers; Face, feet and tail; Bathing; Your first show; Show equipment; On the day; The triangle; The final assessment; The don'ts of showing.

Chapter Ten: JUDGING THE ST. BERNARD   **109**
The changing face of dog showing; Understanding judging list; Understanding judging; Correct mental attitudes; Stewarding; The temperament of a judge; Developing judging technique; Types of judging; Taking your first class; Judging puppies; Hands-on judging; Positive judging; Evaluating movement; Making your choice; The dogs' temperaments; Writing critiques.

Chapter Eleven: YOUR ST. BERNARD'S HEALTH   **121**
Vaccinations; Common ailments and first aid treatment; Specific disorders; Hereditary conditions and disorders; The ageing St. Bernard.

Chapter Twelve: KENNELS IN THE UK   **136**
Old influential kennels; Modern times; Scotland and Ireland.

Chapter Thirteen: THE ST. BERNARD IN AMERICA   **154**
The St. Bernard Club of America; Divergence in type; Breeders' Guidelines; Showing and exhibiting; St. Bernard Rescue; Kennels of note.

Chapter Fourteen: THE ST. BERNARD WORLDWIDE   **166**
Australia; New Zealand; The Saint in Europe; Switzerland; Spain; Scandinavia; The Netherlands; Hungary; Italy; Germany.

Bibliography   **176**

1 *ORIGINS OF THE ST. BERNARD*

How many other breeds of dogs can match the appeal of an eight-week-old St. Bernard puppy? This special quality has been captured by photographers, artists and enthusiasts on greeting cards, posters and a variety of saleable products. The St. Bernard has a wonderful, benevolent expression which is the trademark of this special breed. But behind this cute bundle of joy lies centuries of history and breeding.

EARLY DEVELOPMENT

The earliest identifiable ancestor of the dog has been found in human shelters built within a cave of La Gutte in Lazaret in the South of France some 125,000 years ago. The shelters had been decorated with the skulls of wolves.

There are differing scientific opinions as to when dogs were first domesticated, based upon our knowledge of the physiology and the behaviour of the wolf, as well as the habits of prehistoric man. Some believe dogs were domesticated from wolves in China, in the Near East, in Northern Europe or in North America, that the dog is polygenetic in origin, that the process of domestication took place in various locations around the world. Others feel that domestication was a unique event, that the dog spread from just one home.

What the archaeological records cannot demonstrate is exactly what prehistoric dogs actually looked like. From the physical remains it is difficult to differentiate between what was a wolf

The unique appeal of a St. Bernard puppy. Photo: Steph Holbrook.

and what was a dog. It is doubtful whether the early dogs bore any specific resemblance to any of the current breeds, particularly the St. Bernard.

It is suggested by palaeontologists that wolves and man had been hunting and living in close proximity with each other for thousands of years. Writer Michael Fox, in his book *The Dog – Its Domestication and Behaviour (1983)* suggests that the domestic dog, *Canis familiaris*, is a descendant from the wolf, *Canis lupus*.

The Molossus or Tibetan type of mastiff could have provided a foundation for the beginning of the early St. Bernard. Although stories suggest that the St. Bernard originates from the Hospice of St. Bernard in the mountains of the St. Bernard Pass, it was, in fact, hundreds of years after the Augustinian monk Bernard de Menthon had provided shelter for travellers some 8,000 feet (2,500 metres) up the mountain at this beautiful, sacred hospice, that dogs were used for rescue purposes from this religious base.

EVOLUTIONARY INFLUENCES

By selective breeding, man has been able to transform the wolf in a variety of ways. Systematic breeding, differing climates, geography, predators and parasites have all influenced the production of different breeds.

There seem to be four groups of domestic dog which, it is suggested, developed from around 6,000 BC. It is supposed that the St. Bernard evolved from the *Canis familiaris inostranzewi*. Other groups are the *Canis familiaris metris optimae*, *Canis familiaris intermedius* and *Canis familiaris leiner*. *Canis familiaris inostranzewi* has the same number of chromosomes as the wolf, seventy-eight, whereas jackals have seventy-four chromosomes and the red fox only thirty eight. Dogs were probably domesticated from a small breed of Wolf.

Authors in the period 200 BC – 200 AD addressed all large dogs under the name of Molossus. The Romans brought these mastiff-like Asiatic dogs along with their armies to herd or guard at the military posts and trading stations. It is suggested that these armies travelled over the Mons Jovis (St. Bernard Pass) into the Alpine valleys and the Northern forelands of the Alps. The pass was a paved mule-path over and around the mountains.

Primitive man was known to have lived around the Swiss lakes in settlements built into the margins of the lakes. It is likely that their dogs were much lighter in build than the ancient heavy Molossus from Tibet. The dogs from the Neolithic period were much finer in structure and were used for deer hunting, as they were agile dogs unlike the large-boned, square-headed type from Central Asia.

The civilisations of the Egyptians, the Greeks and the Romans used dogs as household pets, for hunting and as guard dogs. The Greeks and the Romans suggested that dogs were hunters without equal, faithful until death. There is a lot of evidence from Egyptian, Greek and Roman artefacts, such as drawings and sculptures, of the relationships between man and the dog.

When Pyrrhus, King of Epirus, temporarily

Ancestors of the Roman Molossus, from which the St. Bernard has descended.
Bas Relief from Nineveh, British Museum.

conquered Italy, large dogs from Olottia were taken to Rome. It is believed these dogs were used for guarding and herding tasks. There is written information about the dogs being used in the arenas for fighting purposes. This seems very barbaric now but it was part of the accepted culture at that time.

When the Romans conquered Britain, they brought giant Molossus with them. These breeds were crossed with some of the lighter-boned, herding dogs in Britain, which had originally descended from early Asian-type dogs.

The Romans marched into northern Europe along with their dogs, travelling over the difficult terrain of the mountains. The air was light, the Romans felt exhilarated and thankful to their gods, so they built a temple high up in the Alps to Jupiter. At this time, about 40 BC, the Roman invaders introduced the lighter type of Molossus to the Swiss valleys. This was much more like the Sennenhunde.

A second migration of Romans invaded Switzerland in the second century AD, bringing with them the heavier type of Molossus which remained primarily in the mountains, at pass stations, and in the valleys of Aosta and Valais. In time, these mastiff-type dogs reached Berne, Juin and the Bernese Oberland. These dogs were used not only as working dogs but also as guards.

Speculation suggests that there were several types of Molossus; one type was the Illyrian Molossus, which apparently had prick ears, another variety was the Babylonian Molossus, with pendant ears. Historian Professor Albert Heim suggests there were still some specimens of the lighter Molossus in the mountains of Asia around the 1860s.

It was in the seventeenth century that the monks from the Great St. Bernard Hospice started using the heavy Alpine Mastiff to assist in Alpine rescues. The monks probably obtained their original stock from the Valais or the Bernese Oberland. According to Dr. J.M. Paschoud, President of the Standards Commission of the SKG and FCI, the existence of such dogs has been documented in paintings and drawings dating back to 1695 and in official documents at the Hospice dated 1707.

In the early 1800s several chronicles were published in different languages about the large dogs being deployed as rescue dogs for travellers lost in the snow. Soldiers from Napoleon's army who crossed the Great Pass told of the many lives saved by these dogs in the face of the White Death, which is what they called the blizzards.

THE HOSPICE OF ST. BERNARD

It is thought the original Hospice was a structure of cell-like rooms founded by Bernard de Menthon in the 10th century. He was believed to be the son of a wealthy noble family with its residence at the Castle of Menthon, near to the lake of Annecy (Savoy). Bernard probably completed his education in Paris before teaching theology. In accordance with the culture of those times, his wealthy father had selected a bride for his son, who was summoned to return home to wed his betrothed. Contrary to his father's wishes, Bernard fled from Menthon to Aosta in Italy, where he sought solace in the Cathedral. Bernard continued in the theological profession, becoming a preacher and Archdeacon of the Cathedral after the death of Archdeacon Peter. The Cathedral was at the foot of the Pass of Mont Jovis.

The Mons Jovis Pass, at which the Hospice of St. Bernard is located, had inherited the name from a temple that the Roman Emperors had built on the summit of the pass and dedicated it to their god, Jupiter Penninus. At the time, the pass was a principal road connecting Switzerland and Italy. Although this route was used by commercial travellers, the merchants selling their goods, armies also used this route to their advantage. Pilgrims also used the pass to reach the tombs of the Apostles in Rome, where they paid homage to the early Christians.

Merchants and pilgrims preferred to travel during the longer daylight hours to avoid the creeks and to find the easier routes. However, they were unaware of the dangers awaiting them from robbers and heathen inhabitants further up the mountain towards the summit. Archdeacon Bernard made strenuous efforts to eliminate the dangers of robberies by trying to convert the heathens to Christianity.

Bernard was concerned that a lot of the travellers never reached their destination due to robbers, blizzards or intense cold. The pilgrims told Bernard some horrifying tales of agonising deaths. Bernard decided that with the help of some villagers, he

The Hospice of St. Bernard.   *Photo: Munro.*

ABOVE: *The St. Bernard Pass.*

RIGHT: *Statue of St. Bernard at the Hospice.*

would build an appropriate Cloister. The monastery was founded in 1049 AD. Bernard died in 1081, at the age of eighty-five, having been a devout Christian.

Initially the Hospice was dedicated to St. Nicholas, the Patron of children, sailors, captives and pawnbrokers. It was not until one hundred years later that the Hospice became known as The Great St. Bernard Hospice.

THE HOSPICE DOGS
In 1555 a fire at the Hospice destroyed all historical records. There was no written documentation about the existence of large dogs at the Hospice until 1707, when it seems that a dog had been buried there. Most historians accept that the dogs which were brought to the Hospice were descendants of the Roman Molossus.

The monks discovered that the dogs had a very good sense of direction, also a strong sense of smell. Apparently the dogs could locate a man buried in the snow six feet deep and could find their way through the treacherous snow-covered passes in blizzards and when dense fog occurred.

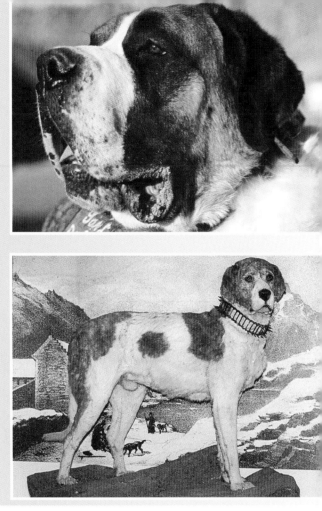

ABOVE: The monks developed a close relationship with the dogs they worked with.

TOP RIGHT: The brandy keg became a hallmark of the St. Bernard.

RIGHT: Barry was famed as a top rescue dog.

There is written documentation from 1774 regarding the work of the monks with their dogs. Travellers wrote that the monks went out daily with their trained dogs to search for people lost, injured or hypothermic from the cold. These strangers would very quickly slipped into unconsciousness. A big St. Bernard is quite capable of digging someone out of the snow unaided, providing the person is not buried too deeply. The dog would then guide everyone back to the monastery. The Saints had to use their minds and all their senses, as well as their strong muscular power, to undertake these remarkable rescues.

There is a romantic image of a big St. Bernard bounding around in fluffy snow, with a brandy barrel around its neck, quickly finding a stranded victim, who opens his eyes and smiles sweetly at the dog. Actually, St. Bernards never did carry brandy barrels, but they did have leather-type saddles which, it is believed, held medicine, and possibly blankets.

In 1787 another written account describes the dogs frightening off an invading band of robbers, thus saving the valuable gold and silver chalices and patens at the monastery. Some of these magnificent treasures can be seen at the Hospice today.

The most famous of the dogs at the Hospice was called Barry, believed to have been born in 1800. According to records, Barry had an instinct for danger and could sense when someone was in trouble. At the onset of snow or fog, Barry would insist on being let out. Once in the darkness, he would begin searching in dangerous or remote places. If he found someone lost in the snow he would start digging, trying to rescue them. If this became too hard, he went back to the Hospice for help and would then guide the monks to the unfortunate victim.

Barry died in 1812, having made his name as a faithful companion to the monks and a wonderful rescue dog for saving the lives of lost or injured travellers. Due to his fame, Barry was given over to

the taxidermist's art, but the first attempt showed this noble dog looking somewhat dejected. However, in 1923 he was restuffed and remounted in a much better stance and can still be seen at the Natural History Museum in Berne.

SAVING THE ST. BERNARD

It is interesting to note that the first dog entered in the Swiss Dog Stud Book in February 1884 was a St. Bernard named Leon. The Swiss St. Bernard Club was founded in Basle on March 15th 1884. In 1856, the Prior, E.R.W.J. Deleglise told Mr Friedrich Tschudi that the Hospice dogs were threatened with extinction. It seems two Newfoundlands were accepted at the Hospice from Stuttgart which were cross-bred with the smooth variety.

The breed gained the rough coat from the Newfoundland. The smooth-coated animal was the original dog used in Alpine rescues. Although it was believed that the long hair would protect the dogs against the cold climate, it soon became apparent that it was, in fact, a hindrance. After walking in the deep snow, a crust of snow and ice would completely cover the dogs and make it impossible for them to carry on as the snow embedded itself into the dense, rough hair, especially on the feathering.

Gradually, the monks found alternative homes for the rough-coated dogs and continued to keep and breed from the smooth-coated variety. There are still St. Bernards kept at the Hospice to this day and they are a great tourist attraction. In the winter period when the temperature reaches well below zero, the snow can become rock hard and the ice hangs down like stalactites, so the dogs go down to the valleys below to be cared for during the coldest weather, to return the following June.

ROYAL CONNECTIONS

Kings, robbers, noblemen, peasants, have all used the route over the mountains; some sought refreshment and shelter from the Hospice. Over two thousand people owe their lives to the dogs at this religious haven. Queen Victoria visited the Hospice, staying for one night. As an acknowledgement of her stay, she gave the monks a portrait of herself. Later Queen Victoria had a dog and bitch St. Bernard sent from Switzerland. The

The smooth coat (right) is the original coat of the St Bernard. It is thought that Newfoundlands featured in the development of the rough coat (left).

daughter of Queen Victoria, Empress Frederik of Germany, in 1832 also visited the region with her husband.

When Edward VII, son of Queen Victoria, was eighteen, he also visited the monastery. The monks gave him a St. Bernard puppy which sadly died on the journey back to England. No doubt other Royals have visited the Hospice over the years, but the luxury which they enjoy is in vast contrast to that of the brothers at this sacred place. Life for the monks is still hard but not as spartan as it used to be.

THE HOSPICE TODAY

The Great St. Bernard Pass becomes a popular tourist route from mid-June through to September. Cars, coaches and transit vans full of eager tourists flock to the Hospice to see the large dogs, the faithful St. Bernards. The Simplon Tunnel, built between 1898 and 1905, now connects Switzerland and Italy, so traffic worms its way around and up the pass to its destination.

There are now a great many souvenir and gift establishments on the way to the Hospice. Along with other tourist attractions comes a sense of commercialism, and the real purpose of the Hospice, where pilgrims visited for prayer and

retreat, could be lost. Many tourists have been moved by the wonderful sense of peace in the chapel. The sanctuary of this church was built by the Master Mason Jean-Antoine of Brissogne. It was consecrated in 1698 by Adrian VI of Riedmattel, Bishop of Sitten. The choir stalls were formed prior to the sanctuary and date from 1681.

To remind tourists of the purpose of the Hospice, a statue of Bernard de Menthon stands on the mountainside with one arm outstretched, the other is holding a staff. With the mountains in the background, it is an impressive sight on a clear day.

The Hospice has a hotel, a restaurant and other facilities for tourists. There is now a museum containing early accounts of the establishing of the Hospice, beautiful manuscripts and early Bibles, as well as treasured chalices and patens in gold and silver used during religious ceremonies. Naturally the museum has photographs and information about Barry, the rescues, and other facts about these famous dogs.

Smooth-coated Saints are still kept at the Hospice but they are behind partitions. These are made of glass so tourists can observe the Saints but not actually touch them. There are also kennels and runs outside for the Hospice St. Bernards. This rather shatters the image of large dogs bounding around in the snow to rescue stranded travellers. Life moves on – the only thing constant in life is change and this applies throughout the world.

With the use of modern technology, helicopters are quickly summoned, should any travellers get into difficulties. There is a lovely prayer for travellers which is kept at the Hospice which is dedicated to the work of Bernard de Menthon.

*"The Mountain Pilgrim's Prayer
O Lord Jesus You have journeyed so far
On behalf of Our Father,
To come and set up Your Home in our midst,
You, who were born by chance on a journey,
You have travelled on every path:
The path of Exile,
The path of Pilgrimage,
The path of Prophecy,
Draw me from my easy self-centred life
And make me a Pilgrim.*

*O Lord Jesus, You who so often followed the mountain path
In search of silence,
In search of the Father,
That You might teach Your Apostles
And Proclaim the Beatitudes,
That You might offer Yourself in Sacrifice,
Send out Your Disciples and return to the Father,
Lead me towards Heaven,
Make me a mountain Pilgrim.*

*Following the example of Saint Bernard,
I must heed Your Word,
I must let myself be moved by Your Love;
For ever tempted to a life of ease
You ask me to risk my life,
As did Abraham, in an act of Faith;
Continually tempted to settle down;
You ask me to travel onwards,
Full of hope towards You,
You, who have obtained the highest summit
In the eyes of the Father.
You, who were created by Love to Love,
Guide my steps, O Lord,
That I may climb amidst the peaks towards You
With all my brothers and sisters
With all creation in reverent adoration...
So be it."*

2 CHOOSING YOUR ST. BERNARD

You must consider whether you are the right sort of person to own a St. Bernard. This is a most important decision which you are about to reach, taking a new puppy into your home which, in a few months' time, will have grown into a large, majestic dog requiring tender, loving care, as well as discipline. Remember that a dog should be for life, not just for a short period.

A St. Bernard's lifespan can run into several years, requiring your commitment, love, care, management and responsibility. The rewards of sharing your life with a St. Bernard are numerous, if given the proper treatment, companionship and discipline. St. Bernards are very loyal and affectionate towards their owners; however, if not trained properly, they can be too zealous in their delight at being reunited with their owners on their return home if they have been out for a lengthy period of time.

Remember that an adult Saint, when standing, can be the height of a table. This height can enable easy access to work surfaces; stolen food can often taste better than that which a dog is supposed to have in his own large dish. Saints usually have good appetites and will eat virtually anything, especially an expensive pair of shoes if these are lying around unattended.

Food is a most important consideration. Generally a large St. Bernard will consume four to five pounds of meat and biscuit per day when adult. Therefore it is vital that you can afford to feed the dog. The amount of money for keeping a fully-grown St. Bernard for a year can vary according to whether you feed a complete food or purchase canned or fresh meat.

DECIDING ON TYPE

After having decided that you are an appropriate person to own a St. Bernard, then the next decision is whether you want to take on a puppy or an adult, a dog or a bitch. Most buyers prefer to take on a puppy as an option so that they can mould the dog's personality and develop the St. Bernard's character around their lifestyle.

There are other options. It can be rewarding taking on a rescue Saint who, often for no fault on the dog's part, has come into the Rescue.

The dog may have some habits which need discouraging; however, by praise and encouragement the dog often settles in extremely well, giving a lot of pleasure to their new owner or family.

Sometimes quality breeders may have an older puppy or young adult who they have been 'running on' as a potential show dog, that may have developed some minor blemish. If the dog is not going to be an outstanding winner, then the breeder would prefer the dog to go into a kind, loving home as a companion, thus leaving space to 'run on' another potential show dog.

Such defects do not stop the dog from being a happy, healthy and attractive companion, one whom the breeder will be pleased to place in a pet home.

MALE OR FEMALE?

Regarding the sex of the dog: there are advantages and disadvantages both ways. A male when mature is bigger, heavier and much stronger than a female. Male St. Bernards, when older, can be affected by their hormones, which in turn has an influence upon their behaviour. Most hormonal activity in the body is controlled by the brain. The brain receives sensory information from the senses. Most of our pet dogs lead relatively quiet lives; nevertheless, the fight or flight survival mechanisms, inherited from the wolf, still exist. Dogs need testosterone in order to develop normal male behaviour patterns; they also need to learn how to be males. For example, an intact male dog (one who has two testicles) that has never mated with a female can find it difficult when young to differentiate between a female dog's head or vulva and an owner's leg. The male dog usually reaches puberty between nine and twelve months of age. This is when a male dog will often challenge his owner by being disobedient. It is most important to let the dog know who is the boss – that you, the owner, are the "leader of the pack" from the moment of obtaining the dog.

Bitches, on the other hand, come into season

The male St. Bernard is big and powerful, and must learn to accept a subordinate role in the family 'pack'. Photo: Steph Holbrook.

The seasonal cycle may affect a bitch's behaviour. Photo: Steph Holbrook.

twice yearly on average. If you live in an area or neighbourhood where there are a lot of male dogs, you could find some unwelcome biannual visitors. Under the influence of oestrogen, when the bitch is in season, she may become more active, and will urinate more, especially if she sees another dog. A female St. Bernard on heat will sometimes cock her leg to urinate and seem to increase her territory marking with urine. Some bitches that live with another bitch may become aggressive prior to their coming into season. Bitches who are not bred from can sometimes have a phantom pregnancy where they guard toys, rags, dolls, slippers, and soft cuddly toys; some can even produce milk. They love to carry something around in their mouths until these maternal urges subside and they return to a normal pattern of behaviour.

The season for a bitch can last in total for a period of three weeks. Initially the vulva swells up prior to there being any sign of blood. In large breeds such as the St. Bernard, there can sometimes be a copious discharge before the sign of blood.

The blood can begin to change colour prior to ovulation, but this is not always the case. After the period of ovulation, which can vary in individual bitches, the colour changes from a pinkish colour to a dirty red, the vulva decreases in size and the discharge then dries up. A white discharge, which is normal, returns after the season.

Bitches do tend to keep themselves very clean and the season should not cause any problems or trouble. Occasionally, bitches may suffer from cystitis if the urine is particularly acidic during their season.

TEMPERAMENT
Both sexes are equally loveable, so it is largely a matter of personal choice as to which would be suitable as a family pet. As well as physical difference in type, there are some variations in temperament. The St. Bernard generally has an excellent temperament, being especially understanding and loveable with children.

Most dogs are territorial and some consider that

The St. Bernard often has a special relationship with children. Photo courtesy: Mr & Mrs J.S. Harpham.

family members are part of their territory. You must remember that the ancestors of the St. Bernard were used as guard dogs. One of the main tasks of the St. Bernard at the Hospice was to guard the valuable items connected with the religious rituals handed down through the ages. According to some experts, the English type St. Bernard tends to be more docile than some of the continental lines. A disadvantage of the heavier-built, quiet dog is that it often does not live as long as the more energetic, lighter-built continental dog.

A lot of the current dogs in America go back to the continental type, as suggested by Joseph H. Fleischli in his book *The Saint Bernard* (1954) and also Albert de la Rie in his book *The St. Bernard Classic* (1971).

THE DOG'S SENSES

St. Bernards are great 'people watchers'. Dogs communicate with each other using all their senses. A two-day old puppy, when separated from its mother, will cry and swing its head to and fro like a pendulum until it reaches its mother's body. Usually the puppy then stops crying and crawls towards the bitch. Touch is the earliest and very important sense in the canine world. It is the primal sense in dogs. A St. Bernard which is deprived of touch will grow to become subordinate, fearful and often withdrawn. As well as its importance for emotional well-being, touch is used by dogs to explore their environment. St. Bernards, like other dogs, have special sensory hairs, vibrissae, above their eyes, under their jaws and most importantly, on their muzzles. These sensory hairs are embedded in areas of skin that have intense blood supplies and numerous nerve-endings. Dogs use this sense to determine the shape and texture of objects as well as to assess the air flow.

The next sense is taste, which is closely connected with smell; consequently, it can be difficult to differentiate between the two. What needs to be remembered in carnivores like dogs is that palatability is based on the odour of the food first, then the texture and finally its taste. A deficiency of calcium and other minerals in the diet can have significant influence upon the mind of the St. Bernard, sometimes increasing aggression.

In the St. Bernard, hearing is more acute than ours, in the 1,000-8,000 cps range. The ability of the dog to hear high-pitched sounds is an aspect inherited from the wolf. The ears catch sound and channel it through to the brain where the significance of sound is determined. The context of the sound determines the St. Bernard's response.

Vision is another important sense. The angle of vision is vital. The more a dog sees laterally, the less well it sees straight ahead. This is why some St. Bernards cannot see something which is practically under their noses. The placement of the dog's eyes will result in differing information being sent to the brain. Some St. Bernards have very deep-set eyes which can affect vision. A Saint with clean eyes has an improved opportunity to visualise what is straight ahead.

Scent is undoubtedly the most important of the St. Bernard's practical senses but it can be the most difficult to comprehend. It is a fact that St. Bernards have around 220 million scent receptors in their noses, whereas humans have around five million. Odours have a powerful influence on both the physiology and the behaviour of the dog. Sensitivity to odours is partly inherited. Smell memories last for life and affect the behaviour of St. Bernards. Barry, the St. Bernard from the Hospice, successfully rescued many people, actually saving the lives of forty travellers, some long distances from the Hospice.

Understanding how these senses contribute towards temperament will help when training the St. Bernard by rewarding appropriate behaviour with treats. Remember, the most rewarding reinforcer is praise by voice accompanied by loving, encouraging hand movements over the dog's head, chest and back.

CHOOSING A BREEDER
Decide on what you want in age, sex, colour and coat variety, then contact a reputable breeder. A good way of finding a conscientious St. Bernard breeder in your area is to visit a breed club show or Championship Show. Look at the dogs people are showing and see which of the exhibitors have Saints which appeal to you. Once the dogs have been judged, approach the particular exhibitor and advise them of what you are looking for. No doubt you may feel as if you are being interrogated, as most caring breeders with the welfare of their dogs in mind will want to ascertain that you are a capable, responsible, caring, appropriate person to own a Saint. Beware of the breeder who states they will "sell you a Champion", that they have just the exact dog for you and asks nothing of your circumstances or of your knowledge of, or interest in, the breed.

If possible, make an appointment at a mutually convenient time for you and the breeder. Remember, dog breeders lead hectic lives: not all have boarding or full-time breeding kennels; some fit this in around their family and other jobs. Some fit their employment and families around their dogs – the Saints take priority over everything else.

Purchasing a St. Bernard is not like shopping at the local supermarket; puppies do not come to order. Discuss what you hope to buy with the breeder. Be prepared to wait; make use of this time

Responsible breeders will be very careful about the homes their puppies go to.
Photo: Steph Holbrook.

17

constructively by reading books on the breed and on training your dog, and look into all the elements of the suggested nutrition for a large dog. The wait will be much better than impulse buying, the results of which can bring about sadness for the owner, when the decision is regretted, and can have upsetting consequences for the St. Bernard, who may end up being rehomed.

PET OR SHOW DOG

If you decide upon a pet puppy, then say so to the breeder. It does not mean you will be sold an inferior puppy, just one with minor blemishes. Should you wish to consider showing, then share this information too with the breeder. There is nothing more irritating to a St. Bernard breeder than to sell a dog or bitch puppy for a pet and then to see it in the ring at a later date. This is not fair on the breeder, or the owner of the dog, who may well be expecting to win top prizes, or the dog.

Should you really wish to consider showing, then attempt to attend smaller shows as well as Championships to observe the way experienced exhibitors handle their dogs to top wins such as Best Dog or Bitch, even Best In Show. A great deal can be learned from observation and by asking sensible, appropriate questions.

In our opinion, it is wonderful to see a dog which carries our affix winning, especially if novice exhibitors have come along for a puppy with show potential. Should another breeder or exhibitor contact us for a show-quality puppy, this too carries a lot of responsibility; as the puppies can change

and develop so much from the age of eight weeks.

PRICE AND TERMS

When purchasing a puppy at eight weeks, you should not expect any guarantees that this will definitely be a stunning quality show dog. At this age, it is difficult to offer any firm guarantees other than that the puppy is really fit and healthy and does not have any parasites. Some breeders offer different price scales, selling a 'pet puppy' for less than a puppy with show potential. We prefer to charge the same for all the puppies at this age, pointing out to prospective owners that the puppy is line bred, has been wormed, has been examined by our own vet and is healthy, often trained to use newspapers and has the early stages of the socialisation process undertaken by regular handling, is accustomed to a variety of noises, and is used to other dogs and cats. If the puppy subsequently develops into a specimen with a large amount of the required breed attributes which meet the KC Standard, as well as a charismatic personality ideal for showing, this is an added bonus.

Some breeders may offer 'breeding terms' for bitch puppies. Different breeders have different definitions for what 'breeding terms' are. This could mean purchasing the puppy at a much reduced rate; then, when the bitch has a litter, giving the original breeder one puppy, or even two puppies. Others may require half the litter, or the cost of one or two puppies once the litter is sold. Initially, this may seem like a good idea, as there is a reduced layout of funds; however, these arrangements can often cause a lot of conflict and distress. More people fall out over breeding terms than you would believe. It is better to purchase the bitch outright; the puppy is then yours, with no one else having control over her future.

LONG OR SHORT-HAIRED?

The original St. Bernards were short-haired dogs. When the Newfoundland was crossed with the Saint to give rough-coated dogs, this proved inappropriate for the snow in the Swiss Alps. However, many St. Bernard enthusiasts prefer the long-haired 'fluffy'-looking Saints. The smooth or short-coated variety is not as popular in Britain or America as the rough-coated variety. This trend

The breeder will help you to assess show potential.
Photo: Steph Holbrook.

The smooth-haired St. Bernard is not as popular as the long-haired variety, but they have their own band of devotees.

The rough-coated St. Bernard requires more time and attention.
Photo: Steph Holbrook.

may well be changing, as increasingly owners prefer a low-maintenance, easily groomed dog, which the smooth-haired is. The rough-coated definitely require much more attention and time spent on the management of their thick coat.

When the smooth-haired or rough-coated dog moults, the soft downy undercoat generally comes out first, with the longer guard hairs loosening as the new coat comes through. A good wire dog-brush, or a dandie/pin brush, is useful for going through the rough coat. A wire glove is handy for grooming the smooth coat, followed by a polish with a velvet cloth or rubber glove.

Remember that with such a large dog there can be a great deal of hair around when the dogs begin to moult. If you are house-proud then it might be better to consider a breed of dog smaller than a St. Bernard; otherwise the amount of work to keep on top of the hair loss, as well as the housework, may eventually become too much.

ASSESSING YOUR PUPPY

Once you have put your faith in a reputable breeder, you should wait until the breeder contacts you again with news of a puppy. Reputable breeders often have waiting lists of potential buyers, so you do need to be prepared to have your name added to their list if you are keen to obtain a puppy from that particular breeder. Having made the breeder aware of your requirements regarding sex and type, it is a matter of looking forward to the telephone call or letter advising you of the birth of a litter.

It may be that you have the opportunity to choose a puppy if there are sufficient in the litter, or the breeder may have a specific puppy in mind for you. In either case, ask to see the whole litter so that you can compare your puppy against the others. It is also important to observe the puppies interacting with each other. There are some questions which you may wish to consider. Is your puppy larger or smaller than its siblings? Is the puppy marked as you had expected it to be? Does your puppy seem extrovert or is the puppy overpowered by the others?

Speaking in general terms, the litter should all seem well-rounded and plump, not pot-bellied or looking as if they have worms. The litter should have bright eyes, good bone and be outgoing. A

It is important to see the dam of the litter.
Photo: Steph Holbrook.

puppy that seems shy and retiring may need a lot of hard work to socialise him properly, especially through puberty. Should there be a puppy that is extremely nervous, he should be avoided, no matter how sorry you feel for him. This type of behaviour is not typical of the breed and may cause problems later in adulthood.

Another important point is to make sure you ask to see the dam of the litter. It may not always be possible to see the sire, as breeders sometimes use a stud dog which is owned by another breeder out of their area. The reputable breeder will definitely have the dam of the puppies and should be delighted for you to see her. This will give you an idea of the temperament of the mother, an opportunity to see her markings and sometimes you can observe her with the litter, depending on the age of the puppies when you visit.

Often breeders have photographs of the sire of the puppies along with other photographs of the ancestors of the litter, so do not be afraid to ask. Genuine breeders are only too pleased to share their love, experience and knowledge of this breed with potential buyers and novices. It is better to have your queries answered than go away with uncertainties.

THE POTENTIAL SHOW DOG

If your choice is to embark on a show dog, you will need to place your trust in the breeder's integrity, as your novice eye may not have the experience to assess what has potential. Even when a breeder makes an assessment of a potential quality puppy for exhibition, things can go wrong. There are,

however, some basic guidelines which may help you evaluate such a puppy.

A promising St. Bernard puppy at eight weeks should have solid bone of quality, with definite 'knuckles' into which the puppy will grow. The front should be straight, the forelegs dropping parallel; there will be quite a lot of looseness and play at that age. The feet should be cat-like, not long hare-feet. St. Bernard heads vary in type, depending on which bloodlines the pedigree contains. We like to see a puppy with well-defined stop, a square muzzle, not long and narrow like a Border Collie, with a slight arch between the ears, not flat-headed but not over-arched so that the puppy looks like a bloodhound. The puppy should not have cheek bumps or too much drop from the lips. The mouth should suggest that when the second teeth come through there will be a scissor bite, not over or undershot. The puppy should have dark, bright eyes, sufficient to give a soft, benevolent expression, not light and somewhat staring.

Ideally, there should not be too much looseness, especially at this age, as this might indicate problems later. The puppy will not have a good length of neck at this age but you do not want to consider one where the head appears to be stuck onto the shoulders. A short back is preferable – not too long so that the puppy looks like a Dane – with a good ribcage, and the tail should not be set on too high. The tail should be carried happily, not too curled over the back, as this could be a fault when adult. Hindquarters should be strong and sturdy with a good turn of the stifle, and thick-set

A typical-looking St. Bernard with show potential.

hocks which should not turn in towards each other with the feet pointing outwards – this is classed as being cow-hocked. The puppy should not turn its feet inwards as this is also a fault.

Markings vary, depending on which country the puppy is from. The perfectly marked puppy should have a white blaze between the eyes, and a white muzzle with a white collar or part-white mantle round the neck. The white collar is important in America, Europe and the Continent; however, in Britain there are Champions with hardly any white collars at all. Show puppies should have white chest, white legs and feet. The tail end should also be white in both the rough and smooth-coated St. Bernard.

The colours on the main body of the puppy can be orange, mahogany, red-brindle; the ears should be black, with black "spectacles" over the eyes. Sometimes dogs on the Continent and in America have white faces. This would be classed as a miss mark in the UK.

Male puppies should have both testicles descended into the scrotum. A monorchid is a dog with only one testicle; it is better not to try and breed from a St. Bernard like this, as the condition can be hereditary. A cryptorchid is a male dog with no testicles and is suitable for a pet only. The testicles can usually be felt at eight weeks of age and should have descended by three months. If there is no evidence of the testicles by this age, it is unlikely that they will descend at a later date. Advice should be sought from the veterinary surgeon, as problems could occur later.

3 CARING FOR YOUR ST. BERNARD PUPPY

St. Bernard dogs will thrive and bring you a lot of pleasure, provided they are given plenty of love, good food and adequate company. They also require physical and mental stimulation, as they can be intelligent, but extremely stubborn if they do not wish to do something. Caring for your Saint involves common sense more than anything else. Firmness combined with affection is the motto. Should you be purchasing a St. Bernard as a first-time buyer, the likelihood is that this will be a house pet. From the onset, you and the puppy need to know exactly where you stand. It is essential to establish from day one that you are the boss, not the puppy. There are certain rules in the house which must be obeyed.

The inexperienced may think the disobedience and waywardness of a St. Bernard are highly amusing, that this cute ball of fluff is funny and should not be scolded. This "ball of fluff" is going to be large and heavy when adult, possibly weighing more than the owner, so it is vital to be in control. Allowing even the youngest of puppies to get away with transgressions unreprimanded will cause unnecessary problems in the future. Think of the puppy as an ambassador for the canine campaign for harmonious living with humans – the newcomer is eager to please and to fit in with the house rules. Naturally, someone has to tell the puppy what the house rules are; it is no use keeping them a secret.

Like children, a most important word which the puppy will become familiar with very quickly is "No". Do not be tempted to use long sentences, it is not necessary. Offering the puppy an attractive chew toy will keep the puppy preoccupied and help it settle down. If the puppy is quietly ensconced with a chew toy in its jaw, let us consider what it is NOT doing. The puppy is not tearing around the house, knocking over plants, jumping on furniture, chewing up magazines, mounting the cat, digging up the garden, or barking at the neighbours. Remember, training should be fun, for you and the dog. Training sessions should be short but frequent as puppies, especially St. Bernard puppies, have a low boredom threshold.

TAKING YOUR PUPPY HOME

When you have chosen your puppy and paid for him or her, the breeder should provide you with a pedigree, a diet sheet and some food for the first few days. The registration documents may not have come back, so be prepared to wait for them. It is also important to check with the breeder that the puppy has been wormed and is insured. The first few weeks in your home are very important for the socialisation process. It is also better for the puppy to follow the diet sheet, otherwise he will develop an upset tummy, possibly having diarrhoea. Usually an eight-week-old puppy will not have been vaccinated, so check with the breeder to make sure.

Once you have taken the puppy home, give him an opportunity to settle in, then telephone your own vet and ask about the appropriate inoculations. Until the puppy has been immunised, he should

The exciting day arrives when you can take your puppy home.

not leave your premises. Your vet will be pleased to give the puppy a thorough examination to ensure he is healthy. This is beneficial for you and the puppy, and the breeder will not be offended as it covers their early care of the young St. Bernard too.

When taking the puppy home, it is useful to have some newspapers in the car in case he is sick. St. Bernards usually enjoy travelling and are not the type of dog which jumps all over the place. Speak to the puppy in a soft voice to reassure him.

Once home, place the puppy in an appropriate area in the garden which you do not mind being used as a toilet area. When the puppy has urinated give him lots of praise so that he knows it is acceptable to do this outside. Allow the puppy to sniff around but do not be tempted to pick him up for cuddles if he cries. Remember, you cannot do this when the dog is older and bigger.

THE FIRST NIGHT

Follow the breeder's diet sheet to the letter and try to stick to the feeding times. Do not be influenced to change the diet, even by vets or other would-be experts – the breeder knows best. After the last meal in the evening, put the puppy outside and make certain you accompany him so that you can observe that he empties both bladder and bowels. Ensure that he is given lots of praise, then return indoors.

Settle him in his own sleeping area with a soft toy or old jumper to cuddle into, perhaps a Bonio-type biscuit and something to chew on. Some people suggest placing a clock which has a loud ticking action somewhere out of reach in the room as this can be like the heartbeat of the dam. We have never used this ourselves; however, we have left a radio on if a puppy would not settle down.

The new addition to the family will be the centre of attention – but make sure he does not become over-tired.
Photo: Steph Holbrook.

When you go off to bed, the puppy may whimper but do not be tempted to return; this is a fatal mistake. If you come back into the room and make a big fuss, the St. Bernard will quickly learn this is a good way of gaining attention. If you ignore the puppy's mournful doggy pleas, he will quickly settle down, realising that objecting noisily has no effect and, eventually, will go off to sleep.

HOUSE-TRAINING

The following morning, get up early and again put the puppy outside as quickly as possible. Once he has urinated, give lots of praise. It may be a good idea to put newspaper near to the door in case the puppy has an accident during the night, or allow him to sleep in a crate, as they do not like soiling the area where they sleep.

During the day, spend time observing the puppy. As soon as the puppy wakes up, put him outside and, again, give lots of praise once he has emptied his bladder. Remember to put the puppy out after every meal when, usually, there will follow a bowel action. These simple tips help save a lot of mess and encourage the puppy to become house-trained. For the puppy that proves more difficult to house-train, give a dog biscuit or some food treat after he has urinated or had a bowel action.

If the puppy has an accident in the house, it should be sufficient to scold him with your voice. Lower the tone of your voice, saying "Naughty puppy, bad dog" and actually scowl at the puppy, then place the puppy outside. Dogs are people-watchers, they pick up signs from adults by our body language so they can quickly identify when something is acceptable as well as our displeasure. We do not believe in rubbing the puppy's nose in the urine, as this is cruel and really does not act as a deterrent. Praise and encouragement are far more likely to have the desired results.

We suggest that fresh water is not kept in the kitchen for the puppy, especially on a tiled or linoleum floor, as pups tend to play with the water. As they grow and take a drink they can make a mess, as one third is actually drunk but two thirds can be shaken or spilt on the floor! A St. Bernard loves to drink out of a large bucket and immerse his head in it. Make sure an old towel, or a special dog towel is kept at hand to wipe the dog's face after drinking; this will save a lot of mess. Obviously, if

the dog has his own kennel and run, a bucket or drinking unit will be available at all times. The house pet will ask to go out for a drink, when required, but do remember to wipe his face and jowl on return!

HOUSE RULES

From the start, you will want to spend time with your puppy. This entails 'quality time', as well as opportunities for rest and basic training. Establish your house rules as soon as possible. For example, if you do not want the dog to go upstairs or into the best room or other 'no-go' areas, it is no use carrying a baby St. Bernard into out-of-bound areas and cuddling him, then a few weeks later chastising the slightly older puppy for venturing into the same place. The puppy should not be allowed to trespass into rooms where he is not welcome.

St. Bernard puppies should be deterred from

Establish house rules and stick to them. What may be endearing behaviour in a puppy may be highly undesirable when your St. Bernard is full grown. Photo courtesy: Mrs L. Byles, Meadowmead.

climbing on to furniture. Do not expect a St. Bernard to differentiate between an old dilapidated sofa and the new three-piece suite. It can be fun cuddling up to a St. Bernard puppy on the settee, but it is no fun when the 13-stone St. Bernard decides it wants a cuddle on the settee with you!

LEAD TRAINING

It is useful to socialise the puppy into wearing a collar for a few hours at a time. Do not leave it on at night, just in case it catches on something, and never leave a choker-chain on a small puppy. After the puppy has had its vaccinations, you can commence lead training as soon as possible. Begin at home in the garden or in the park if dogs are allowed there, remembering to take a plastic bag or poop scoop to pick up any excreta left by the puppy. Give the puppy lots of encouragement when he walks beside you. Puppies are very curious and want to sniff their environment; do not allow the puppy to suddenly jerk forward or pull. Call him by name to gain his attention and clearly say "heel", simultaneously pulling back on the leash.

We believe in training our puppies on a large-linked slip or choke chain; once they pull forward and are given a quick, short, sharp jerk back accompanied by the word "heel" they soon know what is required. St. Bernards should never be allowed to get away with pulling on the leash as it will have disastrous results later – the dog will be taking you for a walk and you will have no control.

USEFUL COMMANDS

Coming when called is essential training; it is surprising how many Saints pretend to be deaf at times. The best way of doing this, initially, is on an extending flexible leash and 'reeling' the dog in. Get the dog to sit by using the word "Sit", backing the dog into a corner. When the dog sits down, immediately give him lots of praise and a treat. Repeat the exercise a few times, always giving a reward by voice and food treat. Walk away from the puppy, say "Come" and reel the puppy in, again giving the reward by voice and food treat. These exercises should be repeated several times daily. A well-trained dog is a happy dog and a pleasure to own. An untrained, unmanageable dog, especially a St. Bernard, is a real nightmare, for dog, owner and society. It is most important to train your dog so

that he becomes a good ambassador for the breed, not a bad example.

"Stay" is another useful command. Once you have taught the puppy to sit, just walk away and delay giving the dog his food treat. Begin by delaying this for a few seconds, gradually increasing the time-span. Remember, give lots of praise when this is done correctly, accompanied by the food treat.

When teaching the recall, it is a good idea to teach the puppy to sit on return, rather than have an adult St. Bernard impact into the groin like a guided missile when fully grown. Remember that pups are enthusiastic and keen to please.

PUPPY PARTIES

Do not keep your puppy a secret, but invite people round on a gradual basis to meet him. The hidden agenda is for your St. Bernard to learn that the majority of people are non-threatening. If friends have puppies from other breeds, once the inoculations are out of the way, it is a good idea for the various pups to socialise together. Often they have great fun; sometimes a dominant puppy may try to be in control, so then common sense must prevail and an adult takes over as 'leader of the pack'. After a period of time, the pups will settle down exhausted, often followed by their owners!

It is a good idea to invite children around to see the St. Bernard as this teaches the puppy that children or little people are fun to be with. Adults can also teach children that puppies are not toys and can encourage them to handle the puppy in a caring, appropriate way. Unless your child-training skills exceed your puppy-training skills, initially invite children in small quantities. One child is wonderful, two are fine; however, three children plus a puppy quickly reach crisis point and emit energy which no scientific gauge or instrument can measure! Puppyhood and childhood are the times the young learn that hugs and cuddles as well as discipline are an important part of life.

PUPPY CLASSES AND ADULT CLASSES

By three months of age, the puppy will be responding to the basic obedience you have been encouraging. Even so, now is a good time to enrol in puppy classes, especially one where the pups can play off-leash. This is good for socialising your

Practise lead training in the garden before venturing into the outside world.

Early recall training involves calling your puppy to you, and 'reeling' him in.

puppy. A dog which will play, rather than hide or fight, is far less troublesome than one which wishes to be aggressive, especially a dog the size of a St. Bernard.

Several large veterinary practices now run classes as well as the Obedience and Ringcraft classes. Information about these can be obtained often from the local vet or the Kennel Club. In America, many Saints go on to win Obedience awards but this is less common in Britain. Both Obedience and Ringcraft classes have experienced instructors who can train you and the dog to work in partnership. This is essential if you are considering showing the puppy when he is older.

If you have purchased an older dog that is badly behaved or untrained, it is really important to commence a basic obedience programme. Lots of encouragement, consistency and assertiveness on your part should bring about some positive responses. It is better to enrol at an Obedience class if the older dog is not responding to the house rules and basic obedience; an expert instructor will be able to offer advice and assistance.

EXERCISE

Exercise is vital for the healthy St. Bernard; however, this needs careful management. Puppies should NOT be dragged around towns or walked for miles. This is extremely damaging to their joints. It is a good idea to take the puppy where there are crowds and sit with the puppy to observe what is going on. Drive somewhere pleasant with the puppy, if possible to a forest, where he can be safe and allow him to have free exercise for about half an hour. Most forests have car parking in appropriate places, so park up, gently walk, or find a large log or seat to sit on and allow the puppy to explore, observing his behaviour, making sure he is safe. Sometimes, when the puppy is tired, he will just flop down and rest for a period of time. When he seems rested, come back to the car and make your return journey. NEVER leave a puppy or any dog in the car and go off shopping or to a business meeting, especially in hot weather. It is surprising how quickly the car can become hot, even when there is just a small amount of sun. The dog will become very distressed: overheating can cause strokes – or, in severe cases, death can occur.

Photos: Mike Trafford.

If your puppy is reluctant to sit on command, apply gentle pressure to the hindquarters.

"Down" is one of the most useful commands to teach.

Free running in the garden or local park two or three times a day is sufficient for a puppy. Combine this with short walks to teach lead-manners, no more than 10-15 minutes maximum. This is ample for the growing puppy. A dog that is over a year old should have regular controlled exercise, walking at a quick pace for half an hour twice a day, along with appropriate free exercise in the garden. For a St. Bernard to be in good physical condition and develop the appropriate muscles when adult, sustained walking is important. This may not be considered important if the dog is just a pet; remember, however, that an under-exercised dog could have extra energy to use up, so could become destructive in the house due to boredom. St. Bernards who do not have any exercise can have obesity problems which can lead to heart problems. A healthy dog is a happy dog.

GROOMING

THE SMOOTH-COATED ST. BERNARD
Grooming is essential for two reasons, to keep the coat free from tangles and to strengthen the bond between owner and dog. Smooth-coated St. Bernards are easier to maintain regarding the care and management of the coat, so this will be dealt with first. The grooming aids which we use on short-haired Bernards are a good-quality, fine-toothed steel comb, a wire brush, a standard rubber grooming pad, and finishing off with a polish with velvet cloth or chamois leather. A pair of quality scissors are used for trimming the hair at the end of the tail to 'round' it off, rather than having long, feathery hair, even on the smooth coats. Usually St. Bernards enjoy being brushed, especially if this is encouraged from the start, when you first bring the puppy home.

When grooming, start at the head and gently work your way down, talking to the dog all the time and encouraging him to stand still. While the dog is in the standing position, use your left hand to stroke the dog gently under the tummy, repeating the words "Good dog. Stand, stand." This will enable him to understand what is wanted when the stand position is required. Pay attention to the area under the ears and comb this through with the dog comb. Check the ears, which can

PLAY AND EXERCISE

It is vital not to over-exercise growing puppies.

There will be days when the delights of walking your dog are dubious...

Playing is a good way of exercising adults and puppies.

Swimming is an excellent way to build up muscle – for both dog and owner. Photo courtesy: Sanflax Saints.

sometimes have excess wax. Gently wipe the ear with cotton wool (cotton) with a small amount of olive oil on, which should remove the lower wax. On no account put the cotton wool deep into the ear canal. This will cause problems, as this is a very sensitive area. Use separate cotton wool for each ear so as not to spread any germs.

Continue with the brush from the shoulders, along the withers and the loin towards the croup, down the flanks and under the tail. St. Bernards do not like having their tails combed, so you may need someone to hold the dog's head while you do that. If the dog stands still, give him a lot of encouragement by praising him. Should the dog be fidgeting, then start the process from the head again and be more firm, as well as encouraging him when you come to the tail. Gradually the Saint will understand what is required and enjoy being brushed and groomed.

THE ROUGH-COATED ST. BERNARD
The rough-coated Saint requires more attention to his coat, as it can become unkempt and tangled, especially when the soft undercoat begins to lift. Extra grooming aids which we use with our rough-coats are: a broad wire brush, a standard-toothed steel comb, a dematting comb which has broader gaps in the teeth, thinning scissors with one blade serrated and the other a solid blade, a stripping knife for the fluffy hair on the outer ears and a normal pair of good-quality scissors.

As with the smooth-haired Saint, start with the head and work towards the tail end and feet. Particular attention must be paid to the area underneath the ears, down the neck, the longer hair under the chest, the feathering on the back of the front legs, the long, thick feathery hair on the flanks under the tail, and last, but by no means least, the tail. When the dog lies down, check the area under the armpits and in between the dog's hind legs near the scrotum. Do take care when grooming this area not to catch the testicles on a male dog, as this will be painful.

Ears can have a lot of thick, feathery, unwanted hair; once again comb this through to remove any tangles, then with your finger and thumb pluck the hair out a little at a time. Some people use a stripping knife but this is best left to the breeder or expert as, when carried out incorrectly, it can make

a real mess. Remember to wipe the eyes with a piece of cotton wool damped in cold tea to keep the eyes clean. Use a separate piece of cotton wool for each eye, moving from the part nearest to the nose towards the ear.

The feet should be well-rounded cat-feet on a St. Bernard, so carefully trim the feet around the toes so that the foot has that all-important 'rounded' look. If the toenails require trimming, go to the breeder or the vet, or use a carpenter's file and file the nails down. It is important not to catch the quick, as this can bleed and is certainly painful for the dog. St. Bernards do not like having their toenails clipped – quite often, as soon as the dog sees the clippers, they do a quick disappearing act. For such large dogs, they can be real 'softies'. It is

The smooth-coated St. Bernard is easy to maintain with regular grooming sessions.
Photo: Mike Trafford.

The rough coat tends to mat and tangle, particularly in the feathering behind the ears. Photo: Mike Trafford.

amazing how Saints can make it seem as if their feet can vanish when you attempt to cut the claws. Remember to check for dewclaws, as these do not receive any roadwork and can sometimes curl right round, which can be painful if the claw grows into the skin. We prefer to remove all the dewclaws on puppies which we breed, as it saves problems later. This is not necessary to fulfil the Breed Standard; the Kennel Club in Britain requires hind dewclaws to be removed, stating nothing about front dewclaws. We believe it leaves cleaner lines on the front legs and avoids damage in later life, as the front dewclaws can easily be caught while the dog is out exercising.

The fur between the toes should be trimmed regularly. All tufts should be removed with a sharp pair of scissors. The best way to do this is to point the scissors the way the hair grows down towards the claws; it should not be done against the hair growth, as this will create scissor marks. The hocks can also have the excess hair trimmed down; again, comb the hair through the cut, towards the back of the foot, not against the hair growth.

BATHING
This can be great fun and a lot of Saints really love being bathed. It is important to get them accustomed to this when they are puppies. Obviously, it is easier if you have a utility room or downstairs shower. It can be achieved by putting the dog in the bath, but this can leave a mess. Some breeders are fortunate to have proper facilities with shower units installed just for their Saints, plus the large dryers, which are invaluable.

We will deal with washing a Saint in a bath. It is a good idea to bathe the puppy when about 16 weeks old, then again at five or six months of age so that he is not afraid of this process. Be fully prepared BEFORE putting the puppy in the bath. Decide which shampoo you require; we suggest a quality insecticidal shampoo which is safe to use on puppies. The best-loved Saint can acquire an unwanted visitor when exercised where other dogs go. Make certain all the doors are closed to prevent the would-be escape-artist from landing on the settee and shaking himself all over granny, or landing on the bed. Ensure you have plenty of towels ready to dry the puppy – there is nothing worse than having succeeded in bathing the puppy successfully and then realising you have left the towels in a drawer! A spray hose attached to the bath taps or shower hose is most useful. Remove all unwanted bottles of moisture cream, shampoo, after-shave, candles, bubble bath, etc., as the puppy may decide to chew these. Place a large towel on the floor beside the bath to absorb any excess water. A non-slip bath mat in the bath is also useful.

Having carried out the preparation work, fill the bath to about six to eight inches of water which is tepid; remember the skin of the dog is more sensitive to heat and temperature than our own.

30

Place the dog rear end first into the bath, talking gently to reassure him. Do not worry if the puppy does not wish to sit or lie down, if possible, have his head at the opposite end of the bath to the taps.

Using the hose, make sure the temperature is correct, then, beginning at the shoulders, soak the dog completely, leaving the head until last. Follow the instructions on the bottle of shampoo and put some onto your hands, then massage it into the hair of the dog, over the shoulders, working up a good lather. Gradually work your way along the dog's back, chest, sides, undercarriage, front and hind legs, and tail. It may be that the insecticidal shampoo has to be left on for a few minutes, so, having succeeded in covering the dog, check the time and leave the shampoo on. Now to the head. Carefully hold the dog's head slightly up, put some shampoo onto the top of the dog's head, making certain that no shampoo goes into the dog's eyes, wash the ears and try not to let the shampoo enter into the ear canals. Work up a lather, leave for a few moments, then rinse off, talking to the dog all the time in an encouraging way.

Make certain that the dog is properly rinsed, as retention of soap in the coat can cause skin problems, such as eczema. Run your hand through the dog's coat to detect any residue of soap – the coat should be squeaky clean; if it is not, give another rinse. Let the water out of the bath. Squeeze the excess water out of the coat firmly but not too roughly and encourage the dog to shake. Place a large bath towel over the puppy and gently pat all over. Change to another dry towel and remove the puppy from the bath. This is often the point where the dog will want to go rushing around like a scud missile to dry himself.

Take the puppy to an appropriate place and give him another towelling. It is possible that you can use a hand-held hair dryer if the puppy is not afraid of the noise. Make certain that you do not leave the hot air too long on one particular area as this can cause burning to the pup's skin. Brush the hair with a suitable brush and the puppy will look beautiful for a short period of time, until the hair flattens again.

If it is a sunny day, the dog can be washed in a tin bath in the garden or yard, as suggested; if not, then the above method is advisable. Good luck!

4 FEEDING AND HUSBANDRY

Having acquired your puppy you need to pay careful attention to your breeder's feeding guide. It should be said that some guides are better than others, and some breeders are better than others at preparing a guide or, indeed, in giving advice on feeding.

In this chapter we do not set out to recommend one or more types of feeding. Your access to food largely depends on your country, area, government regulations and your pocket. We are lucky to live near a small independent abattoir and we can get a regular supply of that which, in our opinion, is the Saint Bernard's favourite food – tripe/offal. We feel that tripe is one of the best foods to feed in bulk as long as it is part of a balanced diet. If tripe cannot be obtained, chopped beef or chicken are bulking foods which have an acceptable protien calorie content.

A balanced diet is essential to your dog's health and therefore it is important to know what constitutes it. A balanced diet is made up of several important ingredients. These are:

Protein	Fat
Carbohydrates	Minerals
Vitamins	Water

We will discuss each of these in turn, but first look at Table 1.

This table shows the protein content of some types of food and their associated by-products.

As you can see, the foods vary quite widely in

A balanced diet is the key to developing good bone and skeletal structure. Photo courtesy: Mrs L. Byles.

	Water g/100g	Protein g/100g	Fat g/100g	Calcium g/100g	Phosphorus g/100g	Energy kcal/100g
TABLE 1. Typical nutrient content of some meats and meat by-products.						
RAW LEAN MEATS						
Pork	71.5	20.6	7.1	0.008	0.20	147
Beef	74.0	20.3	4.6	0.007	0.18	123
Lamb	70.1	20.8	8.8	0.007	0.19	162
Veal	74.9	21.1	2.7	0.008	0.26	109
Chicken	74.4	20.6	4.3	0.01	0.20	121
Duck	75.0	19.7	4.8	0.012	0.20	122
Turkey	75.5	21.9	2.2	0.008	0.19	107
Rabbit	74.6	21.9	4.0	0.022	0.22	124
OFFALS						
Udders	72.4	11.0	15.3	0.26	0.24	182
Fatty lungs	73.1	17.2	5.0	0.01	0.19	114
Sheep lungs	76.0	16.9	3.2	0.01	0.20	96
Spleen	75.9	17.0	6.5	0.03	0.22	126
Kidney (beef)	79.8	15.7	2.6	0.02	0.25	86
Heart	70.1	14.3	15.5	0.02	0.18	197
Heart (trimmed)	76.3	18.9	3.6	0.005	0.23	108
Liver (fresh)	68.6	21.1	7.8	0.001	0.36	163
Green tripe	76.2	12.3	11.6	0.01	0.10	154
Dressed tripe	88.0	9.0	3.0	0.08	0.04	63

their protein content. Of all the foods mentioned, the only raw meats we would tend not to feed are pork and lamb. We feel these are too fatty. However, proprietary dry foods are excellent in combinations of lamb and rice, should you wish to feed this to your Saint.

You can also see that the chart provides a useful table on kcal/100g, allowing you to work out what quantity of food to give your Saint to provide its calorie requirement per day.

PROTEIN

Using the chart to assess what protein is to be used you need to understand the protein's function. Protein contains essential amino acids and the arrangement of them makes up the profile of each individual protein.

The main sources of protein are:

  Animals: meat, fish, eggs, milk
  Vegetables: soya, cereals.

As stated, amino acids are important in protein and are essential to the health of the dog. The animal is unable to make these up from other materials sufficient for good health. These essentials are lysine, methionine, valine, leucine, isoleucine, threonine, histodine, phenyline, tryptophane, arginine.

Protein of good quality, i.e. meat, fish and eggs, provides the essential characteristics for digestion absorption and should have a balanced amino acid content.

If protein is deficient in a diet this shows itself in a lack of appetite, poor growth, loss of coat condition, or impaired immune function.

FATS

The main sources of fats are dairy-producing meats, fish, seeds, oils and nuts. Acid is essential in fat. However, fat is also important for vitamins A, D, E and K, which are soluble in fat. Fat also increases the palatability of food. Fat deficiencies are manifested in: skin lesions (abdomen and thighs), poor coat condition (dandruff, greasy coarse hair and dry skin), poor reproducing ability.

33

TABLE 2. Minerals.

Mineral	Dietary sources	Main functions	Results of deficiency	Results of excess
Calcium	Bones, milk, cheese	Bone formation, nerve and muscle formation	Poor growth, rickets, convulsions	Very high levels – bone deformities
Phosphorus	Bones, milk	Bone formation, energy utilisation	Rickets (rare)	Symptoms of calcium deficiency
Potassium	Meat, milk	Water balance, nerve function	Poor growth, paralysis, kidney and heart lesions	Muscle weakness
Sodium/chloride	Salts, cereals	Water balance, muscle and nerve activity	Poor growth, exhaustion	Thirst, high blood pressure (if intake maintained)
Magnesium	Cereals, bones, green vegetables	Bone formation, protein synthesis	Anorexia, vomiting, muscle weakness	Diarrhoea
Iron	Eggs, meat (liver), green vegetables	Part of haemoglobin (oxygen transport)	Anaemia, low resistance to hookworm infestation	Weight loss, anorexia
Copper	Meat, bones	Part of haemoglobin	Anaemia	Anaemia in other mammals, hepatitis in Bedington Terriers
Zinc	Meat, cereals	In digestion, tissue maintenance	Hair loss, skin thickening, poor growth	Diarrhoea
Manganese	Tea, nuts, cereals	Fat metabolism, many enzyme functions	Reproductive failure, poor growth	Poor fertility in other mammals, albinism, anaemia
Iodine	Fish, dairy produce	Part of thyroid hormone	Hair loss, apathy, drowsiness	In other animals, symptoms similar to deficiency
Selenium	Cereals, fish meals	Associated with Vitamin E function	Muscle damage	Toxic

CARBOHYDRATES

Carbohydrates are found in sugars and form polysaccharides. These are contained in cellulose. This in turn contains starches. Cellulose is not easily broken down but starches are broken down in the dog's digestive tract. Good sources of carbohydrates are meat, milk, sugar, lactose, fruit sugars and starches from cereals and most vegetables. Carbohydrates can form a cheap energy source 3.5 kcal/gr. However, they are thought to be essential nutrients for the dog. The Saint Bernard can maintain blood sugar levels through synthesis from amino acids.

Dogs can utilise high levels of carbohydrate. However, it is essential to ensure that it is balanced in the diet and, if using vegetables and cereals, that these are cooked to allow starch digestion.

Lactose can cause diarrhoea. This is known as Lactose Intolerance (this can be seen in the faeces of very young pups, if the dam is given too much milk of the wrong type). This is caused by absence of lactose. Uncooked cereal or potato starch can also cause diarrhoea.

Too much fibre can interfere with mineral absorption and cause excessive faeces or diarrhoea. So carefully check the carbohydrate content of dried food to assess its suitability for your Saint. Fibre is not generally considered greatly important to the dog and a 1 per cent content in dry matter is adequate.

MINERALS
See Table 2

Minerals are divided into two groups, major and trace. Major: the dog needs large quantities in dry matter. Trace: the dog needs small amounts in dry matter. Minerals are important for the healthy skeleton, fluid balance and metabolism through enzyme function.

VITAMINS

See Table 3

Vitamins form a complex system of molecules needed in small amounts. They form two groups:

TABLE 3. Vitamins.

Vitamin	Dietary sources	Main functions	Results of deficiency	Results of excess
Fat Soluble Vitamins				
Vitamin A	Fish oils, liver, vegetables	Vision in poor light, maintenance of skin	Night blindness, skin lesions	Anorexia, pain in bones (malformation)
Vitamin D	Cod-liver oil, eggs, animal products	Calcium balance, bone growth	Rickets, osteomalacia	Anorexia, calcification of soft tissues
Vitamin E	Green vegetables, vegetable oils, dairy products	Reproduction	Infertility, anaemia, muscle weakness	Not known in dogs
Vitamin K	Spinach, green vegetables, liver, *in vivo* synthesis	Blood clotting	Haemorrhage	Not known in dogs
Water Soluble (B group) Vitamins				
Thiamin (B_1)	Dairy products, cereals, organ meat	Release of energy from carbohydrate	Anorexia, vomiting, paralysis	Not known in dogs
Riboflavin (B_2)	Milk, animal tissues	Utilisation of energy	Weight loss, weakness, collapse, coma	Not known in dogs / Not known in dogs
Niacin	Cereals, liver, meat, legumes	Utilisation of energy	Anorexia, ulceration of mouth (black tongue)	Not known in dogs
Pyridoxine (B_6)	Meat, fish, eggs, cereals	Metabolism of amino acids	Anorexia, anaemia, weight loss, convulsions	Not known in dogs
Vitamin B_{12}	Liver, meat, dairy products	Division of cells in bone marrow	Anaemia	Not known in dogs
Folic acid	Offals, leafy vegetables	As B_{12}	Anaemia, poor growth	Not known in dogs
Pantothenic acid	Animal products, cereals, legumes	Release of energy from fat/carbohydrate	Slow growth, hair loss, convulsions, coma	Not known in dogs
Biotin	Offal, egg yolk, legumes	Metabolism of fat and amino acids	Loss of coat condition (scaly skin, scurf)	Not known in dogs
Choline	Plant and animal materials	Nerve function	Fatty infiltration of liver, poor blood clotting	Not known in dogs

fat-soluble – A, D, E, and K; water-soluble – B group vitamins and C.

It is important to distinguish between these two groups. Fat-soluble are stored in the body and do not need to be supplied daily. Water-solubles are needed daily. Too much fat-soluble vitamins can cause toxicity resulting in a condition of Hyper Vitaminosis.

Table 3 gives a very good breakdown of the various sources of vitamins.

WATER
Every cell in the body needs water to function. The animal does not store water for long periods as it continually loses water through its normal functions. Therefore it is essential that a continual supply of fluids is available.

Metabolic water is produced when proteins and fats are oxidated in the body. The metabolic level of fat can be seen in Table 3. Therefore, a food with a high fat and medium protein content could be ideal for the dog. Water is important for:

1. Easy transport around the body, helping to utilise soluble materials and to aid transportation to the gut and bloodstream. Therefore good water content is ideal in the chosen food.

2. Temperature regulation: Water helps to regulate the body temperature. It has a high specific heat capacity. It is therefore ideal for removing heat from vital organs. It also helps to release latent heat from the body.

3. Aiding digestion: by adding water to the other

major ingredients a vital conduit to aid digestion is created. Enzymes in the body break down complex molecules with the aid of water.

TABLE 4. Metabolic Water.

Class of food	Water yield of 100g on oxidation
Protein*	40g
Fat	107g
Carbohydrate	55g

*Not always completely oxidized

Table 4 shows the metabolic water content of various foods.

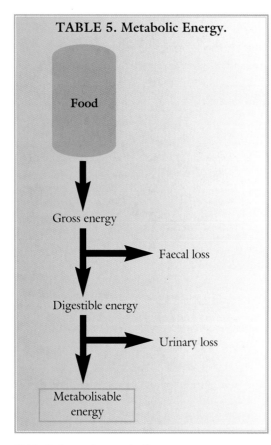

TABLE 5. Metabolic Energy.

Table 5 shows the metabolic energy.

DIGESTIBLE ENERGY
Not all the food you give your dog is available for its needs; some is lost in its faeces. Therefore the digestible energy is that which can be extracted from the food.

METABOLISABLE ENERGY
This is usable energy left after extraction by urine and used by the body during absorption.

Table 6 shows the energy contained in many examples of foods.

Table 7 gives conversion factors.

Table 8 gives weight equivalents.

DETERMINING GROWTH
We now have a broad idea of the ideal constituents and energy contained in our pet's food. So how do you use it to determine the growth of your dog? Table 9 will help with this.

One of our stud dogs, Coatham Smooth Impression, at 15 months was very thin. We had tried several ways to improve his body weight but to no avail. At Crufts 1995, in spite of his lack of weight, he won two firsts in his classes. We consulted with Mr David Watson BV Vet., MEd, MRCVS and, with the help of a leading pet food manufacturer, we developed a feeding regime to improve Bertie's weight. It turned out we were just not giving him enough calories. According to our time-honoured traditions we were feeding him as we fed all our dogs. It was just not enough. He needed over 6000 calories a day. 3.8 kilos of tripe or, to those who work in lbs., 8.36 lbs! We developed a combination of dry complete food and tripe to arrive at his food intake. We used an average of 345 calories per 100g dry food to make the combination. So for Bertie it was 675g of dry food and 5lbs of tripe twice a day. In addition, he was fed 1 pint of goat's milk and 2 eggs per day. The combined food gave him all he required in terms of protein and vitamins. I now use this table for all my dogs. I work out the calories needed according to the dog.

For a puppy the energy needs are greater than those of an adult dog or bitch who is neither used at stud or for whelping. Table 9 is IDEAL to work

TABLE 6. Average energy needs of healthy adult dogs and amounts of prepared food needed to meet them.

Energy requirement (kcal/day)	Weight of dog (kg)	Food to provide this amount of energy		Semi-moist food (g/day)	Complete dry food (g/day)
		Canned food + mixer 3:1 by weight, approx. equal volumes			
		Meat (g/day)	Mixer (g/day)		
115	2	60	20	38	33
460	8	240	80	151	132
806	14	420	140	264	230
1151	20	599	200	377	329
1496	26	779	260	491	427
1841	32	959	320	604	526
2302	40	1199	400	755	658
2877	50	1499	500	943	822
4028	70	2098	699	1321	1151

NOTES: Energy densities of prepared foods will vary depending on the recipe used. For the purpose of this table, energy densities have been assumed as follows: Canned food – 0.7kcal/g; Mixer – 3.5kcal/g; Semi-moist food – 3.05kcal/g; Complete dry food – 3.5kcal/g.

TABLE 7. Conversion factors.

Units	Units Wanted	To Convert
lb (pound)	g (gram)	x 454
lb (pound)	kg (kilogram)	x 0.454
oz (ounce)	g (gram)	x 28.4
kg (kilogram)	lb(pound)	x 2.2
kg (kilogram)	mg (milligram)	x 1,000,000
kg (kilogram)	g (gram)	x 1,000
g (gram)	mg (milligram)	x 1,000
g (gram)	(microgram)	x 1,000,000
mg (milligram)	(microgram)	x 1,000
kcal/kg (kilocalorie/kilogram)	kcal/lb (kilocalorie/pound)	x 0.454
kcal(kilocalorie)	kj (kilojoule)	x 4.2
ppm(parts per million)	/g (microgram/gram)	x 1
ppm(parts per million)	mg/kg (milligram/kilogram)	x 1
mg/kg (milligram/kilogram)	% (percentage)	x 0.0001
ppm (parts per million)	% (percentage)	x 0.0001
mg/g (milligram/gram)	% (percentage)	x 0.1
g/kg (gram/kilogram)	% (percentage)	x 0.1
°F (degrees Fahrenheit)	°C (degrees Celsius)	(°F-32) x 0.5556
°C (degrees Celsius)	°F (degrees Fahrenheit)	(°C x 1.8) + 32

TABLE 8. Weight equivalents.		
1lb	= 454g	= 0.454kg
1oz	= 28.4g	
1kg	= 100g	= 2.2lb
1g	= 1000mg	
1mg	= 1000µg	= 0.001g
1µg	= 0.001mg	= 0.000,0001g
1µg/g or 1mg/kg	= 1ppm	

out this need. All you need to know is your dog's body weight; the rest is easy. Look at the difference between an average 70 kilo adult bitch and a 100 kilo young male.

Feeding the Saint Bernard is not an exact science. You need to manage your dog. Watch how they develop and use your common sense. If your stud dog is going through an inactive period, does he need 6000 calories? If his weight increases and he looks too fat, reduce his food. Young dogs need careful nurturing to get to their optimum weight and condition. Brood bitches need careful feeding and Table 11 shows the energy requirement at different stages.

If you have an adult dog weighing 90 kilos and needing 3,500 kcal, how do you feed it 8,000

TABLE 9. Feeding dogs.

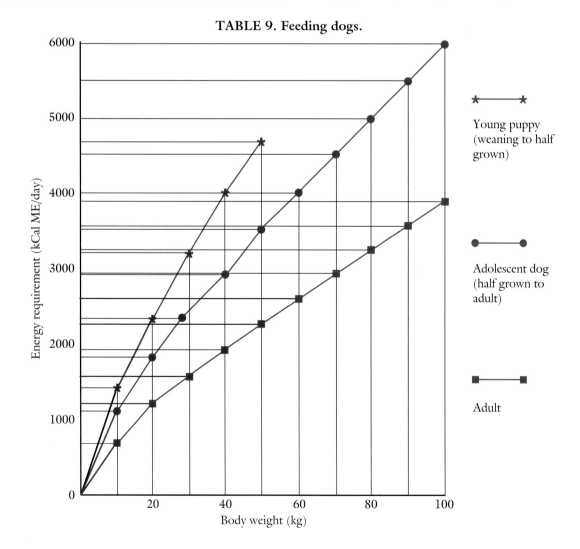

Young puppy (weaning to half grown)

Adolescent dog (half grown to adult)

Adult

calories from 12 weeks to 18 months? The answer is easy, 3 to 4 meals per day at 2,660 or 2,000 calories per meal. You need to work out how much suits your dog.

These meals need to be high in proteins and can be either raw meat or dry complete food. Personally we like to feed two meat meals and two milk and complete dry food per day. When the young dog has reached 9 months we generally start to reduce the meals to 3 per day and omit the milk. At 1 year the food is reduced down to two meals at 4,000 calories per meal. This requires approximately 5 lbs of tripe and 150 grams of junior-style complete dry food. When the dog is 18 months we generally have him or her on their adult diet. The food regime is then dependent on their status, i.e. stud, breed shows or just at home. As long as your food regime is balanced, your dog will be healthy. See Table 10.

You will see that by comparing Table 10 with Table 9 you can calculate whether your Saint is getting the nutrients needed to promote a healthy life.

We tend not to add supplements to our dogs' food. We believe that there are enough vitamins and nutrients in the food to meet the needs of our dogs. You can see by the tables (showing the constituents of the dry food) whether or not the vitamin protein mineral level is good enough for your Saint. Perhaps the only additive we use is SA37, a multi-vitamin supplement for a bitch in whelp of 'teenage' puppies, and we only use this on the young stock. We add gravy, cooked vegetables and eggs to our adult Saints' food.

FEEDING ROUTINE

The feeding regime is not written in tablets of stone. Your Saint will test your patience from time to time. A new puppy, separated form its siblings for the first time, may refuse food. A new owner can worry about this quite unnecessarily. If your new pup refuses food, take the food away. Never feed it by hand. You are asking for trouble in later life. A few days of missed food will soon convince your reluctant dog that food is not so bad after all and it will soon be eating with gusto. We frequently hear that people have difficulties in feeding. The Saint is a greedy dog and if there is one who will not eat it is either ill or has learnt that, by refusing its usual food, its owner will feed it treats or by hand. Be warned!

Adult Saints are happy with their routine once it is established. Woe betide you if you break it. Our Saints usually are looking for their food around 8.00 am and the cacophony of sound is deafening until the food arrives. Thereafter peace descends and contented snores emanate from the kennels until playtime. We use trivets to feed the dogs off

TABLE 10. Factors influencing energy needs of dogs.		
Life stage	Weeks	Energy need as factor of adult maintenance
Growth	Birth to half mature weight	x 2.2
	Half mature weight to maturity	x1.5
Gestation	1-6	x1
	6-9	x1.3
Lactation	1	x1.2
	peaks 3-4 weeks after whelping	x3.5
	6	x1.5
Work		x1.5 – 2.5
Temperature (°C)	-18°	x2
	1°	x1.5
	32°	x1.2

It is important to establish a routine when feeding your dog.   *Photo: Steph Holbrook.*

the ground. We believe it helps to develop neck muscles and to strengthen pasterns. More than once a flat-footed puppy has come up on its pasterns once the feeding off the ground starts. We start this system by placing the food bowl 6 inches off the ground, gradually raising the height to 2.5 feet. Our water bowls are also off the ground and this is a very comfortable way for our dogs to drink their water.

In conclusion, be careful with your Saint's food. A fat Saint will not live too long, and neither will a thin one. You need to manage your Saint's food and, if it looks as though it is gaining too much weight, reduce the food over a period of time until the weight gain has stopped. By the same token, if there appears to be a weight loss, do the reverse; however, in both circumstances, if the trends continue, check with your vet. It is known that some Saints develop intolerance to certain foods; you need therefore to check that such intolerance has not developed in your dog. We feel that well-bred dogs in general do not suffer from such maladies. However, some lines, perhaps not so well bred, can develop an inherent intolerance to normal foods. Buy your Saint from good breed lines, feed good food, and your Saint will give you much happiness and joy for many years.

HUSBANDRY

This section is for those who aspire to develop a bloodline and to build kennels. Most Saint owners are happy to own one Saint; however, some of us have moved on and started a kennel.

Saints are big, hairy, and messy! One or two in a home, in our opinion, is enough. We generally have two – one favourite who is never kennelled, and

then we give each of our nine Saints a turn in the house. With some of them it is a pleasure, with others it is a complete nuisance. You get the bin raider, the kitchen top-raider, the fridge raider and, worst of all, the pooper! Nevertheless, we give each a chance.

THE KENNELS

Our kennels are built around three enclosures. One large enclosure, with a shelter kennel for day use and a smaller, narrower, enclosure with three 8 x 6 stone-built kennels for night-time use, generally in the winter. Finally, we have a smaller pen with a shelter for the young pups and teenagers (that is for teenage dogs, not children!)

The stone kennels are constructed in blocks and plastered inside and outside. This aids cleaning. The doors are strong, with galvanised sheeting halfway up the door to prevent chewing. The windows are of safety glass. The floors are wooden and raised six inches off the ground. This gives a dry, draught-proof environment. In the winter we use blankets, which we buy cheaply, to give added comfort and warmth. Many people have different ideas on kennelling; these are our ideas which we have developed over time.

In our opinion, sturdy, stone-built homes are best suited to this heavy breed. Young and old saints can do prodigious amounts of damage to wooden kennels. While writing this chapter I found a spar of wood from the newly-refurbished shelter kennel in the long run. The spar was 4 foot long and 2 inches thick and had been ripped out of its place. The culprit is still a mystery.

Some people favour the new-style, chain-link, galvanised fencing and galvanised kennels. Personally, we feel these are soulless and cold places. Would you like to live in one? I think not. A pleasant wooden dog kennel can provide a warm place in winter and a cool place in the summer – or, from our experience, just a warm place for a very long winter, 11 months out of 12. It can be kept fresh by regular cleaning and it is easily replaced when bits get chewed off. It is frustrating to find bits chewed off – but, look at the positive side, it is helping to keep the dogs' teeth exercised. This is fine for the day kennel but for the night kennel stone is best. It should be said, however, that in the UK some authorities insist on block.

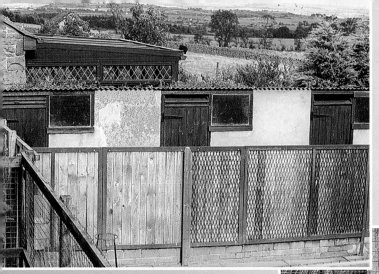
The Coatham kennels.
Photo: Mike Trafford.

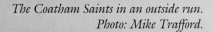
The Coatham Saints in an outside run.
Photo: Mike Trafford.

For the ground surface of the run we favour paving slabs. These provide a good strong surface that is easily kept clean.

The kennel surface needs to be kept clean and well-drained so that, in the most inclement weather, the surface is nice and dry. We feel that concrete is an unyielding surface: one of our smaller pens is of concrete and this always proves the most difficult to keep clean. The base should be well padded to prevent shrinkage and movement. A well-laid surface should last many years before unevenness occurs.

FENCING

The fencing round your kennels should be sturdy and well-built. You can have either the modern galvanised chain link or, as we have, weld mesh. You need strong fence posts set in concrete. We have just renewed some of our posts and fence bars after 17 years. If you use wooden posts you will

need to get used to the chewing marks which will appear. Nevertheless, whichever you use, you must make them escape-proof. I have seen a male Saint trying to scale a 7-foot high fence to get to a bitch in season. Your gates must be double-locked. Ideally a central gate system is best. You can separate your runs, and your dogs, each in their separate runs.

FOOD PREPARATION AND STORAGE

A separate food preparation area is a must for all kennels from the hygiene and convenience point of view. Your kitchen should have hot water and cooking facilities. The hot water is needed to wash your food bowls and food utensils. Food bowls must be kept very clean as infection can occur from dirty dishes. A separate food preparation area is now a mandatory requirement before a licence to breed can be issued in the UK.

Storage of food is vitally important and a fridge

and freezer are very necessary; you can sometimes purchase second-hand units. Some good sturdy bins are also useful for storing dry food.

This will prevent vermin from getting into the food bins. Other ideal equipment can be a mechanical can-opener, a second-hand washing machine (so your clothes do not look like a Saint is hanging off them after washing those blankets!) and a good pair of scales. You now have a well set-up kitchen.

WHELPING AREA

A separate whelping area is also very important as this provides a safe environment for whelping bitches and can also be used as an emergency room for a dog in trouble. The whelping room should be tiled and have a built-in whelping box. An ideal surface for the box is vinyl floor covering, which can be kept clean and disinfected during whelping. Size is not important for your kitchen but it is vitally important for your whelping box. A good size is 4 foot by 5 or 6 foot. Our box is built into the room and is large and airy.

HYGIENE

Cleanliness within your kennels is vital. You need to wash your kennels down at least once a week with a good disinfectant or bleach. Your pen surfaces should be cleaned each day with a good cleaner. Once a week you should bleach your runs. Always make sure your dogs are out of the way when bleaching and make sure all residues are cleaned away. You should be able to take your dog out of its kennel and into a show ring without too much bathing – that is the sign of a good, well-managed kennel.

I once judged a dog, some years ago, and shook the owner's hand; his hand was filthy and, when I looked at his dog, it was filthy too. It is sad to say that some dogs (and owners) can be smelt before they are seen. This would never happen in a good clean kennel environment.

RUNNING A STRING OF DOGS

Running a string of dogs is not easy. It requires dedication, patience and a great deal of time. If you are not prepared for this, you should not take the extra step and go beyond the one or two dog stage. Sadly, the residues from the people who think that they can take that step bedevil our breed. Running a kennel is expensive; you should not enter into this venture if your finances do not permit the outlay. Breeding Saints is not a financial venture which makes profit. We know that there are those who would disagree and say that the kennels should pay for themselves and make a profit. We disagree. Saints are not to be bred from as a money-making venture. This leads to bulk breeding, bad kennels, poor stock and a bulging Rescue. Your kennels should be your pride. They are the home of your dogs. If you would not live in them, why should your dogs?

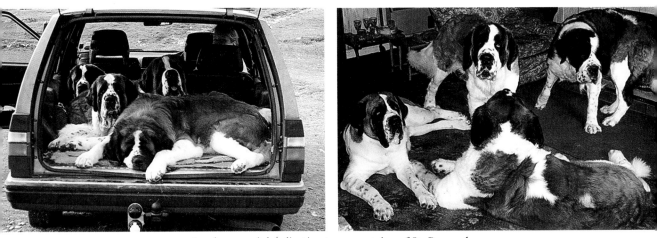

It takes a special dedication to run a string of St. Bernards.

5 THE BREED STANDARD DISCUSSED

When dog showing and breeding grew more popular as a pastime or hobby, it became necessary for every recognised breed to have an accepted formula, or blueprint of the ideal specimen to aspire to. This is the measure against which competing dogs can be evaluated in the show ring. These so-called blueprints were termed Breed Standards.

All judges, in whichever country they are judging, are obliged to judge dogs in the show ring against the relevant Standard for that breed, in that country. This means that a recognised Championship show judge in Britain who is invited to judge St. Bernards on the continent, perhaps in Germany, must be aware of and judge to the FCI Standard which is accepted as the St. Bernard Standard in Germany. If continental judges accept appointments to judge St. Bernards in the UK, it is expected that they will be aware of the Kennel Club Breed Standards for St. Bernards and judge accordingly.

In the United Kingdom the Kennel Club controls the Breed Standards, as do the governing bodies in several other countries. This is not the case in the United States where, as the Breed Standards remain the property of the parent breed Clubs, it is they who maintain ultimate control.

Many of the original Breed Standards in Britain were based on a scale of points, the various components of the dog bearing a certain value in points, their sum totalling one hundred. This is no longer the case with any British Standard. The old St. Bernard show standard carried the total of 40 points for the head, with the remaining 60 points from the remaining parts of the St. Bernard. This did not take into account such important qualities as balance. Movement under the old scales carried only 10 points, which is surprising, when a St. Bernard is supposed to be a working dog! For this reason, many people found these scales and points unacceptable.

ANALYSING THE STANDARDS

GENERAL APPEARANCE

UK **Well proportioned and of great substance.**

FCI **There are two varieties of the St. Bernard, the Smooth-Haired variety (double coat) and the Long-Haired variety (rough coat). Both varieties are of notable size and have a balanced, sturdy, muscular body with imposing head and alert facial expression. Important proportions: Ideal proportions for height to withers to body length (measured from the point of the shoulder to point of the ischium) 5:6).**

USA **Powerful, proportionately full figure, strong and muscular in every part, with powerful head and most intelligent expression. In dogs with a dark mask, the expression appears more stern, but never ill-natured.**

ABOVE: Am. Can. Ch. Stoan's Quincy Of Cabra.

LEFT: Ch. Snoshire Ritches Rich With Chandlimore:
Top winning St. Bernard in the UK 1999.
Photo: Russell Fine Art.

The old Kennel Club Breed Standard stated:
Expression should betoken benevolence, dignity
and intelligence. Movement is most important,
and St. Bernards have often failed in this respect,
the hind legs being especially faulty.

The old KC Standard has been included so that
readers can compare the old wording with the
current Standard for St. Bernards, published by the
UK Kennel Club. In our opinion, the old wording
and the attributes required by the FCI and AKC give
more detail of what is meant by "well proportioned
and of great substance". The UK standard gives no
mention of expression, whereas the FCI and AKC
both refer to expression: the FCI states an "alert"
facial expression, the AKC refers to a "most
intelligent expression".

We would take issue with the AKC, as I believe
the benevolent expression comes from the colour of
the eye; the darker the eye colour, the softer and
more benevolent the expression. The actual colour of
the mask does not make the St. Bernard look more
stern, in my opinion; however, a light, staring eye
does.

CHARACTERISTICS

UK Distinctly marked, large-sized, mountain
rescue dog.

FCI Friendly by nature. Temperament calm to
lively, watchful.

USA No comment on characteristics.

UK previous KC Standard. No comment on
characteristics.

We feel that the FCI Standard reflects the actual
personality of the dog, while the UK Kennel Club
deals more with the cosmetic features.

TEMPERAMENT

UK Steady, kindly, intelligent, courageous,
trustworthy and benevolent.

FCI Friendly by nature. Temperament calm to
lively.

ABOVE: Ch. Saranbeck Spruce: A bebevolent expression is typical of the breed, This dog has good bone, a level topline, and moves well. Photo: Deuchar Fawcett.

RIGHT: A good head of the 'English' type. This dog is eight months old.

USA No comment.

UK previous KC Standard. No mention of temperament.

HEAD AND SKULL

UK Large, massive circumference of skull being rather more than double its length. Muzzle short, full in front of eye and square at nose end. Cheeks flat, great depth from eye to lower jaw. Lips deep but not too pendulous. From nose to stop perfectly straight and broad. Stop somewhat abrupt and well defined. Skull broad, slightly rounded at top, with fairly prominent brow. Nose large and black with well developed nostrils.

FCI Head: Cranial region. Skull: Strong, broad, seen in profile and from front slightly rounded: sideways, it merges gently rounded into the strongly developed high cheekbones, falling away steeply towards the muzzle. Occipital bone only moderately pronounced. Supra-orbital ridges strongly developed. The frontal furrow, which rises at the forehead, gradually becomes less pronounced across the skull until it disappears when it reaches the occiput. The skin of the forehead forms folds over the eyes with coverage towards the frontal furrow. When the dog is

animated, the folds become more pronounced. When alert, the set-on of the ear and the top line of the skull appear in a straight line. Stop: Markedly pronounced.
Facial region. Muzzle: Short with slight groove, even in width. Nasal bridge straight. Length of muzzle shorter than its depth, measured at the root of the muzzle.
Nose: Black, broad and square. Nostrils well opened.

USA Like the whole body, very powerful and imposing. The massive skull is wide, slightly arched and the sides slope in a gentle curve into the very strongly developed, high cheekbones. Occiput only moderately developed. The supra-orbital ridge is very strongly developed and forms nearly a right angle with the horizontal axis of the head. Deeply embedded between the eyes and starting at the root of the muzzle, a furrow runs over the whole skull. It is strongly marked in the first half, gradually disappearing towards the base of the occiput. The lines at the side of the head diverge considerably from the outer corner of the eyes toward the back of the head. The skin of the forehead, above the eyes, forms rather noticeable wrinkles, more or less pronounced, which converge toward the furrow. Especially when the dog is in action, the wrinkles are more visible without in the least giving the

A balanced head in a Junior bitch.
Photo: Martin Leigh.

impression of morosity. Too strongly developed wrinkles are not desired. The slope from the skull to the muzzle is sudden and rather steep.

The muzzle is short, does not taper, and the vertical depth at the root of the muzzle must be greater than the length of the muzzle. The bridge of the muzzle is not arched, but straight; in some dogs, occasionally, slightly broken. A rather well-marked, shallow furrow runs from the root of the muzzle over the entire bridge of the muzzle to the nose. The flews of the upper jaw are strongly developed, not sharply cut, but turning in a beautiful curve into the lower edge, and slightly over-hanging. The flews of the lower jaw must not be deeply pendant. The teeth should be sound and strong and should meet in either a scissors or even bite, the scissors bite being preferable. The undershot bite, although sometimes found with good specimens, is not desirable.

Nose (Schwamm): Very substantial, broad, with wide-open nostrils, and, like the lips, always black.

UK previous KC Standard Large and massive, circumference of skull being rather more than double the length of the head from nose to occiput. Muzzle short, full in front of the eye, and square at the nose end. Cheeks flat; from nose to stop perfectly straight and broad. Stop somewhat abrupt and well defined. Skull broad, slightly rounded at the top, with somewhat prominent brow. Nose large and black, with well developed nostrils.

We feel the current UK Standard is somewhat short in requirements. The FCI has a fuller description of which specific attributes are desirable in the head and which are not. FCI desire the nostrils to be well opened. Flews which are deep and too pendulous are considered a fault, as in the UK and USA Standard. The FCI prefer the length of muzzle to be shorter than the depth. Some UK Saints do have over-developed flews and long ears which suggest more of a hound look, rather than a St. Bernard look. This attribute is difficult to breed out, as the occasional throwback comes along. All the Standards require a well-defined or abrupt stop.

EYES

UK Medium size, neither deep set or prominent, eye lids should be reasonably tight, without any excessive hair. Dark in colour and not staring. There should be no excessive loose wrinkle on brow which would detract from a healthy eye.

FCI Eyes: Medium size. Colour dark brown or hazel. Not too deep set, with friendly expression. Eyelids as close as possible. Complete pigment on eye rims. Natural lightness of lids desired. A tiny fold (angular "pouch") with only a little bit of the conjunctiva showing on lower lid permitted.

USA Set more to the front than the sides, are of medium size, dark brown, with intelligent, friendly expression, set moderately deep. The lower lids, as a rule, do not close completely and, if that is the case, form an angular wrinkle toward the inner corner of the eye. Eyelids which are too deeply pendant and show conspicuously the lachrymal glands, or a very red, thick haw, and eyes that are too light are objectionable.

Good pigmentation and depth of flews.

UK previous KC Standard Rather small and deep set, dark in colour, not too close together, the lower eyelid drooping so as to show a fair amount of haw at the inner corner; the upper eyelid falling well over the eye.

As we all became more knowledgeable about the health and welfare of dogs, it was becoming apparent that, sadly, some St. Bernards were afflicted with fairly severe eye problems. As breeders were endeavouring to breed to the previous Standard, it was more acceptable for Saints to have small, deep-set eyes. We now have evidence that some Saints with small, deep-set eyes suffered from hereditary faults known as entropion and ectropion. Both these conditions are extremely painful. In entropion, the upper eyelid turns inwards and the eyelashes actually rub and scratch the cornea, which can cause ulceration. When ectropion occurs, the lower eyelid turns inward and the lashes rub and scratch the eye. The Saint who suffers from ectropion can also have droopy eyes which can be exposed to infection.

As St. Bernard enthusiasts and responsible breeders, we all need to be aware of hereditary and painful conditions in our breed and aim to breed healthier stock. Breeders should avoid using bitches and stud dogs with obvious incorrect eye conditions, as these are hereditary and can be passed on to progeny. Judges have a responsibility not to place St.

Bernards with sore, incorrect eye attributes in top winning positions in the show ring.

Having judged on the continent and attended several Championship shows in Europe, I have found that the majority of Saints there seem to have a better-shaped eye than some of the British Saints; however, several have hard, staring eyes – not the soft, benevolent expression of the majority of Saints in Britain.

The current KC Standard encourages us to aspire toward a medium eye, rather than a deep-set eye, and to aim for less wrinkle on the brow and side folds, hopefully enabling the Saints to have a healthier eye.

EARS

UK Medium size, lying close to cheeks, not heavily feathered.

FCI Medium size, set on high and wide. Strongly developed burr at the base. Ear lobes pliable, triangular with the tip rounded off. The back edge stands off slightly, the front edge lies close fitting to the cheeks.

USA Of medium size, rather high set, with very strongly developed burr (Muschel) at the base. They stand slightly away from the head at the base, then drop with a sharp bend to the side and cling to the head, whereas the back edge may stand somewhat away from the head, especially when the dog is at attention. Lightly set ears, which at the base immediately cling to the head, give it an oval and too little marked exterior, whereas a strongly developed base gives the skull a squarer, broader and much more expressive appearance.

UK previous KC Standard No change in wording, as above.

We feel the UK Kennel Club Standard does not give sufficient detail regarding the actual set-on of the ear or the shape. Clearly, the FCI and AKC Standards give much greater detail of what are required as positive attributes.

47

Ch. Whaplode Unique showing a stunning head.

MOUTH

UK Jaws strong with a perfect, regular and complete scissor bite, i.e. upper teeth closely overlapping lower teeth and set square to the jaws.

FCI Lips: Edge of lips black. Flews of upper jaw strongly developed, pendulous, forming a wide curve towards the nose. Corner of mouth remains visible. Teeth: Strong, regular and complete scissor or pincer bite. Reverse scissor bite acceptable. Missing PM1 (premolar 1) tolerated.

USA Scissor or even bite, scissor preferable. The undershot bite is not desirable, the overshot bite is a fault. Black roof to the mouth desirable.

UK previous KC Standard Mouth level.

We feel the current KC Standard is an improvement on the older version, as it defines a scissor bite and suggests that strong jaws are important. Although the FCI and the AKC refer to the cosmetic features of the muzzle such as flews on the upper and lower jaw, there is no reference to the bone structure of the jaws, which we feel is of importance. Construction

of the St. Bernard head is the framework on which the other features such as the amount of skin, eye colour and formation, and markings on the face, have their role in the appearance of the dog. Without strong jaws to enable the St. Bernard to chew his food, the cosmetic attributes are not as important as the structure. For example, a St. Bernard with wonderful, benevolent expression and dark eye who can clearly see and smell his food but has difficulty eating it due to weak jaws or poor teeth is not fulfilling the attributes for a healthy dog, let alone a show dog.

NECK

UK Long, thick, muscular, slightly arched, dewlap well developed.

FCI Strong, dewlap not too exaggerated.

USA Set high, very strong and in action is carried erect. Otherwise horizontally or slightly downward. The junction of head and neck is distinctly marked by an indentation. The nape of the neck is very muscular and rounded at the sides which makes the neck appear rather short. The dewlap of throat and neck is well pronounced; too strong development, however, is not desirable.

UK previous KC Standard Lengthy, thick and muscular, and slightly arched with dewlap well developed.

Having observed numerous St. Bernards, as well as other dogs, move on and off the leash at different speeds, we wish to take issue with the AKC in their Standard which requires the neck to be carried erect when in action. When St. Bernards are off the leash or moved on a loose leash, the moving neck contributes towards the kinetic balance of the dog. In my opinion, when the dog is 'strung up' on the leash, this alters his movement and his balance. When dogs move naturally, they do look ahead but the neck is gently moving with the rhythm of the dog. The St. Bernard which has his head forcibly held up on the move alters his movement accordingly. Good necklines merge gradually with strong withers at the base of the neck. If the dog's neck does not feel comfortable when he or she moves, the centre of gravity may not be right for the Saint and his locomotion will not be correct, as he alters the gait instinctively. This is well documented by the American author and lecturer on animal gait, Rachel Page Elliott.

FOREQUARTERS

UK **Forequarters: Shoulders broad and sloping, well up at withers. Legs straight, strong in bone, of good length.**

FCI **Forequarters: General: Stance rather broad, straight and parallel seen from the front. Shoulders: Muscular shoulder-blade oblique, well attached to the chest wall. Upper Arm: The same length or only slightly shorter than the shoulder blade, angle between the shoulder blade and upper arm not too blunt. Elbow: Well fitting. Forearm: Straight heavy-boned, tautly muscled.**

USA **Forearms: Very powerful and extraordinarily muscular. Forelegs: Straight and strong.**

UK previous KC Standard: **As above, no change.**

St. Bernards can have problems moving when the shoulder, the scapula bone, is incorrectly placed in relation to the humerus. The shoulder blade has a lot of mobility as partner in the action of the upper arm. This serves as a lever in lifting and transporting the central body forward as smoothly as possible. The trapezius and rhomboidus muscles, along with the

ligaments and tendons, attach on to the skeleton of the St. Bernard structure, establishing the boundaries within which the scapula is positioned against the chest wall. Muscles as well as bone structure have a part to play in the functioning of the dog. Shoulders must not be too straight or over-angulated, as this affects the gait of the dog.

BODY

UK **Back broad, straight, ribs well rounded. Loin wide, very muscular. Chest wide and deep, but never projecting below the elbows.**

FCI **General: General appearance imposing and balanced. Top line: Withers well defined. Straight from withers to loin. Rump falls away gently and merges with root of tail. Back: Broad, strong and firm. Chest: Brisket moderately deep with well-sprung ribs, but not reaching below the elbows. Belly and Lower Line: Slight tuck up towards rear.**

USA **Back: Very broad, perfectly straight as far as the haunches, from there gently sloping to the rump, and merging imperceptibly into the root of the tail. Chest: Very well arched, moderately deep, not reaching below the elbows.**

UK previous KC Standard **As current Standard**

The KC, FCI and AKC seem to agree on these points. The AKC requires slight tuck-up and the FCI requires the belly distinctly set off from the powerful loin section. All Standards dislike the chest projecting below the elbows.

*A youngster showing good bone.
Photo: Martin Leigh.*

Am. Ch. Cache Retreat Academy: The typical proportions of an American St. Bernard. This typey bitch compiled an outstanding record in the show ring.

HINDQUARTERS

UK Legs heavy in bone, hocks well bent, thighs very muscular.

FCI General: Hindquarters muscular with moderate angulation. Seen from the back, hind legs parallel and not too close together. Upper Thigh: Strong, muscular with broad buttocks. Stifle: Well angulated, turning neither in nor out. Lower Thigh: Slanting and rather long. Hock Joints: Slightly angulated and firm. Hock: Straight and parallel when seen from behind.

USA Hindquarters well developed. Legs very muscular. Hocks of moderate angulation. Dewclaws are not desired; if present, they must not obstruct gait.

UK previous KC standard As current Standard.

The FCI Standard is much more detailed than the UK or AKC, which is useful for the breeders and judges in providing extra guidance as to what the required attributes are. The hindquarters of St. Bernards have not always been as sturdy as they could have been – finer bone and cow-hocks being of particular concern.

FEET

UK Large, compact with well-arched toes. Dewclaws removed.

FCI Pasterns: Vertical when seen from the front and at a slight angle when seen from the side. Forefeet: Broad, tight, with strong well-arched toes. Hindfeet: Broad, tight with strong well-arched toes. Dewclaws tolerated as long as they do not hinder movement.

Ch. Saranbeck Smuggler's Gold: This is an excellent specimen of the breed. A superb bitch, full of quality. She has terrific substance, yet retains feminine attributes. Note the density of bone, good angulation and correct set-on of tail. Photo: Hartley.

Ch. Whaplode Be Our William:
British breed recordholder.
Photo: David Dalton.

Ch. Coatham Good News For Wyandra: A balanced
dog with well laid-back shoulders and level topline.
Photo: David Dalton.

USA Feet: broad with strong toes, moderately closed, and with rather high knuckles. The so-called dewclaws which sometimes occur on the inside of the hind legs are imperfectly developed toes. They are of no use to the dog and are not taken into consideration when judging. They may be removed by surgery.

UK previous KC Standard **As current Standard.**

An area which none of the Standards mentions is the importance for large dogs like St. Bernards of having good, strong, spongy pads. If dogs have poor pads, then their 'shock absorbers' are not serving the purpose intended. St. Bernards with cat-like feet look much better than long, hare-feet, which are undesirable.

TAIL

UK **Set on rather high, carried low when in repose; when excited or in motion should not curl over back.**

FCI **Set on broad and strong. Tail long and heavy. The last vertebra reaching at least to the hocks. When in repose the tail hangs straight down or may turn gently upward in the lower third. When animated, it is carried higher.**

USA **Starting broad and powerful directly from the rump, is long, very heavy, ending in a powerful tip. In repose it hangs straight down, turning gently upward in the lower third only, which is not considered a fault. In a great many specimens, the tail is carried with the end slightly bent and therefore hangs down in the shape of an 'f'. In action, all dogs carry the tail more or less turned upwards. However, it may not be carried too erect or by any means rolled over the back. A slight curling of the tip is sooner admissible.**

UK previous KC Standard **Slight change only.**

Gay tails are considered a fault in most countries. The tail is one of the ways in which a dog communicates. If a St. Bernard has the majority of attributes required to comply with the Standard and is given a lower place, or not placed, due to having a gay tail, in my opinion this is fault judging. The dog should be judged holistically with the gay tail being taken into account, then assessed for a place along with all the other attributes. The gay tail does spoil the kinetic balance when the dog is in full locomotion.

GAIT/MOVEMENT

UK **Easy extension, unhurried or smooth, capable of covering difficult terrain.**

Am. Ch. High Chateau's Yuri; This dog is having a big influence on the breed in the USA.

FCI Gait – harmonious striding movement with good hind drive. Front and hind feet move forward in a straight line.

USA No comment on movement.

UK previous KC Standard No comment on movement.

My comment on movement is that some exhibitors move their dogs far too quickly; this is not necessary. The actual KC wording for the UK St. Bernards is "unhurried or smooth" movement. Dogs tend to be moved at a more gentle pace on the continent.

COAT

UK In roughs, dense and flat, rather fuller round neck, thighs and tails well-feathered. In smooths, close and hound-like, slight feathering on thighs and tail.

FCI Smooth Haired Variety (Stockhaar, double coat): Top coat dense, smooth, close lying and coarse, plentiful undercoat. Buttocks lightly breached. Tail covered with dense coat. Long Haired Variety (rough coat): Top coat plain or medium length with plentiful undercoat. Over the haunches and rump usually somewhat wavy. Front legs feathered. Buttocks well breached. Short hair on face and ears. Bushy tail.

USA Coat – very dense, short-haired (Stockhaarig) lying smooth, tough, without,

however, feeling rough to the touch. The thighs are slightly bushy. The tail at the root has longer and denser hair which gradually becomes shorter toward the tip. The tail appears bushy, not forming a flag.

UK previous KC Standard In Rough specimens should be dense and flat, rather fuller round the neck; thighs well feathered. In Smooth specimens, it should be close and hound-like, slightly feathered on thighs and tail.

Our only comment is that there is a variety of rough-textured coats – all roughs are not the same. This also applies to smooths. Some are like Labrador-textured coats, others are slightly longer.

COLOUR

UK Orange, mahogany-brindle, red-brindle. White patches on body of any above named colours. Markings: white muzzle, white blaze on face, white collar, white chest, white forelegs, feet and end of tail, black shadings on face and ears.

FCI Ground colour white with smaller or larger reddish-brown markings going to reddish-brown blanket covering back and flanks (blanketed dogs). A broken reddish-brown blanket is of equal value. Red-brindle permissible. Brownish-yellow tolerated. Dark brown shadings on head desirable. Slight black shadings on body tolerated. Markings: Chest, feet, tip of tail, muzzle band, blaze and patch on neck must be white. Desirable – white collar, symmetrical dark mask.

USA White with red or red with white, the red in its various shades; brindle patches with white markings. The colours red and brown-yellow are of entirely equal value. Necessary markings are: White chest, feet and tip of tail, noseband, collar or spot on the nape; the latter and blaze are very desirable. Never of one colour or without white. Faulty are all other colours, except the favourite dark shadings on the head (mask) and ears. One distinguishes between mantle dogs and splash-coated dogs.

UK previous KC Standard As above – no change.

In Britain, some St. Bernards with white faces would be classed as a miss-mark, whereas on the continent and in America these specimens can be shown. White patches on ears are also undesirable in the UK.

SIZE

UK Taller the better, provided symmetry is maintained.

FCI Height at shoulder of the dog 27.5 inches minimum, of the bitch 25.5 inches. Female animals are of finer and more delicate build.

USA Minimal height – dogs 70 cm, bitches 65 cm. Maximum height – dogs 90 cm, bitches 80 cm. Dogs which exceed the maximum height will not be penalised, provided their general appearance is balanced and their movement correct.

FAULTS

UK Any departure from the foregoing points should be considered a fault and the seriousness with which the fault should be regarded should be in exact proportion to the degree. Note: Male animals should have two apparently normal testicles fully descended into the scrotum.

Reproduced by kind permission of the English Kennel Club.

FCI (Effective from 1st January 1993) Every departure from the foregoing points should be considered a fault which will be assessed according to the degree of departure from the Standard.
Lack of sexual features.
Unbalanced general appearance.
Strong wrinkles on head, excessive dewlap.
Muzzle too short or too long.
Flews on the lower jaw turning outward.
Under or overshot bite.
Missing teeth other than PM1 (premolar 1).

The white-faced dog (middle) would be faulted in the UK, but not in Europe or the USA.

Low set on ears.
Light eyes.
Entropion, ectropion.
Eyelids too loose.
Sway back or roach back.
Rump higher than withers or falling away.
Tail carried curled over back.
Crooked or severely turned out front legs.
Poorly angulated, bowed or cow-hocked hindquarters.
Faulty movement.
Curly coat.
Incomplete or totally absent pigment on nose, around nose, on lips and eyelids.
Faulty markings (e.g. white with reddish-brown ticks).
Weak temperament, aggressiveness.

DISQUALIFYING FAULTS
Coat totally white or totally reddish-brown.
Coat of a different colour.
Wall eye.
N.B. Male animals should have two apparently normally developed testicles fully descended into the scrotum.

USA Considered as Faults: are all deviations from the Standard, as for instance, a sway back and a disproportionately long back, hocks too bent, straight hindquarters, upward growing hair in spaces between the toes, out at elbows, cow-hocks and weak pasterns.

(Reproduced by kind permission of the American Kennel Club.)

6 BREEDING ST. BERNARDS

Having acquired an adorable, fluffy St. Bernard puppy and managed to rear the bitch without too many problems, the owners then decide to visit a dog show. Often they engage in conversation with a variety of novice exhibitors as well as breeders. Someone suggests to the pet owner to give the dog shows a try. This they do, win a prize, and feel that it would be a great idea to have a litter of puppies.

Another reason why some people consider having a litter of puppies is that they mistakenly think they will make a fortune. Let us say this is entirely the wrong reason for having a litter – and you certainly will not make a fortune!

We have also been told by an enquirer wanting the use of one of our stud dogs, that letting their Saint have puppies would be good for the children. This would teach them about birth, attachment and the care and development of the puppies. This seemed fine until the comment was made that when all the puppies were sold, the children could all have brand new mountain bikes. Another prospective 'breeder' told us openly that they wanted a litter to pay off their credit card. The list goes on.

We feel that the only valid reason for having a litter of St. Bernard puppies is that your bitch has something special, some qualities to contribute towards the breed. Many St. Bernard breeders, lots of whom are still successful today, started with indifferent stock, gradually improving it with each generation. The days when mainly one or two kennels kept a predominance of male Champions

Many St. Bernard owners are tempted to breed from their dogs – but the potential pitfalls are all too many.
Photo courtesy: Judy Teniswood.

for stud, where the majority of breeders went to have their bitches mated, have gone.

APPRAISING THE BITCH

When contemplating breeding from the St. Bernard bitch, do try to be as honest and objective as possible. Unless you are prepared to be constructively critical, the fact of being 'bitch-blinded' could have an influence upon the progeny which is detrimental to the breed. In our opinion, the bitch needs to be sound in mind as well as body – free from any major faults.

The bitch should be typical of the breed, from proven stock and with a good temperament. She does not have to be a top-class winner, but sound. You will find that, for whatever reason, top Champion bitches do not always have the best quality puppies; it is often a litter sister who does not have all the qualities of her sister that proves to be the better producer of quality St. Bernards. To quote from the writer and show judge Andrew Brace: "The best sort of brood bitch is one that has a body of a charwoman and the face of a lady!"

TRACING PEDIGREES

In our opinion, dog breeding is a combination of knowledge, art, science and a modicum of luck, as well as the irrepressible optimism of the St. Bernard enthusiast. Remember, the perfect St. Bernard has not yet been bred and this is what the majority of caring breeders are aspiring to achieve – the St. Bernard which has all the attributes of the 'perfect' St. Bernard.

The Breed Standards were discussed in the preceding chapter, so these are the required guidelines which breeders are striving to meet. When studying a pedigree, it is helpful being able to recall the attributes of the ancestors of the bitch, as this enables you to focus on complementing attributes in the possible stud dog. If, as a novice, you have no idea about the history and qualities of ancestors, then you should be prepared to carry out some research and find out all you can about the dogs featured in the pedigree. Senior breeders should have first-hand knowledge of these St. Bernards and be willing to share their perceptions with you. Lots of senior breeders will probably have collections of photographs and be willing to show them to you.

Remember to ask about the personality of the Saints, as well as type, strain, movement, structure and temperament. Enquire if any litter siblings did any winning or produced winning progeny. Tracing through a pedigree can be really fascinating. Discussing the names on the paper with knowledgeable breeders and judges brings them to life. With time and experience you will learn to be able to 'read' a pedigree, being able to recall the dogs. Through current technology a lot of St. Bernards who are now sadly deceased had their pride of place recorded on videos at Crufts and various Club Championship Shows, so do ask around to see if any of these are available. If someone is good enough to loan a treasured photograph or video, please ensure its safe return.

Some top winners are what are known as 'one-offs'. This is when they do exceptionally well in the ring but never produce as good as themselves. Invariably, they come from a pedigree which is a mish-mash of different bloodlines and strains, with no dominating line or ancestors. The majority of current lines in the UK can be traced back to Cornagarth, Burtonswood, Bernmont, Whaplode, Snowranger, Coatham, Lindenhall, Swindridge, Marlender, Saranbeck, Schnozzer and Finetime.

If you feel your own bitch is not really good enough to be bred from, or has a pedigree which is less than promising, it would be better to rule out mating this bitch and look around for a bitch specifically as a brood bitch.

A FEW WORDS ABOUT GENES

To understand breeding, some knowledge of genes proves helpful. Unfortunately genetics is an extremely complicated science on which there are lengthy, appropriate books to study. Some important points will be examined to raise awareness of the 'dominant' and the 'recessive' genes. Breeders who breed from common sense and their own personal observations may well breed fine dogs, but their experience will improve if there is an understanding of why faults and virtues have been perpetuated.

The founder of modern genetics was Gregor Johann Mendel. The importance of Mendel's work only came to be recognised after his death. Interestingly, like Bernard de Menthon, founder of the Hospice, Gregor Mendel turned to religion and entered the Augustinian Monastery at Brno as a novice and was ordained priest in 1847. For several years he attended the University of Vienna before returning to his beloved monastery. He became Abbot between 1857 and 1868 and worked on his experiments on peas in the monastery garden. Mendel discovered the laws of heredity and how characteristics are transmitted.

In the dog, there are 76 sets of chromosomes, 38 from each parent. Each chromosome in turn consists of thousands of genes threaded out in a specific way, rather like a string of beads. When cells divide and reproduce themselves, these genes do so in the most amazingly exact way. Every living cell has a data bank for the DNA, the blueprints of life. Geneticists calculate that there might be one mistake in one single gene for every million copies! Genes use four sites, or states, commonly referred to as A, T, C and G for their data bank. The common scientific name for a chain is a 'polymer'.

The chemicals which make up the genes A, T, C and G are known as nucleotides which come in four-state information technology chains named polynucleotides. The polynucleotides pass information from one generation to another, in the form of deoxyribonucleic acid, more commonly known as DNA. This information is stored in the memory of germ cells, eggs and sperm, reproduced millions of times over as cells multiply, thus reproducing the St. Bernard puppy and keeping it going into adulthood.

Genes are classified as 'dominant' and 'recessive'. Breeders need to be aware of the dominant-recessive relationship, because the recessive characteristics of these genes can suddenly appear in future generations, although they have probably been masked by the dominant gene and did not show. The genetic influence upon behaviour is more difficult to understand than the genetic influence on morphology, as many more genes are responsible for behaviour, while coat colour might be under the control of a few genes only.

Recessive Genes Recessive genes can skip one or more generations; they will not appear unless there is an identical recessive gene from each parent. Only a relatively small number of the progeny will carry the trait, and only a dog which has the recessive gene in a double dose will show the characteristic.

Considerable research should be undertaken examining family pedigrees. This is Ch. Coatham Praise Be Smooth, grandmother to the puppies featured below.

Coatham Heaven Blest, mother of the puppies featured below.

Four-day-old puppies

56

Dogs which have only one recessive determiner will not show the character or trait, as it is masked by the dominant gene. When the recessive gene appears in a double dose, it cannot produce a dominant gene.

An example of a recessive gene is if a dog or bitch has one brown leg at the front; the progeny can produce all their puppies in consequent litters with white chest and clear white front legs. It can be several generations before one puppy in a litter from two correctly marked parents can throw a puppy with one brown foreleg.

Dominant Genes Unlike recessive genes, dominant genes do not skip a generation. A large number of the progeny affected by those that show the traits can carry them. The dominant gene traits can usually be seen.

To make matters more complicated, not all genes are wholly dominant or wholly recessive. Some are more dominant than others and vice versa, for example, coat colour can still be dominant but not shown.

Matings will not always produce genes paired up in averages as expected. The recessive gene, if not fully recessive, can show itself to lesser or greater degree in combination than the dominant gene. A large number of progeny have to be produced in order to establish an average. Other factors or traits may be due to multiple genes or polygenes, not merely Mendelian dominant or recessive genes.

For St. Bernards to have female progeny, the sex cells must be XX, which is one X chromosome from the mother (the dam) and the other X chromosome from the father (sire). The male sperm carries the X or the Y chromosome, but not both, so it is the male who determines the female as well as male progeny. Male St. Bernards are thus XY chromosomes.

Lethal Genes: Lethal genes are recessive. The following are some of the examples of lethal genes: Cleft palate, Haemophilia, Wall eye.

Semi-lethal genes: Bilateral cryptorchids, Entropion, Ectropion. Some abnormal whelpings can be hereditary.

Selective breeding of St. Bernards is not an exact

The breeder seeks to establish a similarity of type within their line. This is Ch. Coatham Suffragette and her son Ch. Coatham Good News for Wyandra.

science. It is a precarious balancing act which brings together a highly selective gathering of genes from the available gene pool, so care should be taken to select healthy St. Bernards with a good temperament who meet the required attributes of the Breed Standard. Environment can also have an external influence on how the St. Bernard develops, so this needs to be taken into account, as well as the biological and genetic knowledge.

THE PRACTICALITIES OF BREEDING
Introducing a new litter of puppies into the world demands careful thought, time, money, dedication and, most importantly, responsibility. For at least two months constant love, care and management must be devoted to the bitch and her progeny.

Questions which ought to be addressed are: Do you have an appropriate place in which the St. Bernard bitch can whelp? Remember that with a large dog, there can be a great deal of mess when the bitch whelps. Is the place you have considered effective for the puppies to grow and develop in peace? St. Bernard puppies require a great deal of

The next generation: Ch. Coatham Good News for Wyandra and Coatham Saxon Monarch.

peace to be able to sleep without too much disturbance. Puppies are NOT toys; they require handling and nurturing, but are not to be the subject of curiosity by all the neighbourhood and its children! If and when the litter arrives, do you have any guarantees that you can sell the puppies? You do need to have some potential homes before you mate the bitch since, if you are a novice breeder, it is unlikely that you will have a queue of would-be St. Bernard enthusiasts banging on your door, as you will not have built up a reputation.

Being stuck with a litter of eight or nine St. Bernards who are eating large quantities of food by eight weeks of age, is no fun. What should have been a pleasurable experience can turn into a nightmare, for the puppies as well as yourselves. You must endeavour to ensure that these bundles of fur do receive loving, caring, responsible homes where they will be looked after properly. Sometimes a puppy will go off to what is considered to be a desirable home, only to return two or three weeks later when the people have changed their minds. You must be willing to take the puppy back.

Sadly, far too many breeders will not accept any responsibility for the puppies once they have been sold. All too often, they become another St. Bernard welfare problem, as the hard-working dog lovers who run and help with the St. Bernard rescue take the puppy in, thus increasing the rescue statistics. This is not good breeding practice and certainly not the attitude of a genuine dog lover.

Although a remote shed with adjoining run is suitable for an adult St. Bernard, it is not appropriate for a first-time St. Bernard mum, who needs tender loving care. A suitable place would be a utility room or conservatory (if it is not too hot) for mother and babies to have reassurance and to be near the family's comings and goings, yet spacious enough for the bitch and her babies to be left in peace.

SELECTING THE STUD

You will need to select carefully a stud dog for your bitch. Meticulously analyse your own bitch. Which attributes need to be improved? What are the worst faults in your bitch? Will these faults be recessive or dominant genes coming through into the next generation of St. Bernard puppies? Examine the bitch, keeping the Breed Standard in mind. Does your bitch have balance? In your opinion, does she fulfil the requirements of the Breed Standard? Write down her negative attributes as well as the positive qualities. If the negative attributes outweigh the positive, then ask yourself if it is a good idea to breed from this bitch.

Look for the points in the stud dog where he excels and see if these complement your bitch. Do not fall into the trap of thinking a St. Bernard dog with a broad over-done head may compliment your fine, narrow-headed Saint. Never breed extremes and opposites, but look for examples of the desired head. Once you have identified a few possible suitors, look at their breeding. Ask stud dog owners if they would object to you having a look at the dog's pedigree. Endeavour to look at other progeny which the stud dog has sired; does it have soundness and personality conducive with the line and strain, qualities which reflect the Breed Standard. Carry out as much research as possible. Do not be tempted to ask to use the St. Bernard down the road, just because it is near; the dog could have a variety of unwanted traits.

*Coatham Smooth Agent: Sire
of Coatham Smooth Liaison.*

Having obtained a few pedigrees, photographs, etc., compare these with the pedigree of your bitch, endeavouring to see if some of the ancestors match up – in other words, do some of the same ancestors appear on both pedigrees? If so, try to find out more about these St. Bernards. This is considered to be looking for line breeding in the pedigrees.

THE MALE ORGANS

Having considered the attributes of the stud dog, we will consider his reproductive organs:-

The Prostate Just below the bladder is situated an important gland known as the prostate gland. This is a secondary sex gland developed in the dog, which produces the bulk of semen. Semen fluid is a greyish milky white colour and when fresh is odourless. The purpose of semen fluid is to flush the sperm along to their journey's end. Continuing from the prostate gland is the urethra, which is a tubular passage connecting the prostate gland to the penis. This passage is used for urine and seminal fluid.

The Scrotum The scrotum is a pouch of skin situated between the thighs and this is divided into two separated compartments where the two testicles are descended. The testicles can differ in size. A hormone known as testosterone is secreted in the testicles which is responsible for the development of the male dog. Spermatozoa are formed and secretions of fluid protect and nourish the sperm until they are required. Ducts leave the testicles and join the main organ, the vas deferens, which connects the urethra at the opposite end.

The Penis The penis continues down from the urethra and is constructed with erectile tissue. This has a bulbous enlargement at the base which contains a small bone. The tissue is covered by the prepuce, forming a sheath. When mating occurs, a reflex action is caused by pressure on the penis and the bulb at the base becomes engorged with blood. This then swells to about five times its normal size and becomes three times the size of the penis. During mating, the contents of only one testicle are used at a time, the semen being pumped into the vagina in spurts.

Spermatozoa Spermatozoa possess astonishing mobility. A sperm consists of a head, body and tail. By their long tails, sperm can reach their objective, the ova of the bitch, in a matter of twenty-five seconds. It is the semen fluid which helps flush the healthy sperm along to their goal. In one mating, millions of sperms are released. The male dog is not responsible for the number of puppies in a litter; however, he is responsible for the sex of the puppies.

A dog which has not been used for a long period produces a variety of sperm, some of which will be aged and degenerating. He may also produce some immature sperm. A stud dog used regularly will vary in time as to how long it takes the spermatozoa to be replaced; this can lead to a lower sperm count.

The Testes The testicles in the male dog generally descend into the scrotum just before the birth. The male pup's brain is masculinized by male sex hormones. Testosterone has a dramatic effect upon the pup's neonatal brain and subsequent surge of sex hormone at puberty. Spermatozoa thrive in the scrotum due to the difference in temperature to the rest of the dog's body. When both testicles have descended into the scrotum, the St. Bernard is considered to be 'entire'. If for any reason the testicles do not descend into the scrotum, remaining in the abdomen, no spermatozoa will be produced. Should this occur, it is better to seek veterinary advice, thus avoiding problems later.

THE BROOD BITCH

Ideally, this bitch should be a paragon of the breed, free of as many faults as possible and with excellent temperament. The foundation of any St. Bernard kennel is a good brood bitch. Since fertility is strongly inherited, it is important that the St. Bernard bitch is from strong, healthy stock, preferably from quality breeding lines.

FEMALE ANATOMY

When genuinely interested in showing or breeding it is essential in our opinion to have an awareness of the anatomy of the dog and bitch and where the organs are within the St. Bernard.

The ovaries These produce the female sex cells known as ova. The vagina, the uterus and the uterine tubes are the passages through which the spermatozoa pass on the way to fertilise the ova. The ovaries are situated inside the bitch's abdomen, high up behind her last ribs, and just below the kidneys. The right ovary lies above the duodenum (small intestine) and the left one near the colon (large intestine). Each ovary in a St. Bernard would be slightly bigger than a fat broad bean. This is covered by a capsule, having a slit on one side which has a spongy edge known as the fimbria. From this tissue a tube known as the fallopian tube runs in a roundabout course across each capsule, continuing to the upper end of each horn of the uterus. The ovaries produce the ova.

The Uterus The uterus itself is shaped like a letter Y, so that it is quite different in shape from the human uterus, which tends to be pear-shaped. The first part of the Y is approximately one fifth of the length of the two extending horns, which carry the St. Bernard whelps. The whelps from both horns have to pass through the body of the uterus during birth. Until a bitch is in whelp, the uterus is comparatively small; however, when in whelp, the horns of the uterus fold back, the ends are then at the rear of the bitch. The St. Bernard puppies are carried in what could be described as two layers, one above the other.

The bottom of the uterus is known as the cervix, which is the neck of the womb; this is tightly closed except during the bitch's season or during parturition (birth). The cervix extends into the vagina.

The Vagina The vagina in a St. Bernard is very long, ending in the vulva, which is the external genital part. There are often variations in the angle of the vagina from the vulva upwards in St. Bernard bitches. Occasionally there might be a constriction. In cases where this inclination is gradual, there may be more difficulty in mating.

The Vulva The vulva is situated below the anus and contains erectile fluid in a bitch who has had a season. The vulva enlarges during the season. The bitch can protrude her vulva to facilitate the entry of the dog's penis during mating. The vulva also enlarges for a whelp to be born.

OESTRUS

This is the period during the season when the St. Bernard bitch will accept the male. By this period in her season the colour or discharge should have gradually diminished and the vulva also becomes softer and spongy. This phase can very considerably between four and twenty four days. It can vary from one St. Bernard to another and can last up to three days in larger breeds. The bitch's behaviour changes during this period. Blood tests can now be undertaken to measure the level of oestrogen in the system to determine when ovulation is taking place. Oestrogen is a female hormone which male dogs can detect when a bitch in season urinates. This gives a male dog the message that the bitch may be ready to accept his advances and his own male hormone, testosterone, stimulates the hypothalamus to secrete fluid, releasing factors which cause the pituitary gland to increase luteinizing hormone back to the testicles.

METOESTRUS

This follows oestrus, if conception has taken place. The duration is two months. If there is no pregnancy, the changes in the uterus still continue. During this period the size of the vulva can return to almost normal. Progesterone, another female hormone, has a surge at this time; this can have a 'sedative effect' upon the bitch. Indeed, some St. Bernards can appear to become depressed for two months. They separate meat from their biscuit, often leaving the biscuit, a fondness for brown bread often becomes apparent. They will sometimes guard toys, slippers or something soft which they focus upon. Progesterone, like oestrogen, influences behaviour by acting upon the brain of the St. Bernard.

ANOESTRUS

This is a period of 'resting' which can last upwards of three months and then the menstrual cycle commences again. These cycles are controlled by various glands and hormones. Environment, nutrition, temperature, health and light also have an influence upon the cycle.

TYPES OF BREEDING

Outcrossing This is where you mate a dog and bitch with no common ancestors for at least five generations. This is generally resorted to when some particular feature from another strain is required, or perhaps to correct a fault which has crept in either in physical characteristics or in temperament. This type of mating may produce a varied litter in which the puppies are rather uneven. There may be a 'flyer'; however, the chances of this are small. Should you produce a 'flyer', the likelihood is that any offspring may lack the ability to reproduce their own attributes consistently, unless mated back to a dog or bitch of their bloodlines which has the dominant genes for the features required.

A quick rule of thumb which may be helpful is, if offspring display a characteristic which is not visible in either parent, then this is a recessive gene. For example, if both parents have dark eyes and noses, and then produce progeny with light eyes and dudley noses, then in the background of both parents there must be recessive genes for light eyes and dudley noses. Subsequently, if any of this progeny with the light eyes and dudley nose is then mated to a similar St. Bernard with light eyes and nose, this bitch will not produce dark-eyed Saints.

Line Breeding This is where a St. Bernard dog and bitch are mated which have one or more common ancestors quite close up on the pedigree. It is considered that this type of breeding should produce relative consistency, which should endorse both the virtues and the faults of the dogs which repeatedly appear in the puppies' pedigree.

The term 'line breeding' is used to cover the breeding back to an outstanding dog in the pedigree of one's bitch, or to close relatives such as grandfather, half-brother, cousin, where the gene make-up should be similar. A line-bred stud dog should usually be more dominant than one resulting from more distant breeding. Remember that faults as well as virtues can be doubled up when line breeding, so endeavour to avoid serious, undesirable faults. Line breeding is widely used in all livestock breeding, especially in herds of pedigree cattle, some dating back to the 1880s. It is an acceptable way of retaining attributes and, hopefully, improving upon previous generations. Senior St. Bernard breeders may well keep records and photographs of dogs featured a few generations back in the pedigree. We are privileged to have shared our lives for over thirty years with St. Bernards. Some of our current Coatham stock look and have similar personalities to our original dogs which were direct descendants from Cornagarth and Burtonswood. Over the years we have carried on line breeding, with the occasional out-cross to

The fruits of a successful breeding programme – mother, father and son. They are Ch. Whaplode Be Our William, Ch. Whaplode Be Smart and Ch. Whaplode Beyond Valour.

Maggie Greene with four generations of her Copper Mountain Saints – puppies, dam, great dam, and great-great-dam.
Photo: Munro.

increase the gene pool. Having used an out-cross, we have then returned to line breeding, as the pedigrees demonstrate.

In-Breeding In-breeding is the mating together of extremely close relatives, such as mother and son, father to daughter, brother to sister. This should only be contemplated after serious consideration and research, and where thorough knowledge of the breed is available. We feel breeders who undertake this should be prepared to cull when necessary. This form of mating is a method of discovering fairly rapidly if there are "any skeletons in the St. Bernard closet", metaphorically speaking. This type of breeding does not cause defects but increases the probability of doubling up on any recessive genes carried by both parents. In-breeding can be a way of bringing to the fore faults which may be in the line. It can also produce outstanding virtues which can be strongly emphasised in the resulting stock. Such dogs should then be out-crossed.

I cannot stress how important it is to know exactly what lies behind the St. Bernards intended for in-breeding. The parents must obviously carry the minimal amount of faults possible. It is essential when in-breeding from outstanding stock to go out at the next mating, in our experience. Prolonged in-breeding can, in fact, reduce size and vigour, and sometimes progeny can become infertile, or aggressive. A novice breeder should avoid this type of breeding until they have gained more knowledge and experience. In-breeding with poor quality specimens can do untold damage to our breed.

'Kennel blindness' is one of the tragedies which some breeders and would-be breeders suffer from. This term basically means that the breeder cannot see faults in their own stock. Honesty in recognising faults, and sharing the information in a constructive way with other breeders, will help the welfare of this amazing breed.

Do not rush off to use a dog just because you like the look of him and he is winning everything in sight. Consideration should be given to a dog which is of the basic type you require and which has even better stock behind him. This dog may well have common ancestors with your bitch's pedigree. At the end of the day it is your decision, and breeding St. Bernards is a continuous learning curve. As breeders, we are merely 'custodians' of the St. Bernard lines until other potential breeders take over, as we have done with previous lines. With this comes a lot of responsibility to ensure the breed remains as healthy as possible. We all learn by our mistakes; hopefully this makes us better prepared for the future.

Once you have decided upon the stud dog, write to or telephone the owner, for confirmation that they will accept your bitch. Not all dogs are 'at public stud'. Many discerning stud dog owners may refuse to accept a bitch if they feel it lacks quality or has certain lines which are known to carry undesirable faults or if the breeding will prove incompatible. Make sure you discuss the stud fees BEFORE the bitch is mated, then no-one should be under any misunderstandings about the contract.

TIMING THE MATING
Most bitches come into season every six to nine months depending upon their menstrual cycle. Six months will usually be the minimum period between seasons, so after six months observe your bitch

closely for the first signs. Generally, the vulva will swell and there will be a heavy, bloody discharge. This should gradually become paler to a more pinkish colour in between the twelfth and seventeenth day. St. Bernard bitches differ, so this is just a guide; some St. Bernards are successfully mated while still showing full colour.

The best guide is when a St. Bernard begins to 'flash' her tail from side to side and appears to be ready to stand eagerly for the stud dog. There are exceptions to this. Bumble, our Champion smooth bitch, is a real 'tart' and she will stand for any dog, especially the younger males.

When a bitch is ready and with no male around, just tickling her around the tail area will often give the same result. If you intend travelling a long distance to the stud dog, we strongly recommend having blood tests after the sixth day of the season, to establish more accurately when your St. Bernard bitch is ovulating.

THE MATING

It is a matter of courtesy to inform the stud dog owner when your St. Bernard has come into season so that an estimated time may be discussed. If you are intending to have blood tests undertaken, the time of the mating very much depends upon these results. Kennel and stud dog owners are generally very busy people and do not appreciate owners and their bitch arriving at 11.00 p.m. for a mating! Endeavour, where possible, to arrange a specific appointment when the bitch is actually ready.

On arrival, the stud dog owner will probably wish to have a look at the bitch and possibly give her an internal examination to ensure there are no abnormalities or restrictions which could prevent mating. Should there prove to be any problems, then please do accept their advice and the integrity of the stud dog owner. No-one would wish to lose a stud fee, but if it is inappropriate due to a medical problem, then it is better not to proceed.

Most stud dog owners will provide you with some refreshments, especially after a long journey, so having stretched your own legs, allow the bitch a small drink of water, then allow her to relieve herself before being introduced to the dog. It is quite a good idea to stop at a lay-by or services before getting to the stud dog's residence so that smells are not picked up near the kennels.

It has already been discussed that dogs communicate by touch, taste, hearing, vision and scent. Bruce Fogle in *The Dog's Mind* (1990) points out that the dog has around 220 million scent receptors in his nose and to put this into perspective, the human only has around five million. Little wonder then that a quality stud dog can literally smell a bitch in season a mile away. Flirting is an important part of the mating process in our opinion; dogs in the wild would enjoy a courtship ritual and domestic dogs are no different. Allow the stud dog to sniff the bitch; he may wish to lick her ears. The bitch should be gently encouraged if she is a little apprehensive, especially if this is her first mating. This foreplay is a valuable aid to mental and physical preparation for the mating.

Stud dog owners vary considerably in their attitude to stud work and to managing the stud dogs and in what their expectations are of the owners or handlers of the bitch to be mated. Some may be keen to remove the bitch and have someone else hold her. Personally, we do not like this method as, if the owners are sensible, they can reassure the bitch and, when necessary, hold her firmly. The bitch is generally more likely to stand still if her owner is with her once the dogs have tied. Other breeders may well disagree with us.

We would advocate that some harmless play is encouraged, provided it is supervised, to allow dog and bitch to become acquainted. Given that the bitch is ready and the St. Bernard stud dog keen, the dog should soon wish to mount the bitch. Owing to the size of our breed, my husband and I have a routine of managing the mating once the dogs have become familiar with each other. The owners or handlers of the bitch are asked to hold her while George has a stool which he sits on to support bitch and dog, then I manage the stud dog. With a well-trained, experienced stud dog who trusts you, the mating can be easy, as the dog will respond to commands such as "down" or "off" if the positioning is not correct. In a young or inexperienced stud dog, it is often by trial and error that the young dog learns what is required. A mature St. Bernard bitch who is a 'tart' makes a good teacher for the adolescent St. Bernard.

Back to the mating in question. Once the bitch is standing firmly, the stud dog will grab her with his front forelegs, bring her closer towards him, then begin a thrusting movement. If the stud dog knows his job, he will persist until such time as he penetrates the bitch. This is the time when she should be held really firmly, ideally by means of a leather collar, as there may be some discomfort during penetration. There is the risk that the inexperienced bitch may suddenly panic and endeavour to bite the dog. If the bitch moves, it could damage her or the dog at this point.

Some stud dog owners may insist on the bitch being muzzled from the onset, especially if she has been showing any anxiety and snapping, as this may turn into aggression later. This is understandable; however, we have found with an experienced stud dog that they generally do not take any notice of these protestations. If we have to muzzle a bitch, then we only use a tape bandage which does not cause the bitch additional distress.

Pet bitches, who can become very spoilt by their owners, can be difficult to mate. Should yours fall into this category, it is best to be guided by the stud dog owner. They may prefer you to sit in the lounge, then once the mating has taken place with another experienced handler, you can witness the actual tie. This does not suggest that any malpractice has occurred; any responsible, caring stud dog owner will be keen for you to know that your bitch has been mated to the stud dog which you are paying for.

The tie involves the male swelling up considerably inside the bitch, preventing her from breaking loose. This can last from as short a period as ten minutes to over an hour. Once the pair are relaxed the stud dog owner will invariably lift one of the male dog's hind legs over the bitch's rear so that the dog and bitch can both stand comfortably in a 'back to back' position. The tie is effected when the bulbous base of the engorged penis of the male is held by the strong constricting muscles of the bitch's vagina. When this muscle completely relaxes, the dog is released. By the time copulation has ceased, some of the sperms may have travelled up the whole of the uterus and right through the fallopian tubes, entering the capsules which surround the ovaries where fertilisation generally takes place.

The dog's ejaculation takes place in three stages: initially a clear fluid containing no semen flushes the bitch's passage; the second stage is that fluid which is rich in semen flows through the passage carrying the spermatozoa; in the third stage, the clear fluid from the prostate flushes the semen forward into the St. Bernard's uterus.

It is not necessary for a 'tie' to take place to ensure fertilisation has taken place. Penetration is only required for a few moments, while ejaculation is taking place, for a mating to be successful.

There is a lot of discussion regarding one or two matings. One mating should be sufficient if the bitch is ovulating on the correct day when she was mated; however, if owners have travelled a long distance, it is perhaps better to have two matings. We do not mind if the owner of the bitch requests two matings – the stud dogs certainly enjoy it!

I have been asked on numerous occasions why the dog and bitch, when mated, end up back to back. There is a reason suggested by behaviourists that this stems from the ancestors of St. Bernards, when dogs were wild. If the dog and bitch faced opposite directions, they were in a position to ward off an attack by the enemy while they were locked together in such a vulnerable position. Personally, I feel the dogs would have been somewhat hampered by their position for a while. You will no doubt have your own thoughts on this matter.

DIFFICULT MATINGS

I am a great believer in mother nature. If a healthy dog and healthy bitch who is in the optimum stage of her season will not mate readily, there may be a very good reason for this. The chances are that the lack of enthusiasm stems from a clinical problem which humans have not identified. "Survival of the fittest" is the rule when nature is allowed to run its course. We are quite old fashioned and do not believe in forced matings as it can mean such a lot of problems later. In fact, a forced mating is very difficult to accomplish in dogs with the size and strength of St. Bernards.

It is usually pet bitches who create the problems, so if an above-average level of control is necessary and it still does not work, the bitch does not get mated. We find it hard to justify what is tantamount to rape being encouraged and perpetuated; it is very unfair to the bitch and not what breeding St. Bernards is about. We endeavour to be reputable stud dog owners, breeders and, first and foremost, dog lovers and St. Bernard enthusiasts.

STUD FEES

Having achieved a successful mating, you will need to pay the agreed stud fee. Please remember that a stud fee covers the actual service, not the resulting puppies, as some believe. Most breeders will offer a repeat mating if the bitch fails to conceive; however, this is courtesy on the stud dog owner's part and is not your right.

In Scandinavian countries, it is the practice to pay a nominal fee for the actual mating, followed by a set fee per live puppy born. This is logical and satisfactory to both parties. Forty years ago it was traditionally the accepted 'norm' to pay a stud fee which was the equivalent cost of a pick-of-the-litter puppy. While puppy prices for St. Bernards have steadily increased, stud fees have not done so proportionately. As a consequence, you can use a quality stud dog for half the cost of the average pet puppy.

In the UK, the stud dog owner will sign and give you the KC registration form once the stud fee has been paid. This form verifies that the mating took place and without this you will not be able to register your litter of puppies; so ensure you pay and retain the form.

ARTIFICIAL INSEMINATION

I am indebted to Andrew Brace for the following up-to-date information on artificial insemination which is most interesting.

The showing and breeding of pedigree dogs becomes a more and more international hobby with each passing year. Judges travel worldwide to officiate at major shows, while breeders increasingly visit such shows, notably national breed Specialty events, and thereby get the opportunity to see many of the best dogs in the world. This is invaluable to breeders, as they can then gauge the level of quality found in a breed from country to country, and can identify where certain virtues and weaknesses prevail. Sometimes outstanding dogs are located and may be for sale, but usually they are not.

In such cases, the technique of artificial insemination (AI) can be a successful alternative, so that instead of buying the dog, some doses of semen are collected and shipped. Also, for countries which still have strict quarantine regulations, the possibility of AI is of great importance as a method of increasing what may be a restricted gene pool. Should you ever consider embarking on the AI route to breeding, it is vital that you consult both the relevant government Ministry and also your national Kennel Club, which may have certain restrictions regarding the registration of puppies resulting from AI – and do so well in advance.

To obtain good results with AI it is important to use semen of the best possible quality, to handle the semen properly, and to inseminate the bitch at the optimum time during her season, using adequate techniques for the actual insemination. Only dogs and bitches with normal fertility should be used for AI because it is not a method of improving fertility; rather it should be expected to result in a pregnancy rate slightly below that obtained by a natural mating, especially when using thawed frozen semen.

Dog semen can be used freshly collected if both dog and bitch are present and it is used immediately. It may also be chilled, extended, or frozen, if it is to be shipped or stored for any length of time. From countries not too far away, chilled, extended semen (which can retain its fertilising capacity for 12 to 48 hours or even longer) can be used. From more distant countries, the semen must be frozen and stored in liquid nitrogen at –197C. This is also convenient in case semen enough for several bitches is required. Frozen dog semen can be stored practically forever (1 to 2,000 years).

Should you decide to import a particular dog, or even semen from it, it is of fundamental importance that you get as much information as possible about the dog and, if possible, its forebears. To make such decisions, which will have far-reaching effects on your breeding programme, based solely on photographs of a dog, may result in you getting some unpleasant surprises. Such things as temperament, bites, testicles, movement and eye colour, to mention just a few, may be looked upon in totally different ways in different countries. What may be acceptable in the country from which you are thinking of importing, may be totally taboo in your own. In these days of amazingly inexpensive air travel, flying to see a dog in the flesh is infinitely preferable to a very costly mistake.

Most artificial inseminations are performed with fresh, or chilled, extended semen. Fresh semen is used when both dog and bitch are present, but for some reason cannot, or are not permitted to, mate naturally. To collect semen from a dog is quite simple, and to inseminate a bitch with fresh or chilled, extended semen is not that complicated, as long as the inseminator has a good knowledge of the genital anatomy of the bitch. The semen is usually deposited in the cranial vagina, and the bitch held with elevated hindquarters for ten minutes or so to facilitate the transport of sperm through the cervix and uterus to the ovarian tubes, where fertilisation takes place. Care has to be taken, however, not to cause damage to the bitch and not to use semen contaminated by bacteria – for instance, from a dog with prostatic infection (which may well be the reason for his refusing to mate naturally in the first place). Semen quality should always be checked before using it for AI, which is why contact with a veterinarian specialist in canine reproduction is advisable.

If the semen is to be shipped, it should always be diluted with an extender to provide nourishment, and to protect the sperm membranes from the shock of shaking during transport, and the semen should be chilled to slow down the sperms' metabolism and thus encourage them to retain their fertilising capacity for longer. Dog semen treated in this way can often be successfully used after two days or more. It can be shipped in an ordinary vacuum flask, which is cheap to buy and does not have to be returned. Shipments of chilled, extended dog semen between Europe and the USA have been successful.

If the transport takes more than two days, or semen for several bitches is to be sent, the semen should be frozen. The freezing of dog semen also makes it possible to store it in a semen bank, to be used at some stage in the future. This technique is rather more complicated and is best left to the experts. A special freezing extender has to be used, and the semen cooled at a certain rate, then finally frozen in liquid nitrogen at a temperature of –197C. The semen has to be shipped in a liquid nitrogen container, a costly piece of equipment which will have to be returned.

There are various ways to freeze dog semen, and considerable commercialisation has developed in this field, notably in the USA. Unfortunately, many companies are very secretive about both the

methods they use and, more importantly, the results they obtain. The breeders have not put enough pressure on them to come forward with their success rates, but, hopefully, this will change as the use of AI becomes more commonplace.

The Swedish Kennel Klub has decided that, for a litter to be eligible for registration, the AI has to be reported to them within two weeks, i.e. some time before it can be established whether or not the bitch has conceived. Only veterinarians with special training in canine AI may perform the inseminations; the results of such breeding are reported each year, and are available for breeders to study.

This system has been in operation since 1990, and, during the ensuing six years, approximately 1,500 AI breedings have been reported with the SKK. A large number of vets have performed the inseminations and/or collected and preserved the semen. The average success rate, using both fresh and frozen semen, is around 50 per cent. Whelping rate after natural mating has been reported as between 80 and 90 per cent in the species. This discrepancy in results after AI and natural mating depends partly on the fact that a number of AIs are performed on dogs with problems, and also that sometimes the semen is of poor quality, or the bitch has not been inseminated at the optimal time of her season. If only semen of high quality is used, and on bitches at the right time of their season, the results are around 80 per cent with fresh semen.

Frozen dog semen should be deposited directly into the uterus of the bitch, because this can also result in an 80 per cent whelping rate when using high quality semen, as opposed to only 40-45 per cent when semen is deposited in the cranial vagina. In the Scandinavian countries a method of non-surgical intrauterine AI by catheterisation of the cervix was developed during the early 1970s and has been used routinely ever since.

The bitch is not sedated, and the technique is neither painful nor dangerous. It takes some time, and dedication, to learn, which is why in many countries the intrauterine AI of frozen semen still involves full abdominal surgery. Again, the breeders should put pressure on those performing AI in dogs to apply more modern, less invasive techniques.

STERILITY

Many diseases, including prostatitis, may cause a dog to become sterile, but over the years some male St. Bernards have become sterile without any obvious cause. Sometimes their testicles can be seen to have degenerated, becoming small and hard, or softer than normal, but in many cases, the testicles appear to be perfectly normal. Yet the dog does not produce sperm.

Sometimes these dogs have produced some litters before becoming sterile, but that is not always the case. In one family of Saints, this tendency in the males has been connected with a tendency for the bitches to suffer uterine inertia, indicating that the central hormonal system may be involved. The problem on the male side eventually will prove self-eliminating, but this again emphasises the importance of selecting breeding stock from healthy, self-whelping lines.

Infertility Syndrome

Many breeders have problems from time to time with bitches "missing", i.e. failing to conceive having been mated. Sometimes the problem can be due to a deep-rooted infection within the kennel. This is known as BHS, Beta-haemolytic streptococcal (Lancefield type G and L), and the problems caused by these bacteria are encountered in show dogs in many countries of the world. The following information has been supplied to me by Andrew Brace and is an account by Eleanor Bothwell (Norcis Beagles) of her experiences over a period of nearly thirty years breeding dogs. Eleanor originally wrote it with the intention of informing and helping breeders such as herself, who had experienced the heartbreak of Infertility Syndrome in their kennels. She felt that breeders tend to keep problems of this nature hush-hush, but realised that it is only when you are faced with a problem of this magnitude, with no forewarning, that you realise the importance of sharing experiences and knowledge. Subsequently she has delivered the information as a paper to various breed clubs.

Beta-haemolytic Streptococcal (Lancefield type G and L) Infection in the Bitch and Dog

The obstacles and problems the seriously dedicated dog breeder can face in the pursuit of the ideal are many. Anyone who has bred dogs over a number of years will have had their setbacks. Breeders, however, are a resilient lot, so most of the seemingly awesome obstacles are overcome. However, it matters not whether you have the best dogs and bitches in the world or merely "also rans"; if the ugly problem of infertility arises and your bitches are not producing puppies, it is absolutely heartbreaking. All of your carefully planned breeding programmes can be seriously set back or even brought to a halt.

Infertility can be permanent or temporary. The former cannot be aided, the latter can usually be cured if diagnosed speedily and corrective treatment given. The problem of infertility does not happen overnight. It creeps up over some time. One bitch misses – how easy it is to find a convenient reason for that to happen. Another bitch misses. Still philosophical, you accept the setback and make more excuses. By this time, a third bitch may have been mated to no avail, and only now that niggling thought in the back of your mind has to be accepted: "Perhaps there is something wrong with the bitches." Even for you to begin to reach this conclusion three bitches have missed and some 18 months may have passed. All this before investigations have begun. By now the infection has had plenty of time to become deep-rooted.

The most common cause of failure to conceive, for abortion, foetal absorption, stillbirths and early puppy mortality, is a uterine infection caused by the bacteria Beta-Haemolytic Streptococcal Lancefield Type G and L, sometimes called BHS infection or fading puppy syndrome. The infection can occur in both sexes but is most common in bitches. Rarely does it affect the testicular tissue of the dog. Other forms of Streptococci found in the bitch's genital area have little or no pathological significance.

SYMPTOMS AND DIAGNOSIS

Abnormal Seasons: Infected bitches often have irregularly timed seasons. Instead of the six or seven month cycle, she may have seasons with two to 12 month gaps. Others may show seasonal activity every few weeks; some just do not come into season for one or two years. Young infected bitches may have a very late first season, sometimes missing the first season entirely. The season itself varies from the normal 21 days – in some cases only two to five days, or as long as four to six weeks. The discharge is also different from normal – profuse or scant, heavy or pale throughout the entire season. If the bitch is having abnormal seasons, then BHS should be suspected. Another symptom is a lack of sexual interest shown by the stud dog for mating the bitch.

Sterility Syndrome: Failure to conceive is a common result of BHS infection. It may be due to ovarian infection and inflammation which may cause non-development of the ova, production of misshapen or infertile ova, or a failure to ovulate; or the ripe ova are shed at abnormal times, too early or too late in the season. If there is inflammation of the fallopian tubes, this makes it nigh impossible for the ova to travel down. Inflammation of the uterine walls retards or stops the embryonic process of implantation. Also, the secretions from the inflamed uterus are often lethal to live sperm. So BHS should be suspected when successful matings do not produce results, especially after repeated attempts.

Absorption – Abortion Syndrome: In spite of having BHS, the bitch does conceive and a seemingly normal pregnancy ensues for about four to five weeks. Abortion happens when the foetus can no longer maintain its attachment to the uterine wall. If this happens before 21 days, then the only symptoms the bitch will exhibit are those of being slightly off-colour and having a profuse dark, bloody discharge. Later on in the pregnancy, the symptoms are similar but more dramatic. Dead foetuses can be seen in the discharge.

Bitches can show mild or severe distress. Foetal absorption happens when the blood supply from the mother to the foetus is lost. Those foetuses become detached from the uterine wall. Instead of aborting, they remain in situ. Mummification occurs, followed by re-absorption. In most cases these bitches show little or no discharge or distress. Sometimes there can be a rise in temperature, loss of appetite and a general feeling of being off-colour. Such bitches recover in a week or so. Occasionally the bitch can develop severe symptomatic reactions. Therefore BHS should be suspected when bitches who seem to be pregnant fail to complete the pregnancy, when bitches have abnormal discharge at any stage of pregnancy, and when bitches have periods of general malaise along with a rise in temperature during pregnancy.

Fading Puppy Syndrome: This is the most common and the most heartbreaking result of BHS infection. There is a normal pregnancy, normal whelping and healthy new-born puppies. Puppy deaths start to happen at about four or five days. The puppies weaken from about three days old and lose the desire to suckle. They develop a bluish/purplish colouring on the belly, they dehydrate, lose weight and cry incessantly. Unless remedial action is taken immediately they will die very quickly.

The bitch that has been perfectly healthy at first becomes emotionally distressed by the crying of the pups. Her mammary glands become engorged as the pups stop feeding, leading to discomfort and pain. That requires remedial treatment to ensure that she does not develop a systemic infection.

It is important to realise that puppies born of bitches infected with BHS are healthy and normal at the time of birth. The puppies become infected by suckling the infected milk from the bitch. It is the milk that contains the BHS. The ingestion of this infected milk causes severe generalised disease usually resulting in death.

If the puppies from the infected bitch are removed quickly and fostered or hand-reared, they do not develop the disease. If Fading Puppy Syndrome is suspected, and immediate removal of the pups from the bitch plus treatment with antibiotics is carried out, they stand a fair chance of survival. They should be hand-reared or fostered. The important thing is early diagnosis and treatment. So, if puppies whine and weaken, seek immediate veterinary advice.

Confirmation of BHS can be made by growing a sample of the bitch's vaginal discharge in culture and identifying the bacteria. A suitable antibiotic can be prescribed. This can take a few days, which can be too long for the survival of the pups. A broad-spectrum antibiotic could be given, thus saving valuable time while the culture is growing. The presence of BHS can also be confirmed by a post-mortem examination of any dead pups in the litter and by bacteriological testing of the bitch's milk.

SOURCES OF INFECTION

The most common way for a bitch to pick up this BHS infection is by direct contact of the external genital organs, particularly during her season, when the cervix is dilated. As she sits to urinate or defecate, the vulva lips come into contact with the ground. If the bacteria are present, infection can take place. It is also thought possible for infection to take place when the bitch licks her genital area, thus ingesting the bacteria, if present.

The stud dog can act as a carrier of the disease. If he has mated an infected bitch, the BHS infection can survive on his penis and genital area for some 48 hours, and it is possible for him to infect the next bitch. Only rarely does the infection in dogs affect the testicular tissue, but when it does, the ejaculate of such dogs contains BHS organisms. These dogs should not be used at stud until completely recovered.

TREATMENT

Unfortunately, sensitivity in BHS strains varies from one patient to another. If time is available it is important to use specific drugs on specific patients after laboratory testing. The vet should advise you on this. Antibiotic treatment is effective, which can be given by injection or orally. The bitch and her puppies are usually treated for five to seven days, after which the pups could, theoretically, go back to the bitch. During treatment, careful nursing and high-quality feeding to both bitch and pups is essential. In order to clear up infection in the breeding kennel, each bitch, whether she is to be mated or not, must be swabbed and treated with antibiotics as soon as she comes into season. She should be swabbed on the first day of each season and this is to be carried out until she proves clear of infection for two successive seasons. The antibiotic treatment is given orally and has been found to be

successful only if started when the bitch is in season. When the bitch is not in season the treatment is useless. Generally speaking, for the first five days of her season, the bitch has 500 mg Ampicillin Trihydrate in two daily doses of 250 mg. Obviously the dosage varies, depending on the size of the breed. The treatment is repeated four-and-a-half weeks later, and again about five days before whelping is due.

There is another method of treating BHS and that is by the use of autogenous vaccines, which have proved to be successful in some kennels, but they can only be prepared under licence, when requested by a vet. The procedure is that all dogs and bitches in the kennel are swabbed. The swabs are sent off to the laboratory for culture, where the micro-organisms are identified and sufficient vaccine is prepared to treat the whole kennel. It is a lengthy, difficult and complicated process, but it is an alternative if antibiotics have failed.

PREVENTION

Floors of kennels and exercise runs should be made of an impervious material which is easy to disinfect. All bitches, as they come into season, should be kept isolated for the full season period. Infected bitches should be isolated and the kennel and run sterilised before any other animal is housed there. A stud dog should not be used on different bitches within a five-day period, unless it is known that they are free of infection. In this way the male's role of passive vector is minimised. Bitches should not be taken to dog shows during their seasons. And a breeder should not ignore any small indication that all is not right – never ignore "gut feelings". A brood bitch's breeding years are few, and seasons are usually only twice yearly. So time is of the essence when there is the least suspicion of BHS infection, and you and your vet need to work together fast to counteract it.

7 WHELPING AND AFTER CARE

The normal gestation period for bitches is sixty-three days. With St. Bernards it can vary from sixty to sixty-eight days, with perfectly healthy puppies making their debuts. If a bitch is having a large litter she may whelp early, so it is important to be prepared and keep a watchful eye on her behaviour.

FEEDING THE PREGNANT BITCH

DO NOT be tempted to pump lots of additional additives into your hopefully pregnant bitch; this is not necessary. However, quality protein and a balanced diet are important. The nutrient demand of a bitch rises during pregnancy, increasing rapidly towards the end of the gestation period. This actually peaks during lactation. The maintenance energy of a St. Bernard bitch can be estimated to be approximately 110 x body weight.

A growth or lactation type diet should be fed throughout pregnancy. This provides a natural form of calcium without the need for additional supplementation. There are vitamins A and D in milk which will encourage absorption of the calcium. An inbalance can create growth and bone problems. During the last four weeks of pregnancy, as foetal size increases rapidly, the quantity of the bitch's intake should be 15-25 per cent greater than her maintenance diet.

During the last ten days of the gestation period when the stomach capacity is limited by the extremely enlarged uterus, food should be supplied to the bitch ad lib. As long as the bitch maintains a good body condition, it can be assumed that she is receiving adequate nutrition. Although the number of foetuses will affect nutrient requirements during pregnancy, it is not necessary to take into account the litter size. Overfeeding will not significantly affect the pups' size, as the amount of nutrition they receive is dependent upon the placental size.

During peak lactation, between three and six weeks, 200 kcal of extra energy is required per day. This can be provided by increasing the amount fed by 25 per cent for each puppy. An alternative method is to provide 1.5 times maintenance in the first week. A St. Bernard bitch with an average litter will generally require 1.5 times maintenance for the first week, twice maintenance for the second week, increasing up to four times maintenance during peak lactation. It may be appropriate to feed the dam ad lib, with clean water available; however, a word of caution, St. Bernard puppies have an extra sensitive sense of smell, so it will be no time at all before they climb into their mother's bowl!

In order to achieve the high-energy intake required during lactation, a high-energy and nutrient-dense diet, which is also digestible and palatable should be given. If canned food and biscuit mixer are used, it may be necessary to increase the biscuit component. Feeding puppy foods, semi-moist or complete dry foods will increase energy levels for the same volume of food eaten; all are appropriate.

We still prefer to use a mixer of fresh-meat protein mixed with biscuit for the adult dogs, with fresh eggs added when a bitch is pregnant.

According to Dr Bryn Tennant, BVSc., PhD, Cert VR, MRCVS, bitches that are not in good body weight and condition, and on a balanced diet prior to mating, will tend to lose body weight and condition during pregnancy and lactation. Bitches in poor body condition and/or fed an inadequate diet prior to oestrus will have insufficient resources of protein, energy and some vitamins to see them through to weaning.

MALNUTRITION
This may develop if:
• The diet is insufficient. An appropriate diet must be given in sufficient quantity. Diets of insufficient energy density and protein can result in nutrient depletion, which may not be clinically evident until lactation.
• Food is of poor quality (e.g. contains poor-quality protein, low energy density and is deficient in one or more essential nutrients) or of low digestibility (i.e. only a small proportion of the food that is consumed is actually absorbed from the intestinal tract).
• The diet is not balanced. This is particularly a risk with home-produced diets. Such a diet may not cause problems when fed for maintenance but does do so during lactation because of the greater nutrient demand (see lactation tetany below).

Clinical consequences of malnutrition include:
• Up to 30 per cent neonatal mortality, usually as a consequence of starvation when insufficient milk (agalactia/hypogalactia) is available. Death in these pups may be directly due to, and is often blamed on, bacterial infections or rejection by the bitch rather than on malnutrition. However, the underlying problem of malnutrition results in weak pups with a reduced ability to prevent and combat infection and also to compete with littermates for milk. Even if pups do not die, reduced availability of milk will slow growth rates.

WORMING
The bitch should be wormed prior to mating and again when she is approximately four weeks in whelp. This is to alleviate the amount of worms transmitted to the whelps. Most puppies do have worms; however, worming the bitch can reduce the quantity of worms the puppy is likely to have.

SIGNS OF PREGNANCY
One of the first signs that the bitch is in whelp is that her nipples become enlarged and can be much more pink in colour, with a puffiness around the base of the nipple. This usually occurs around the second to third week. The bitch can also have a thickening around her abdomen and look 'rounded'. Sometimes St. Bernard bitches that normally enjoy eating may go off their food at this stage and may even prefer a change of diet due to their hormones. We have found a couple of tablespoons of tinned cat food spread over the normal food will tempt the bitch to eat. Like humans, their taste buds can change too.

The bitch can be taken along to the vet's at this stage. Between three and four weeks, it is feasible for the vet to ascertain if the bitch is pregnant, unless she has a deep rib cage where the uterus has tucked up, in which case it can prove more difficult to diagnose a pregnancy. With modern technology, many large veterinary clinics have scanning machines which can detect if the St. Bernard bitch is pregnant from four weeks onward. What the scanner does not detect accurately is the number of whelps. It is staggering the variations between the number of foetuses reported to be shown on the scan and the actual number of puppies born.

PREPARATION FOR THE WHELPING
Two weeks before the bitch is due to whelp, the area where the St. Bernard is going to have her puppies should be thoroughly cleaned with disinfectant or the bacterial cleaning aids which are now available. The whelping box in particular needs to be thoroughly scrubbed out to ensure the birth area is as clean as possible.

Make sure there is an appropriate area for the equipment which may be needed when the bitch begins to whelp. You will need some basic equipment such as:
• An ample supply of towels
• Pair of sterile scissors
• Cotton wool (cotton)
• Iodine or wound powder
• Dettol or Savlon solution
• Strong cotton thread
• Artery forceps
• An abundant supply of newspapers
• Fleecy-type bedding

• Old candlewick bedspread
• Whelping stimulant for the puppies in case of need
• Pair of scales for measuring the weight of the puppies
• Pen, small writing-pad and the vet's telephone number
• Animal carrying basket.

The towels are to dry and rub the puppies for stimulation to get their circulation and lungs going after the challenge of birth. A pair of scissors is useful for trimming the hair around the bitch's rear end. Some people use the scissors to cut the umbilical cord; we prefer, when necessary, gently to tear the umbilical cord and place artery forceps on it to stop any bleeding. Cotton wool (cotton) is useful for dabbing wound powder onto the umbilical cord if there is some bleeding. Cotton thread can be used to tie the cord if necessary. Diluted iodine can also be used to prevent bacteria getting into the cord.

The newspapers are a good way of providing a covering over the whelping box for the bitch to whelp on. They can then be picked up and disposed of. Fresh newspapers can then be used as a replacement in readiness for the next whelp. Fleecy bedding can be used to keep the puppies warm.

The scales are useful for keeping track of the puppies' weight and development. Usually puppies weigh from as little as 10 oz up to 2.5 lbs when born. Just like human babies, puppies can lose some birth weight over the next twenty-four to forty-eight hours. After birth, note down any identifiable marks, the birth weight and gender of each puppy, and, by weighing them each day, you will be able to monitor their progress or identify a problem or area of concern.

In case there is a problem or you want to have direct advice from the vet or the breeder of your own Saint, make certain you have their telephone numbers nearby for quick reference.

Should the bitch be having a large litter, it is useful to place some of the whelps in an appropriate 'cat' basket or cardboard box so the novice mother does not accidentally lie on one of her new-born puppies when having another. An important point to remember is not to remove all the puppies but leave one, or possibly two, with their mother. The suckling action of these puppies

encourages the hormones to influence the birth of the remaining whelps and stimulates the milk glands into action.

The antiseptic is to wipe the bitch around her feathering and vulva once she has finished whelping. It is important to have a heat lamp if the bitch is whelping in a kennel, to maintain the required temperature.

PRE-WHELPING BEHAVIOUR
Sometimes bitches that are approaching the actual whelping date may try to escape their normal surroundings. This can happen a week or even ten days prior to whelping. The bitch wants a safe, secure place to have her puppies, and she can decide that this is away from her favourite surroundings. Pet bitches can go and dig an enormous hole in the garden or endeavour to dig under the garden shed – and also dig up the best carpet! Kennelled St. Bernards can commence digging up all their bedding, even digging at the floorboards or plasterwork.

Bitches may also decide to bury their food or store it for later, especially if they are fed on tripe, fresh meat or chicken. They are less likely to bury complete food but may tip their dish over and nudge the contents under the cupboards, refrigerator or other available spot. Sometimes the bitch will guard her food, not wanting anyone to go near the dish, then eat her meal later.

This behaviour is consistent with that of their ancestors. Bitches living in a pack would find a dark secluded place, possibly a cave or unused 'earth' as an appropriate safe 'nest' for their potential litter, leaving the security of the pack. Some domestic dogs try to remove themselves from the family, while others much prefer the reassurance from their owner. St. Bernards are no different. Over the past thirty years, we have found a variety of behaviours adopted by the bitches in whelp.

One particular bitch, Coatham Goodness Gracious, would not have her puppies if anyone was around. As soon as the 'sitter' left their observation post, out popped a puppy. Another bitch, Ch. Coatham Suffragette, pulled the hair away from her vulva, inside legs and teats by licking and tugging until the undercoat came away two weeks prior to the birth of her litter.

An important task to undertake is settling your

bitch into the prepared whelping room or area at least seven days before the earliest date of delivery. Make sure the whelping box is thoroughly cleaned and has plenty of newspapers or old candlewick bedspread for the bitch to 'dig up'. Also ensure there is plenty of fresh clean water for the dam, and remember to change this regularly so it is not full of 'slobber'. Bitch's own milk is constituted from water, which is a point to be mindful of when feeding the expectant dam. However, half-a-pint to a pint of milk and one egg can be given during the last three weeks of pregnancy.

Do not be too alarmed if your bitch appears to be digging her way to Australia! This may be your first time as an 'expectant' St. Bernard 'breeder', so take our advice, this behaviour is quite natural. Remember, St. Bernards are great observers of human behaviour and body language, so if the bitch realises you are anxious it is a great way for her to receive extra attention by becoming restless, scratching, standing up, lying down, to gain the affection which she feels she needs. Remain calm and speak softly to the bitch in a reassuring way, giving her TLC (Tender Loving Care), then leave her alone, occasionally checking on her. If you are really worried or feel something could be wrong, contact the breeder of your bitch or the stud dog's owner for their comments and reassurance.

If you have been taking the bitch's temperature then an obvious sign that the bitch is ready to whelp is that her body temperature will dramatically drop from the normal temperature to 98° Fahrenheit or less about twenty-four hours before whelping. Some Saint bitches go off their food, others do not. Some Saint dams will expel milk if their teats are gently squeezed; for other Saint bitches, especially first-time dams, the milk comes through slightly later, when the whelps are born.

THE WHELPING (PARTURITION)
Parturition ('parturio' means 'I bring forth') is the expulsion of the foetus and its membranes from the uterus through the maternal passages by natural forces. Although this act is a continuous one, it can be divided into four stages:
The Preliminary Stage
The Dilatation of the Cervix Stage
The Expulsion of the Foetus Stage
The Expulsion of the Membranes Stage.

1: The Preliminary Stage
Usually the teats of the bitch will swell and become tender and there may be a waxy fluid from them. The external genitals, i.e. the vulva, become swollen, enlarged and flabby. The lining is reddened. A clear, straw-coloured, stringy mucus is secreted from the vulva which can stick to the bitch's tail and feathering on her hindquarters. The abdomen drops, becoming pendulous. The quarters droop and the muscles and ligaments of the pelvis slacken then relax. This is when your St. Bernard bitch will really begin in earnest to make a bed for her babies.

If your bitch is absolutely determined to have her litter in a totally inappropriate place in the house then, rather than distress her, let the first puppy be born in her chosen spot; then when she is preoccupied with her rear end, encourage her to move with her new baby to your chosen spot!

2: Dilatation of the Cervix Stage
This merges with the preceding, uneasy stage. This

Coatham Amazing Grace just prior to whelping.

uneasiness gradually increases and the early stages of mild labour pains commence. Your St. Bernard can sometimes become distressed, or may begin to breathe more quickly and display a slight coughing. There may be signs of pain in the abdomen. This may fall and rise again several times. Meanwhile, the labour pains become more powerful, the intervals between the contractions shorten. The expression upon the St. Bernard's face can become anxious, almost imploring, so speak softly and reassure the bitch. The pulse is quickened and the breathing distressed and rapid. When a pain has passed, the Saint calms down, remaining so until the next contraction takes place. The length of time of this phase can vary from a half to two-and-a-half hours, until the 'water-bag' appears at the vulva. At this stage the cervix is fully dilated, and Stage 3 occurs.

3: Expulsion of the Foetus Stage
The "water-bag" usually bursts and is quickly followed by the head of the first puppy, wrapped up in a clear membrane. If the bitch is obviously licking the membrane away from the head of the puppy, allow nature to take its course and do not interfere. Let the bitch break the cord.

If the puppy lies motionless, take a clean towel from the pile and rub the puppy vigorously to stimulate the lungs and encourage it to breathe. Once this whelp has taken several steady breaths,

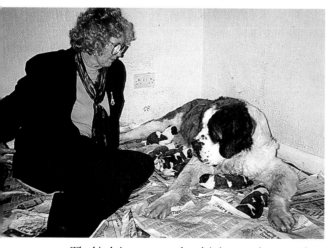

The bitch is encouraged to drink some glucose and water. She is halfway through whelping.

place the puppy on one of the teats of the bitch. Should the puppy be born with its legs first instead of the head, it is referred to as a 'breech delivery'. If it is apparent that the bitch is having problems and you can actually see the front legs, then when the bitch bears down and pushes, carefully take the front feet in a towel and pull GENTLY. Several contractions may occur before the foetus is safely delivered, so be patient.

It is most important that the bitch is encouraged to lick her baby, as this establishes bonding and attachment between mother and offspring.

Should the bitch not have broken the umbilical cord, clip the artery forceps onto the cord, then sever it with a sharp pair of scissors and tie cotton thread around the cord to prevent bleeding and any infection setting in. Allow the bitch to lick and become acquainted with her new-born baby, and then place the puppy on the teat.

After a period of respite, which could be a half to two-and-a-half hours, the process commences again and the next whelp is on the way. Saint bitches can be slow whelpers, so do keep a record of the time between delivery of the whelps.

4: Expulsion of the Membranes Stage
The length of time before the afterbirth is delivered can vary from bitch to bitch. Sometimes it can follow on from the foetus almost immediately, while in others it can be retained for some time. This afterbirth is dark green in colour and jelly-like. After each St. Bernard puppy is born, the uterus contracts and becomes smaller, a process known as 'involution', so that its capacity is decreased. The attachment between the membranes and the mucosa of the uterus becomes loosened and the placenta is ultimately separated from the uterus. These contractions also serve to force the membranes outside through the cervix.

The importance of the pituitary and other hormones involved in the birth process cannot be overestimated. The amniotic fluid acts as a lubricant during birth, while helping the cervix to dilate. The fluid also protects the whelp to some extent during birth.

The placenta is a structure from which the whelp obtains its nutriment and oxygen supply. The oxygen and nutrients pass through the umbilical cord from the maternal blood supply to the whelp's blood supply. The whelp excretes the waste products through this same organ, although the two circulatory systems are separate. The umbilical cord connects the whelps to the placenta and contains two umbilical arteries and one vein. The arteries carry deoxygenated blood from the whelp and the vein conveys the oxygenated blood and nutrients direct from placenta to whelp.

St. Bernard bitches will usually swallow the afterbirth. Do not become alarmed, this is normal. The afterbirth will provide the bitch with energy during the whelping process, as it contains nutrients, so let her get on with it. If the bitch does not wish to eat the afterbirth, remove it. Do count the afterbirths to make sure all have been expelled.

REMOVING THE PUPPIES

Should the puppies be removed from the bitch during whelping? This depends on the bitch, the number of puppies and how quickly the puppies are arriving. It also depends on whether the bitch is whelping in a proper whelping box or in a corner in a utility room. The whelping box should have a 'pig-rail' round it, so that puppies can have some protection from their mother during whelping. If your St. Bernard bitch is extremely restless, up and down, turning round, digging, when the second puppy arrives, it is probably a good idea to place the first whelp in a suitable basket or cardboard box, on a hotwater bottle covered by a fleecy blanket.

It is far better to allow the bitch to do everything for herself if possible; allow nature to take its course – the "survival of the fittest" philosophy. However, humans tend to interfere and often look at the whelps in terms of 'commercial enterprise'. Often a weak puppy would just quietly pass away; however, some people see this as the loss of a large number of £££s, or dollars, so are determined not to allow the puppy to die. A large litter can be exceptionally hard work for a bitch.

It is really a matter of discretion and observation as to whether all the puppies are left with the bitch, or removed, or just some of them; a lot depends on how many live puppies the bitch delivers. In the wild, African dogs, Dingos and Wolves usually have litters of around four or five puppies, which are not too much of a drain on their mother.

The first milk from the teats contains colostrum, which is thought to be a mild laxative. and it also contains important antibodies for the puppies' protection against infection. When the puppies suckle, this stimulates a peristaltic action, ensuring that the puppies evacuate their bowels. The meconium which the puppy discharges from its bowel is made up of waste product from the mucous membranes lining the intestines. Once this has been discharged, the digestive system will begin functioning in an improved manner.

If the bitch is having a large litter, it is acceptable to let her go out in between delivering her whelps to urinate. This will help her feel more comfortable and give her the opportunity to stretch her legs. Do not worry, she will not want to be away from her whelps for very long and will come running back. Bitches can be really protective of their puppies. Make sure she does not drop another puppy while she is doing this; however, if a pup should be born outside, wrap it in a towel and take it and the bitch back to the whelping area as quickly as possible.

POST-WHELPING

Giving birth to a litter can be an exhausting process for a St. Bernard. In the main, we have found this breed do make excellent mothers; however, there are some that will prove to be exceptions to this rule. The bitch should be given some warm milk with beaten egg in it once she has whelped. It may be appropriate to place some glucose in this to give her some extra sugar to help her energy levels which will have been reduced by the whelping process.

The bedding should be completely replaced and fresh newspapers, blankets, bedspreads or fleecy bedding put down for the bitch and her new-born litter to settle down upon. It never ceases to amaze me how the whelps quickly seek out the teats and how bodily functions respond accordingly. Having observed a lot of St. Bernard bitches, I find from their expressions that they really do appear to have a sense of satisfaction and maternal love for their tiny offspring.

After whelping, the bitch should be allowed some peace and quiet to recuperate and become familiar with her puppies. Just keep a watchful, unobtrusive eye on her to make sure she is all right. There will be a certain amount of discharge coming from her vagina; this again is normal for a few days post-whelping, so do not panic. The colour may also be very dark, almost black, like charcoal; again, this is normal.

In most cases, the St. Bernard bitch will have a good appetite after whelping. We advise feeding a lighter diet for the first couple of days, such as chicken or fish mixed with a mixer meal, rather than a rich diet, to allow her stomach to regain some of its tone. The bitch should be offered a continual supply of fresh water to sustain her milk supply. After the third or fourth day post-whelping, the uterus returns to half the distended size that it was prior to whelping. Gradually, it becomes smaller, returning to its normal size. It may never return to the exact size prior to mating, especially after a large litter.

Allow the bitch the opportunity to go and relieve herself several times per day, just for short periods only. It is most important that she does not contract any infections. We have found that garlic pills boost her own immune system and do not have any adverse effect on the puppies. Make sure a temperature of 21°C (70°F) is maintained for the puppies.

The bitch and her puppies need careful observations but not too much interference during the first week. Sometimes novice St. Bernard mothers are so keen to return to their puppies that they can be too zealous, accidentally standing on one. This is the time to help by moving the brood out of the way, enabling her to lie down, and then placing the puppies towards the teats. They will quickly latch on and commence suckling. I do enjoy observing puppies at the "milk bar" and the way mum watches over them with pride at this age. Do not be tempted to bring strangers to show off this lovely litter; it is unfair to the bitch. No strangers before they are two weeks old, unless it is the vet! Do be careful that the Saint does not over-react towards the vet, especially with a very maternal dam; this professional is only doing his job, so do not give the bitch a chance to get her own back on him.

DEWCLAWS

These are not a deformity in the St. Bernard; however, they are a useless appendage. Often St. Bernard puppies can be born with double dewclaws on their hind legs. The Breed Standard does not require dewclaws, unlike the Pyrenean Mountain Dog where it is desirable that they display double dewclaws on their hind legs. The dewclaws should be removed around the third or fourth day. A lot of people have this carried out by the vet, although it is possible to do it yourself, provided proper care is taken. It is useful to have the following equipment:

• A pair of sharp scissors
• Artery forceps
• Cotton wool
• White or surgical spirit or bacterial spray
• Savlon or similar antiseptic
• Permanganate of potash crystals
• Wound powder
• Warm boiled water
• A box containing hot water bottle covered by a fleecy blanket.

Encourage the bitch to suckle all her puppies for ten to fifteen minutes, then take her for a walk or place her where she cannot hear the puppies crying. Collect all the equipment together. Make certain all the tools are clean and free from bacteria. Modern sprays are good; however, standing the scissors and artery forceps in surgical spirit for ten minutes is a good way of eliminating some of the germs.

Take one puppy at a time; we do the small front dewclaws first, then the dewclaws from the hind legs. Wipe the area with cotton wool dipped into the antiseptic solution. Take the artery forceps and clamp them around the dewclaw, making certain you have the entire appendage. This will cut off the blood supply if left on for a few seconds. Remove the artery forceps and then take the sharp pair of scissors and quickly cut off the dewclaw. Take another piece of cotton wool, damp it with warm water, dab it onto the permanganate of potash crystals and press onto the area where the dewclaw had been. This seals the area and prevents any bleeding. The puppy may cry a little, but it is worth the discomfort to avoid a full anaesthetic and problems at a later stage.

Follow this procedure on each foot until all the dewclaws have been removed. Check for bleeding. If one area still seems to be bleeding, place another piece of dampened cotton wool into the potash and press onto the small wound. Place the puppy onto the hot-water bottle covered by fleece or clean towel.

Do each puppy in turn until the litter have all had

their dewclaws removed. Bring the bitch back and settle her into the whelping box or area. Place the puppies on her teats and they will quickly forget their traumatic experience. If done properly, there should be no need for the puppies to have any stitches and the pain subsides very quickly. It is essential that the scissors are sharp and free from hair or bacteria.

The bitch may lick the puppies all over, paying extra attention to the small wounds where the dewclaws were. This should not do any damage and aids the healing process. If any of the wounds do appear to be inflamed, bathe with antiseptic solution and dab permanganate of potash crystals on the wound. Within a few days the wounds will begin to heal from inside out.

Reassure the St. Bernard bitch, as she may be anxious about her brood, then mother and progeny will soon settle down again. The following is a quick guide for a normal whelping, which may be useful.

A QUICK GUIDE TO NORMAL WHELPING
Lots of digging, restlessness, more frequent than normal.
Drop in temperature from the normal to 98°F or below, 24 hours before whelping.
The bitch lies with her feet outstretched and with her head between her paws or forelegs.
The bitch becomes progressively more restless, sitting up, lying down. This is indicative that early stages of labour have occurred.
Bitches often look at their rear parts, licking profusely.
May refuse food, but not always.
Occasionally, the bitch can bring up some froth. Nothing to worry about.
The vulva becomes swollen with soft, clear mucous discharge.
The bitch begins to push and strain, may make grunting noises.
The second stage of labour begins.
Make a note of the time from this point onwards.
The breathing becomes noticeably quicker; may dig up the bedding again.
The dam begins intermittent, irregular pains, and pants. This can last between one and three hours – if any longer, call the vet as there may be a problem.

Appearance of the water-bag; this must not be mistaken for the actual whelp.
The bag should break of its own volition, or is broken by the bitch.
The whelp appears soon after this, hopefully head first, forelegs facing forward and tucked under the chin.
The actual first St. Bernard arrives. Remain calm.
If necessary, break the membrane over its nose; or, if the bitch is managing, allow her to undertake this task.
Draw the placenta out.
The bitch should chew the umbilical cord, if not, break, tie off and dry the puppy with a towel.
Place the puppy onto a teat if it has not already found its way there.
The afterbirth should now have been discharged; allow the bitch to eat this if she wishes to.
Weigh the puppy and note the figure down, together with any specific distinguishing marks and the gender.
Clean up any mess; prepare the whelping box for the next delivery.
Allow the bitch to rest after each puppy.
If the bitch is getting tired, give her some warm milk with beaten egg and glucose added.
Take her out to relieve herself.
Endeavour to establish if the bitch has completed her litter, as sometimes inertia can occur; an injection of oxytocin can help the proceedings, so it may be necessary to contact the vet.
Check that all the placentas have come away.
Mother should settle down to a good sleep, often snoring loudly once all the litter are born.
Have a cup of tea and relax!

DANGER SIGNS
Strong contractions over a two-hour period with no visible result, or the cessation of contractions for several hours, are really warning signs that something is amiss. Contact the vet, as it may be necessary for the bitch to have a Caesarean operation.

EXAMINING THE PUPPIES
The litter of puppies should all be checked thoroughly for any abnormalities, such as hernia or cleft palate, and to ensure that the anus functions properly. When I was working as a

veterinary nurse, there were a few occasions when some deformities of the anus were diagnosed, such as not having a full opening to the anus. This resulted in distressed whelps being really blocked up with waste matter and having to be put to sleep after a week or two, as no treatment was possible.

When the bitch has completely settled for a rest after parturition, you have an ideal opportunity to examine each puppy from head to tail, making sure the litter are all fit and healthy. If any abnormalities are visible, it is better to deal with these as soon as possible, before the bitch becomes attached to each puppy, or rejects the whelp which is deformed or has some malfunction.

Examine the nose and lips to check and see that there is no harelip. Open the mouth and look at the roof to ensure there is no cleft palate deformity. If the roof of the mouth appears to have a large gap in the structure of the palate, this will probably be a cleft palate. The puppy will be unable to suckle and artificial feeding will not be satisfactory.

Make sure that you examine the fore and hind legs, check that the puppies have the correct number of toes and none of the pups have clubfeet. Turn the puppy over and check for any signs of hernia. Lastly, check the tail and gently look around the anus; it is not always possible to see a hole, so observation is required to make sure that each puppy passes a motion.

Bitches who push out and reject a whelp do so for a reason. It is much better to allow Mother Nature to deal with this than to try to save the puppy. In the majority of cases the dam has an insight into some malfunction or disability which may not present itself until the St. Bernard is older. From experience both as a breeder and as an ex-veterinary nurse, I can tell you that it really is a case of "mother knows best!" Some enthusiasts may see that the rejection of a whelp as the loss of several hundred pounds. This is a very materialistic, commercial stance, and in the long run it will prove to be false economy: some unsuspecting St. Bernard purchaser could be taking on health problems in the future through your uncalled-for intervention. A good reputation is built up over a number of years; remember it

can all be lost in one litigation case, so do listen to our advice.

If any puppies have to be put down for health reasons, the kindest way to do this is to take the tiny whelps along to your vet. NEVER try to drown the whelps, as this is extremely cruel.

INFECTIOUS DISEASES
Canine Distemper
Canine Distemper is an infectious disease mainly of younger dogs, characterised by a high rise in temperature, listlessness, and loss of appetite. In the later stages, a catarrhal discharge from the eyes and nostrils is evident. The disease is often complicated by broncho-pneumonia; sometimes nervous symptoms develop, such as twitching. In severe cases, fits occur. Consult the vet as a matter of urgency.

Canine Hepatitis
Canine Hepatitis usually occurs in younger dogs from twelve weeks to twelve months, although occasionally older dogs can be affected. The virus attacks the liver, often producing symptoms of jaundice, with yellowing of the mucous membrane in the mouth, and the white of the eye can also appear yellow. Puppies are vulnerable to this contagious disease. Their temperature will rise and diarrhoea occur. The blood clotting mechanism in the circulatory system is affected. If the St. Bernard survives, the infection remains for a long period, causing risk to others. The virus may be excreted in the urine for up to six months after the infection has been diagnosed. On-going veterinary treatment and quality nursing are essential.

Leptospirosis
Leptospirosis is caused by the bacteria Leptospira Icterohaemorrhagiae and Leptospira Canicula, which can be transmitted to humans. Rats are the hosts for Leptospira Icterohaemorrhagiae and it is passed in their urine. It is a good idea to remove empty dog dishes from kennel runs, or tip buckets upside down at night to prevent any rats from urinating in these vessels. Although you may not have rats on your premises, a stray rat may find its way to any tempting food deposits.

Leptospirosis Canicula is transmitted when a

St. Bernard puppy sniffs the urine of an affected dog. The symptoms are a high rise in temperature, abdominal pain, usually a tremendous thirst, diarrhoea containing blood and vomiting. Jaundice can be present. The puppy will be really listless and depressed. Veterinary treatment is vital.

Canine Parvovirus
This highly contagious virus came to prominence about twenty years ago. Puppies can be vulnerable to it. Symptoms include severe sickness which can be accompanied by diarrhoea containing blood. The St. Bernard puppy will be listless and really miserable. The odour from the vomit is very marked. Once you have smelt it you will be able to detect Parvovirus again if it should ever re-occur. The St. Bernard will quickly dehydrate, so it is vital to seek veterinary advice as soon as possible, and an intravenous drip may be necessary to aid recovery. Death can occur rapidly with this infectious disease, so seeking early diagnosis from your vet is essential.

Remember, prevention is often much better than cure, so do be careful and have your St. Bernard puppy vaccinated against these specific diseases. It is also important to have a booster inoculation every two years. St. Bernard puppies can be vulnerable to Parvovirus from the age of five weeks. When you obtain your puppy from the breeder, it is essential that you have insurance cover from the minute it leaves the breeder, as the next two to three months are a critical time for the young St. Bernard.

Most reputable breeders will ensure you take away a fat, healthy puppy from their establishment, along with quality insurance cover. However, the dealers of this world will not care whether the puppy is fit and healthy.

In the majority of cases, dealers do not give any insurance cover, and you will not be able to see the mother and father, so do contact the St. Bernard Club Secretaries for advice about genuine, caring breeders. BE PREPARED, rather than acting on impulse because you want a St. Bernard immediately or are pressurised into it by the children. Carry out your own research. Visit a few kennels, ask awkward questions, and test out the breeders' genuine motives for breeding, caring and management. It is all worth it in the end.

If you are a first-time breeder, ensure that all your litter are insured; it is worth it for peace of mind that the puppy is covered once it leaves your care.

WHELPING COMPLICATIONS
Unfortunately, there are complications which do arise during and after whelping, so it is better to be prepared, to know what the signs and symptoms are and to respond accordingly for the benefit of the bitch and the whelps. There are some complications which can be dealt with by the owner; others which are more serious will require veterinary attention as soon as possible. It is important to realise that if one puppy is causing an obstruction and is not delivered in a reasonable time, then it can cause the death of all the whelps lying behind it. When a difficult St. Bernard whelp has eventually been born, the remaining whelps can still be born naturally and easily, provided the bitch is not totally exhausted from fruitless straining.

The over-sized whelp in relation to the size of the birth canal is fairly rare in St. Bernards. Older St. Bernard bitches tend to have smaller litters, so their puppies are bigger than those from a larger litter.

Another complication can be two whelps arriving simultaneously, in the majority of cases a St. Bernard can pass these along the birth canal and through the cervix without too many difficulties. If the bitch is continually straining and nothing happens, get the vet.

Circulatory Embarrassment
This can occur when an exceptionally large litter is expected. The bitch can collapse a week, or just a couple of days, before the earliest day of delivery. She may have great difficulty breathing, the hind legs could be extended, with the feet facing backwards. This is caused by cramp due to the lack of circulation, owing to the pressure of the over-extended uterus. This causes lack of oxygen on the lungs and the bitch will experience laboured breathing. The vet must be contacted immediately.

Dystocia (Abnormal Labour)

The St. Bernard is a 'normally' constructed breed, with no exaggerated breed requirements which cause concern during whelping. There should be no reason for bitches to experience difficulties delivering puppies, yet some lines do suffer from dystocia. Uterine inertia is when the whelps do not seem to respond to the strong hormonal response to the pituitrin which is necessary to begin the whelping process. An injection of additional pituitrin may be required if the contractions do not occur or are weak.

Our theory is that, considering the size of some St. Bernard bitches, comparatively speaking the puppies are very small. If a smaller bitch is whelping larger puppies that weigh over two pounds, there is often a quick whelping without any problems. As a veterinary nurse, I had the opportunity of observing a variety of breeds having litters. Terriers in particular seemed to put a lot of effort into the process, really pushing when the contractions occurred. St. Bernards do not seem to put any effort into having puppies, sometimes a few gentle strains and, hopefully, the healthy puppy arrives fairly quickly. St. Bernard bitches can be very lazy.

One cause of dystocia can be due to a single puppy, the 'one puppy syndrome', where such a small litter will not trigger the hormonal response. Another factor is the large litter which exhausts the uterine wall by over-stretching it, and the resultant distension renders the uterus unable to contract.

Another cause of inertia which can be hereditary is a hormone imbalance, such that the contractions are weak and finally cease altogether. In strains where this condition is known to exist, it is better not to breed from the bitch. An injection of oxytocin will probably help. Another method is to put the bitch in the back of the car and take her for a half-hour drive over a bumpy country road – this often does the trick.

Complete inertia is when the water bag breaks and the only sign or evidence is a dampened place on the bedding. The bitch may still dig and part-make a nest, but there are no other visible signs of contractions. This can occur after a caesarean section for a previous litter, owing to adhesions. If the Saint bitch does not go into a normal labour within a short period of time, then it is better to consult the vet.

Absorption of Whelps

The majority of healthy St. Bernard bitches, mated at the right time, should conceive unless they are infertile. Bitches rarely abort a puppy. In early pregnancy, the whelps can be completely absorbed, causing no problems to the bitch. Sometimes these whelps become mummified and are only found during a caesarean operation being performed for the other puppies. Occasionally, one of these mummified whelps will be passed normally without there being any unpleasant odour. Sometimes these tiny things just look like 'Jelly Babies'. Absorption can be caused by some traumatic event early in the pregnancy.

Manual Manipulation during Whelping

This must be carried out after having made sure that you have removed any bacteria from your hands; if possible, use surgical gloves. Should a puppy be visible at the vulva but there is no progress with its expulsion, a finger can be inserted very gently into the vagina. Then hook the finger around the whelp, preferably over the back of the neck; when the bitch strains, gently but steadily pull the whelp downwards and outwards. This will help the bitch (especially if it is going to take time for the vet to come out) and provide a better life-chance for the puppy.

Difficult Head Presentations

If the head is born but the back is uppermost and there is clearly a problem, the membranes need to be removed from the nose of the puppy. It is best to grasp the puppy at the top of the neck just below its head, between the first two fingers and then, when the bitch strains, try to pull the head downwards and forwards between the legs of the puppy, keeping a steady traction. If the whelp does not move immediately, gently move the head from side to side; this should release the shoulders. Once the shoulders are through the pelvic brim, the whelp should come through the cervix without too many problems. Sometimes a small cloth or a large piece of cotton wool strip can aid the grip on the whelp. Grip the whelp firmly and continue pulling with a gentle but firm traction. Remember that the head and shoulders are the heaviest part of the whelp, so that if they come first, the centre of gravity is forward; this aids the uterine contractions to expel the whelp more quickly.

Breech Presentations

If it is discovered that the tail and hind legs are presented and the water bag is intact, the feet should be grasped when they are first sighted, so that they do not disappear up the bitch again. If the bag has broken, every second counts, but DO NOT panic – remain calm. Keep a steady traction on the feet, try to pull the puppy out by steady, gentle movement. Unless the puppy receives oxygen quickly, it will be dead.

Stomach Uppermost

This can occur if the whelp has had its abdomen nearest to the dam's spine. A little warm liquid paraffin can be syringed into the vulva, making the whelp more slippery; then turn the whelp so that its back is uppermost and parallel to the bitch's back. When the whelp has been turned, generally it will be born quite easily. If a whelp is only partially incorrectly presented, it is better to turn the puppy to the correct position if possible, as it will make the birth a lot easier and improve the life-chance for the whelp.

Neck Presentations

The neck can be presented at the brim of the pelvis, and since the crown of the head and the nose are the widest part of the head, they may become impacted in the brim of the pelvis. It is better to push the pup's head back, so that the nose can present at the brim of the pelvis. It is preferable for the vet to do this rather than an amateur, but if there is a delay in the vet coming out, gently try this procedure.

Limb Presentation

If a forelimb is protruding, try to pull it forward, in order to encourage the corresponding shoulder free, then try to pull the other limb, possibly using a 'corkscrew' movement. This should always include a strong, gentle traction round and towards the bitch's nose, never straight out behind the root of the tail. Once the placenta begins to separate from the uterine wall, the blood and oxygen supply to the whelp will be cut off and as a consequence, sometimes the whelp will have blue or even white paws. Gently breathe oxygen into the puppy's lungs and rub it vigorously with a towel, stimulating the circulation. A tiny drop of brandy on your finger placed on the pup's tongue may help the pup to rally, or other specially prepared products advertised in the dog press. If the puppy is still rather limp and lifeless, hold it firmly and then swing it downwards several times. This may cause it to gasp for air. Keep repeating this process for about five to ten minutes.

Retention of the Afterbirth

Often the last placenta can be left in a horn of the uterus. Generally, if the St. Bernard has undergone a post-whelping examination, the vet will give an injection of pituitary extract to ensure that the uterus contracts and this will expel the afterbirth. The bitch may also require an antibiotic as a precaution against an infection. We have found that a course of garlic pills seems to aid the immune systems of our own St. Bernard bitches.

Retained Whelp

A retained whelp is a great source of infection, particularly if it has been dead for more than twenty-four hours. The longer the whelp is retained, the more poorly the bitch can become, with her temperature rising increasingly. She can go off her food, septicaemia can occur and she can die unless appropriate veterinary treatment is sought as soon as possible. Usually, an injection of pituitary extract can be given; sometimes it is necessary for a caesarean operation to be performed to remove the dead whelp and completely cleanse the uterus.

The new-born puppies would require substitute feeding, so ensure they do have a suckle from the dam before their mother goes in for the operation so that they have some colostrum, which helps build up their own immune systems.

Eclampsia

After whelping, possibly due to a fall in the level of calcium in the blood, this condition can occur. The exact cause is not properly known. The control over the calcium mechanisms, the internal secretion glands such as the pituitary glands and the hormones, is a delicate balance. If the level of calcium falls below a certain level this delicate balance is upset. Eclampsia is sometimes referred to as milk-fever, as it can occur within a few hours after whelping or three to four days after. Sometimes it can occur in the third or fourth week of post-whelping.

The symptoms of eclampsia start with the St. Bernard bitch being extremely restless, sometimes nervous, with a real expression of apprehension on her face. Another early symptom can be stiffening of the legs, which can develop into jerking movements consistent with having a fit. The bitch needs to be given fluids of calcium as soon as possible. It is probably better to take her along to the vet, rather than call the vet out, as all the equipment necessary will be at the clinic. The temperature of the bitch will be subnormal and she may try to vomit.

These convulsions are caused by a condition in the brain, possibly set off by an irritation of the uterus, and need to be treated as quickly as possible. Once the bitch has been on the necessary fluids, she can recover quickly. This condition can be extremely worrying for owners because of its unpleasantness, but it responds to treatment.

Metritis

This can result from a prolonged whelping, or the retention of a placenta or of the membranes. Chills and exposure can also cause this condition. Inflammation of the uterus occurs within a week of whelping, the vulva becomes swollen and is painful. This is a condition which requires early treatment. Check the dam's temperature which will have risen, and the pulse could be much quicker. The bitch is in a lot of pain after crouching in an upright position balanced on her hocks. There is a greyish/white discharge with an unpleasant smell and the bitch can occasionally vomit.

Other signs are that her milk could dry up and, in severe cases, the bitch can fall into a coma, have convulsions and die. Nursing care and treatment with antibiotics are essential, along with plenty of TLC. Extra nourishment which is easily digested is helpful, for example something like Complan.

The puppies would need to have substitute care from a foster bitch, or hand-rearing using the tube feeding method for the best results and to avoid air going into their stomachs.

Mammary Glands

When a puppy is born, its cry will stimulate the pituitary gland to release the hormone oxytocin, which in turn acts upon the bitch's mammary gland to release the milk. Interestingly, the growth hormone is released by the pituitary only after the pup has gone to sleep. Mammary glands are closely connected to the oestrus cycle.

There are generally five pairs of teats, not necessarily opposite each other, nor do they always run in pairs, so sometimes there can be an odd number. When the bitch is lactating (producing milk), the rear teats are often larger and can hold more milk than the other teats. Keep a close watch for introverted teats as these can create problems.

Mastitis

This is the inflammation of a milk gland. It occurs in bitches with an excess quantity of milk. The milk accumulates in a gland due to there being insufficient whelps to drain the milk, or because the puppies are weak, or the teats are introverted. Mastitis may also be caused by a bacterial infection.

Mastitis can often be prevented if the bitch has her teats examined daily. A teat which appears congested should have a strong, vibrant puppy placed on it to suckle. The gland could be massaged with warm olive oil to draw the milk off if there is a shortage of whelps. If the condition persists, contact the vet for further advice and treatment.

Prolapse

Fortunately, this is a rare occurrence in St. Bernards; however, should it happen, early diagnosis and treatment from the vet are essential. It can involve prolapse of one horn or the prolapse of the vagina. The latter is visible; however, the prolapse of the uterus horn is not. Wherever there is a suspicion that something is wrong with your bitch, a telephone call to the experienced breeder or vet describing the signs and symptoms should be made. A physical examination will probably be necessary.

Pyometra

This is an infection of the womb. It can sometimes occur about three to four weeks after the St. Bernard has been in season, though not all pyometra infections arise then. Generally it affects older bitches. Like metritis, there is distension of the abdomen and a foul-smelling discharge from the vulva. Usually the bitch has an excessive thirst and can drink a full bucket of water. This can make her vomit. The pus or discharge from the vulva is a pinkish colour and it can turn brown in some cases. Usually the only effective treatment is for the bitch to have a hysterectomy (removal of the womb). Older bitches can receive a new lease of life after recovering from the operation. There is a tendency for the bitch to put weight on and her coat may change its texture and require more grooming. This is a small price to pay for the quality of her life being improved.

Remember, a healthy St. Bernard is a happy dog. St. Bernards do make caring mothers, so they need to feel loved and cherished by their owners, and this includes attending to their medical needs.

FOSTERING AND HAND-REARING

Occasionally, when unforeseen circumstances occur, it may be necessary to hand-rear puppies. Some bitches' own milk can be too acid and, instead of nourishing her new-born puppies, it actually kills them. This is unusual but it does happen. We had a St. Bernard bitch, Ch. Coatham Hermes, who was the mother of Coatham Britania. Sadly she poisoned two of the litter before we realised that her milk was not constituted properly. Instead of the milk being white and slightly creamy, the milk from Hermes was yellow with an unpleasant smell.

Fortunately, we had another bitch that had whelped two-and-a-half weeks previously, Topvalley Blyth Spirit at Coatham, known as Carly. We took her babies and mixed them in a box with the three-day-old puppies from Hermes, then put the tiny puppies with Carly, who readily

accepted them, washing their faces. We started to give the larger puppies, which were two weeks older, porridge and more solid food, as they had been able to obtain some colostrum from their mother, and we gave them Lactol milk.

We observed that the urine of the tiny puppies was very yellow in colour, with a strong smell of ammonia. Although Carly would allow them to suckle and would wash their faces, she would not clean their genitals, as she disliked this strong urine; her nose would twitch in disgust. Thankfully we managed to rear both litters successfully, thanks to the maternal instinct of Carly.

Obviously it is much better to obtain a foster-mother if possible, as it helps socialise the puppies, as well as saving a great deal of hard work and commitment. It does not have to be another St. Bernard as long as the bitch can cope with Bernard puppies. Often the vet's is a good place to start to find a foster mother; the practice may be aware of bitches which have lost a litter or only had one or two puppies. The vets are also likely to know other breeders in the area, so do give it a try.

Composition of different kinds of milk.						
	Fat	Casein	Albumen	Sugar	Ash	Water
Dog	10.00	6.00	5.00	3.10	0.70	75.20
Cow	3.70	3.00	0.50	5.00	0.70	87.10
Goat	5.00	3.20	1.00	4.50	0.70	85.60
Cat	3.65	7.90	0.20	5.20	0.70	82.35
Sheep	5.20	4.70	0.10	4.95	0.60	84.45

THE FOSTER MOTHER

It is apparent from the above chart that the bitch's milk contains a lot of fat, as well as casein. The next best thing, if you are unable to obtain a foster mother, is to try goat's milk. If you have condensed milk in the house, this can be used as a substitute for bitch's milk by using four tablespoons of boiled water to five tablespoons of condensed milk, depending upon the number of puppies in the litter. Currently there are quality substitute milks on the market, so obtain packets of this as soon as possible. Follow the instructions carefully.

Presuming that you have obtained an

appropriate foster mother, the puppies must be introduced carefully so that the substitute carer will take them on. We believe it works well if the puppies are mixed in a box along with the birth puppies of the foster bitch. A little butter can be put on the backs of the newcomers to encourage the foster mother to lick them. Observe the foster mother when she gets into the whelping box, then carefully place the 'new' puppies on a teat next to one of her own babies. If the bitch begins to lick one of the newcomers, then she is probably going to accept the St. Bernard babies. This will be a relief as it can be rather worrying if you feel the life chances of your litter are slipping away. Do ensure that the bitch cleans the puppies to encourage them to use their bladder and bowels. This is to get rid of the meconium in their bowels.

As time moves on, the foster bitch and the puppies will form bonds and an attachment to one another. The bitch will start teaching the puppies in a natural way to prepare them for adulthood. When the time comes to wean the litter, carry on with solid food, as dealt with in the next chapter. We have known of a litter of St. Bernard puppies who were fostered successfully by a keen, maternal Dalmatian who, sadly, had lost all her own puppies.

BOTTLE FEEDING

When puppies have to be hand-reared due to unforeseen circumstances, a strict routine is required. It is advisable to have a tray laid out with all the equipment ready, such as feeding bottle, cotton wool swabs and wound powder to dab the umbilical cord if that is still necessary. It is most important to hand-rear puppies SLOWLY and not to overfeed them. The secret of effective hand-rearing is to avoid lethal mistakes happening in the first place. Hold the puppy in your left hand securely, with the head up. In your right hand place the feeding bottle and gentle encourage the puppy to suckle. The bottle needs to be tipped up so that the milk can flow. You will be able to feel the puppy suckling as well as seeing the milk reducing. The puppy needs to have his tummy gentle rubbed after feeding.

A satisfactory way of ascertaining that the Saint puppies are having sufficient food is if they sleep

contentedly between feeds without crying. Their stools will be properly formed without any undigested curds. The puppies will gradually gain weight, which can be monitored by weighing regularly. Initially, the puppies should be fed every two hours; this can be reduced to three hours after a few days. Fortunately, with the size of St. Bernard puppies, it is fairly easy to get them onto a premature baby feeder.

If the feeding is unsuitable, the puppies will cry continually and their stools, instead of being brown and of a good consistency, may become yellowy-green in colour, accompanied by undigested curds. Should this happen, the next feed should be cut down in mixture. Puppies can be fed on goat's milk. However bitch sustitute milk is better. As the fluid is vital for the puppy, dilute the mixture but maintain the level of fluid. Obtaining the balance for the puppies between correct and under or overfeeding comes with experience. Each litter is different. The milk substitutes now available are much improved, so there is an improved likelihood of the litter surviving, provided you can follow the directions and provide genuine commitment and time. Remember to feed the puppy by its body weight, rather than its age.

TUBE FEEDING

This can be useful if there are a large number of puppies to feed. Doing it, however, can be daunting but a vet could demonstrate how it can be done safely. Tube feeding is, basically, inserting a catheter, which is the length from the St. Bernard whelp's mouth to its stomach, into the puppy and then, using a syringe, inserting the puppy's food into the catheter. A hairclip spring can be clamped to the tube where the required amount of food has been poured, ensuring that the puppy does not receive too much of the mixture. This also prevents the catheter from being pushed too far into the puppy.

The formula of substitute milk should be ready-mixed and at the correct temperature. A little more than the puppy requires should be drawn up into the syringe (minus the needle) before you insert the catheter into the puppy. Place the puppy upon a flat surface with its tummy downwards, lying on something soft, such as a towel, to keep the puppy warm. Gently open the pup's mouth, the tip of the catheter should then be inserted into the mouth, causing the pup to start to swallow it on its own. It is most important to keep the head of the St. Bernard forward and downwards while inserting the catheter, so that it is directed into the stomach. If the head is held back the catheter could go into the lungs instead of the stomach, with disastrous results. This could be fatal, so do be extra careful.

As soon as the clip reaches the mouth of the puppy, the hand which is holding the puppy across the back can support the clip in order to prevent the catheter from slipping down the throat of the whelp. The puppy and the syringe can be lying flat on the towel or tray. Ensure that the end of the catheter is not kinked. Press the plunger of the syringe slowly with your thumb, until half the mixture is in the stomach. Allow the puppy to rest for a moment or two, then continue to feed. You can feel the pup's stomach extending. When full, it should not be taut, but have some "give" left. The puppy should then have had an adequate amount. Leave the catheter in place for a few moments then withdraw it carefully. Wipe the pup's mouth clean. Follow the normal after-feed procedure, encouraging the puppy to urinate and defecate. This is what the bitch would normally do from instinct to ensure that the waste products are expelled.

Repeat the process with each single puppy until all the litter have been fed, ensuring that the utensils and catheter are clean and free from any bacteria, so that you do not cross-infect these vulnerable Bernard babies. If in any doubt, consult the vet. Tube feeding a litter should only be carried out once the vet or an experienced breeder has demonstrated exactly what to do.

8 WEANING AND SOCIALISING THE LITTER

St. Bernard puppies in an average-size litter will be quite happy with their mother's milk until the age of three weeks. If the bitch has a particularly large litter, it may be necessary to start weaning at two weeks of age. We have found that a recent porridge-type mixture, introduced by a major pet food manufacturer, is ideal for St. Bernard puppies. It is palatable and easy to administer, and is a balanced food specifically designed for weaning puppies. However, the puppies' nutritional requirements develop simultaneously with their minds and their early socialisation.

NEONATAL PERIOD
The neonatal period is from zero to two weeks. The puppies are with their dam and their communications by touch, taste and smell are developing. The eyes of the St. Bernard puppy open between ten to fourteen days from birth, so the tiny puppy has to rely on its other senses. During this period, we find it is important gently to stroke every puppy for a few moments, carefully checking that each one is developing as normal. The gentle action of the stroking should feel comfortable, like the bitch's tongue. Through being handled on a daily basis the puppies should become accustomed to the human smell, and they should feel safe when handled. Do not be too rough with the puppies, as it can give them a sudden shock, especially if they have been sound asleep.

Back to feeding. Prepare the porridge mixture as

For the first couple of weeks, the puppies will sleep for the majority of the time.
Photo courtesy: Sanflax.

per the manufacturer's instructions. Take the bitch away from the puppies for an hour or so until the pups feel hungry but have no 'milk bar' to turn to. Offer a small amount of the mixture by pushing each pup's nose towards the dish. It is amazing how quickly St. Bernard pups get the idea and generally start lapping without any further encouragement, unlike some of the smaller breeds. On the first day of weaning this porridge mix could be given to each puppy twice, and the same amount given for two more consecutive days. On the fourth day introduce another substance, a proprietary complete puppy food, either from a can or dried. The dried complete puppy-food preparation would need to be scalded or soaked; we feel the tiny puppies prefer this. Be careful not to give the enthusiastic St. Bernard babies too much or they will develop colic. We would generally give this more solid food to our litter between 5.30 and 7.30 pm, so that we can observe the litter after eating. The bitch will be delighted to clear up any left-overs and wash her pups' faces.

TRANSITIONAL PERIOD

The transitional period is when the puppies' sensory abilities come to the fore, usually when their eyes are fully opened, their teeth have appeared and they begin to be stimulated by the sights and sounds of their surroundings. This generally starts between two and four weeks. The early life of the St. Bernard is so important – and the importance of the socialisation of such a large breed must not be underestimated.

During this transition period, pups start to wag their tails. They growl and bark for the first time and their world opens up, with the sounds of their environment having a dramatic effect upon their development. They will be aware of human contact and their temperature regulation mechanism improves. Their hearing begins to sharpen as their ear canals open up, so that brisk, startled responses can be seen if a door is banged.

By four weeks, the vision of the puppy will be similar to that of the adult dog; however, another week or two of development is required before the St. Bernard puppy will be able to recognise its own mother from sight. Also, by four weeks of age, the brain of the St. Bernard puppy is myelinated and ready for complex learning.

During this stage, a particularly maternal bitch may regurgitate food for her litter. We have had several bitches which have done this, particularly if the pups have licked the face of their mother. It is in the best interest of the dam to get her pups weaned as quickly as possible as, in the wild, the suckling process inhibits the bitch's "fight or flight" response, and this instinct remains even in the domesticated animal. However, her maternal influence on her young is very strong during this period and the influence of the other littermates begins to kick in too.

COAT TYPE

Genetics have already been dealt with in an earlier chapter, but it is important to point out here that, at around four weeks after a pup's birth, it should be possible to distinguish between the two types of coat. If you have mated a rough bitch to a rough dog then all the puppies will be rough-coated St. Bernards. If your bitch is rough-coated and has been mated to a smooth-coated male St. Bernard, a proportion of the puppies will also be smooth-coated like the sire. However, if you have mated two smooth coats that have long or rough-coated ancestors, then there is a one in four chance that some of the puppies will have long coats.

The transitional period is when the senses begin to function.

The puppies take an increasing interest in what is going on.

The method we use to identify a rough – the long-haired in comparison to the smooth or short-haired coat – is by feel as well as appearance. At around four weeks the smooth-haired tends to have straight hair on its ears and the texture of the coat will actually feel like cotton wool. The slightly longer hair on the smooth, which will end up as the top coat, glints or shines in the sun or the light in the kennel. The rough, or long-haired, St. Bernard, has waves on the hair on their ears, and their coat feels much more like velvet or silk, softer to the touch. On the forelegs the long-haired St. Bernard will have slightly longer feathering than the short-haired. The hindquarters also have slightly longer wavy hair on the long-haired St. Bernard, whereas on the short-haired the coat tends to be 'spongy' on their hindquarters.

Obviously, by the time the pups are six or seven weeks old, it is easy to distinguish between the two types of coat just by appearance. Sometimes, however, even with experience and knowledge of this marvellous breed, it is possible to have a problem with the occasional Saint to determine whether it is a long-haired or a short-haired until the puppy is about eight weeks. Thankfully this is a rarity rather than a norm.

WORMING THE LITTER
This can be carried out at four weeks of age. There are various preparations on the market but the veterinary surgery is the best place to obtain quality worming products. It is essential to ensure that St. Bernard puppies do not have an infestation of worms, as it can affect their growth. Worm the

By four weeks of age, the rough-coated and the smooth-coated can be detected.

Feeding should be a social as well as a nutritional task. Photo: Steph Holbrook.

litter again at six weeks of age. We believe in worming our own litters at least twice before the puppies move on to their prospective new homes. We advise that the puppy should be wormed again at twelve weeks, and then every six months, especially if there are children in the household.

WEANING

When the puppies are five weeks old and eating regular balanced meals, they should be weaned off their mother in a gradual way. Be mindful of the fact that your St. Bernard bitch, when lactating between three to six weeks, will require 7.5 kcal of extra energy per day to meet the needs of her litter. This can be provided by increasing the amount of her food by 25 per cent for each puppy. Alternatively you can provide the extra food ad lib so that the bitch can help herself when she needs to. The puppy will begin to ask the dam for food during the transition period. It is during this period that the building blocks for the dog's life are laid down. What the puppy learns now, and the experiences which the St. Bernard pups are given from birth, will affect the rest of their lives. Encouragement and praise is required, not leaving the litter in total isolation. Human contact is vital to the development of the individual pups.

Feeding the pups is a social as well as nutritional task which the breeder generally carries out four to five times per day. By now the puppies should be having two milky or porridge meals and two meat or complete puppy food meals per day. Follow the manufacturer's instructions for giant breeds and you will not go far wrong. We usually add beaten egg to the morning feeds and attempt to feed the puppies in pairs. At times this is easier

said than done, especially with a large litter. Remember that how the St. Bernard behaves, at any given time in its life, is a result of constant interplay between the genetic potential and the environment. What tiny puppies experience can affect the adult St. Bernard.

The puppies will gradually increase their growth and appetite. We ensure that the mother still sleeps with the litter until they are six weeks old. By seven weeks the litter should be completely weaned. The milk from the dam will begin to dry up and should not cause her any problems.

THE SOCIALISATION PERIOD

This starts between four to six weeks with littermates and possibly other dogs. Their attachment to humans, I have found, is generally important from four to twelve weeks, to establish strong bonds. It has been observed that any type of social relationship that a pup develops begins as a problem and ends with solution. The main relationship which the puppy St. Bernard has experienced has been a care-dependency with its mother. During the socialisation process this relationship evolves into one of dominance–submission. We have observed many bitches with litters of puppies for over thirty years; it is fascinating watching St. Bernard puppies develop. Maternal care, as we are aware, is based on several factors such as genetic, hormonal, sensory and environmental. The following list shows the type of behaviour we have observed over the years in our St. Bernard bitches when caring for puppies.
• Licking the faces of the whelps and grooming their bodies.

• Licking the pups' ano-genital region, then consuming their waste products.
• Gently pushing the pups with their nose, positioning them for feeding and warmth.
• Carrying "lost" puppies back to the nest.
• Lying on their sides so that the pups can suckle, then the next time on returning to the whelping box, lying on her other side.
• Regurgitating food for puppies.
• Carrying tripe, chicken and pieces of meat around for the pups.
• Guarding the litter if any strangers have approached.

In fact, one bitch, Sheba, actually tried to put her fifth puppy into the cardboard box with the others after she had whelped! This was her first litter and Sheba was clumsy. We were concerned that she might inadvertently lie on her newly-acquired two bitch puppies so we placed them on to a fleecy cover in a cardboard box, allowing her to clean and look after number three. When the next puppy was arriving, the previous one was safely placed in the box. By the time her last puppy arrived, Sheba clearly thought this was the correct procedure to have them all in the box.

The tiny puppies, when seeking care from their mothers, will initially whine, then use their sense of touch and smell to root around their mother for warmth and food. St. Bernard puppies are adept at crawling forward with their necks extended searching for food and warmth, quickly latching onto a vacant teat like a limpet on a rock.

During the socialisation process, care-seeking behaviour in St. Bernard puppies becomes more complex. This occurs between four and six weeks. Examples are:

• Wagging their tails and holding them low over their backs like a pug.
• Yelping.
• Licking their mother's face, nose, lips and flews.
• Jumping up.
• Pawing their mother.
• Biting her tail.

The dam begins to teach her puppies some lessons in life by withdrawing her milk bar, and scolding the puppies by biting them if they persist in nibbling at her teats when she has withdrawn this service. The way the St. Bernard dam alters the care dependency relationship is fascinating. Puppies often show passive submission by lying on their backs, feet in the air, to be licked earlier than the other pups. 'Growls' and mouth threats are all part of the teaching process for determined puppies. The litter have to learn compromise, so sub-dominance occurs.

THE IMPORTANCE OF PLAY

I am certain anyone who has a litter of St. Bernard puppies will spend hours of 'puppy-vision' and learn a lot about how pups develop and interact with one another. It is far more rewarding than watching TV. The litter of pups is a temporary society where play activity has a number of functions.

• Play stimulates communal behaviour, creating social bonds with the other dogs. These bonds will be necessary for the future well-being of any 'pack', not that there would be a pack in the majority of cases, only humans. However, in St. Bernard kennels where a particular puppy may be run on, the dog has to learn his or her place in the established hierarchy.

It is fascinating to watch the interaction between bitch and puppies.

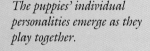
The puppies' individual personalities emerge as they play together.

• Play affects and moulds adult social behaviour. Through trial and error of play, the foundations are laid for communication skills.

• Careful observation of the litter playing and interacting is a good guide as to which are going to be the more dominant St. Bernards and those who are sub-dominant or more submissive. Through play, they learn how to manipulate inanimate objects and social objects, including us!

• Play promotes physical dexterity and mental flexibility.

• Play helps the puppy to become more co-ordinated.

• Play encourages experimentation under safe conditions. It teaches the puppy how to time him or herself, how to intervene or intercept and how to maintain their ground.

• Play teaches action patterns and how to carry out sequences of events.

• Play allows for safe exploration.

• Play stimulates inventiveness and teaches problem-solving.

• Play is a life-long activity in dogs, especially in kennels, where older St. Bernards will respond to the 'invitation' to play from the younger Saints.

In St. Bernards, instincts passed on from generation to generation still come to the fore during social interaction between one another. Classic canine play, normal behaviour such as sexual, predatory and some aggression, take place, but not out of context. Play is a source of information about littermates; it encourages the St. Bernard to develop certain skills and deflects natural aggression. Play teaches co-operative behaviour, and adversaries can be tested in a ritualistic manner through play fighting. A single puppy brought up on its own can sometimes be aggressive towards other dogs as it has not learned how to inhibit this behaviour.

St. Bernard pups need to be exposed to a lot of

noises before leaving the litter, such as vacuum cleaners, radio, TV, cats, cars and so on. We try to take each one of the litter out for a short ride in the back of the estate car so that they can become accustomed to this prior to going off to prospective new homes. I feel it is less disturbing for the puppy.

DOMINANT BEHAVIOUR

St. Bernards are usually gregarious, sociable dogs. Due to their size and strength when adult, it is most important for you to be in control over your St. Bernard, not the other way around. A well-behaved dog in any breed is a pleasure to own; a disobedient dog, especially a St. Bernard, is a nightmare.

New owners must carry on the training and socialisation programme where the breeder left off, so knowledge and awareness of aspects of training and understanding your eight week-old puppy are vital. Owners need to establish with their puppy that they are very much the pack leader.

The St. Bernard puppy learns a lot during play. He learns to use weapons, for example his sharp teeth. These milk teeth can be as sharp as razors. A dominant puppy can display 'threat' by raising his hackles, feign an attack or startle an adversary by barking or growling loudly. He can intimidate a littermate by staring or standing over the puppy, then possibly attack. It may seem comical to observe these fat bundles of fur play-fighting but it is not comical to the littermates. The pup learns to signal dominance and must equally learn to signal friendliness, lack of aggression, submission, tolerance and co-operative behaviour if he is to be balanced and trainable.

Dominant activities to look out for during the socialisation stages are:
• Stalking other pups with head and tail down, hindquarters raised and ears alert.
• Chasing, ambushing or pouncing upon littermates.
• Standing over the littermate with head and tail erect and neck arched.
• Circling the littermates while stiffly wagging the tail and walking imperiously.
• Actually biting and attacking the neck, ears and face of a littermate.
• Hackles up (piloerection).
• Baring of weapons, snarling and displaying incisors and canines.

• Direct stare at other St. Bernard pups with dilated pupils – "showing eye".
• Shoulder or hip slams to other pups.
• Standing with forepaws on the littermate's back.
• Male pups mounting other siblings.
• Wagging only the tip of an erect tail.
• Ears very alert or completely flattened back against the head.
• Play fighting to excess.

By using these displays, the dominant dog implies power to the other St. Bernard siblings. As owners and managers of this breed, we need to do exactly the same later in the pup's life when we begin formal training. If a pup has learned the importance of these body signals during the socialisation stage, the likelihood of later fighting and dominance is largely reduced. The pup's hormonal feedback system is still being developed.

SUBMISSIVE BEHAVIOUR

Just as important as the dominance behaviours are the defence and submissive behaviours. These surrendering behaviours are vital to prevent unnecessary injuries.

St. Bernard puppies show submission in the following ways:
• St. Bernard puppies put their tails between their legs, ears flattened, head hung low and eyes averted from the dominant sibling.
• The puppy may adopt a submissive 'grin' with lips retracted.
• Licking lips, sometimes sneezing and showing their incisors at the same time.
• Rolling on their back.
• Lying on their side, lifting their hind leg and exposing the genital region.
• Urinating.
• Defecating.
• Remaining stationary while aggressor circles or places paws on their shoulders.
• Remaining stationary while aggressor mounts.

GROUP ACTIVITIES

During this socialisation period up to twelve weeks, the St. Bernard's mind is at its most impressionable. The puppies learn to participate in group activities with their mother. Other exploratory behaviour occurs along with care-giving and care-receiving activities. Group activities which St. Bernard

Companionship between puppies gives a sense of well-being. These Wardana pups are 10 weeks old.

puppies enjoy are sleeping together, walking or running with each other, grooming each other by licking the faces of their siblings after drinking milk, barking or howling together, sniffing, pawing and nosing each other and feeding together.

These group co-ordinated behaviours developed during the socialisation period as normal litter or pack activities are either perpetuated by the dogs or co-opted by us when we, as owners, exhibitors, enthusiasts or custodians become members of the 'pack'.

THE PACK LEADER
It is important for new owners to be the pack leader, the 'alpha' dog for the St. Bernard puppy being taken into your home. Physical activities, such as walking or running, St. Bernard puppies love and they will keenly follow their new 'alpha' leader. This is a marvellous opportunity to teach the puppy to 'come'. Simply find a large open space, leave the puppy, then walk quickly or run ahead, turn round and wave your arms, shouting the pup's name, followed by the word "Come". The likelihood is that your Saint will be delighted to be reunited with you, so will respond immediately.

The socialisation of the litter has been based on observation of maternal, environmental and peer pressures. It provides would-be breeders with a little insight into what to expect from breeding a litter of St. Bernard puppies. Remember the puppies love to play, so ensure they have pull-type toys to play with, as well as softer toys to chew. This will help to develop the Saint's mind.

POTENTIAL OWNERS
A most important task, which holds a lot of responsibility for breeders, is to ensure that the right people obtain one of your Saint puppies. It is a good idea to have a set of questions to ascertain if potential St. Bernard owners know just what they will be taking on.
• Do these people have adequate time to spend with the St. Bernard puppy?
• Do these people have the commitment to meet all the needs and requirements of a large dog?
• Is the dog going to be part of the family or outgrow its usefulness?
• Are they prepared for all the dog hair when the St. Bernard moults?
• Can they cope with the saliva – or "slobbers", as the majority of Saint enthusiasts name the long drools?
• Can they really afford to meet the cost of food and veterinary expenses?
• Are they prepared for this delightful ball of fluff to grow into a stubborn, possibly 14-stone, giant dog?
• Do they have somewhere the Saint can go when non-doggy friends or family arrive?
• Have they ever owned a large dog before?
• What is going to happen to their Saint when they go on holiday?

• Ask prospective owners to go away and think about it if you are unsure about their commitment or motives in wanting to own a Saint.

• Encourage the unsure prospective St. Bernard owner to write down a list of 'for' and 'against' reasons for having a St. Bernard, taking into account their current lifestyle.

These are just a few of the questions which should be considered before selling anyone a St. Bernard, in our opinion. As a breeder, you have the responsibility to ensure that each one of your puppies receives the best possible home. This can only be achieved if you are totally honest with potential Saint owners and point out the disadvantages as well as the advantages.

If a person is extremely house-proud, then quite honestly the last thing they need is a St. Bernard, who is not the cleanest of dogs. Within a short space of time, their stress levels will have risen and the dog possibly placed on the Rescue, which is very sad for the poor dog. Spending extra time with potential owners to educate and raise their awareness about some of the problems which may arise is well worth the time and trouble in the long run, especially for the future of that delightful puppy.

Remember, a dog must be for life. This could be from as little as five years to over ten years. Are you really prepared to ensure new owners can meet this task?

We have known people really devote their lives to one Saint, going to extraordinary lengths to make certain the dog is happy. One family up in Scotland who purchased a puppy from us after their Newfoundland died, moved home so that their Saint had more room! Other families have changed their cars so the St. Bernard is more comfortable. These are often super homes where the dog is loved way beyond the call of duty. St. Bernards respond by being extremely loyal, loving and faithful to their kind owners. The invisible bond is most important in the life of St. Bernard and owner.

Somehow this chemistry must work, as we are delighted to say that several people over a thirty-year period have now been back for a third St. Bernard, after their dogs have died from natural causes. Others have gone on to have lines or kennels of their own, starting off with Coatham stock. This is very rewarding, especially if the St.

Potential owners should be picked with the greatest care.

Bernards go on to become Champions. We are just as pleased when the pet owner contacts us at Christmas, often sending a lovely photograph and letter. It is so wonderful to know that the bundle of fluff that you saw come into this world, carefully nurtured and loved, and with which you carried out early stages of socialisation, has gone on to become a majestic, well-behaved Saint who is the pride and joy of the couple or family.

St. Bernards and children are definitely a winning combination, in our opinion, provided children are encouraged to handle and help care for the St. Bernard in a caring, appropriate way. St. Bernards also need to learn some basic obedience to be sociable around the children. We have found this breed to have an amazing affinity with children, particularly those who are vulnerable or have a disability. Although Saints can be clumsy and extremely rough when playing with older teenagers, with toddlers or with children with a disability they seem to have a natural instinct that they must be gentle and careful.

Newspaper articles, and the evidence from the

Typical St. Bernard puppies from the Ravensbank kennel.

Hospice regarding amazing rescues of children and adults carried out by Barry and other St. Bernards, clearly support these findings. All of this reinforces the importance of early socialisation from birth, within the litter, then the continuing process within the St. Bernard pup's new home. This ensures the St. Bernard has a positive place within the family and enjoys quality of life, rather than being some kind of status symbol or mere kennel dog.

KENNEL CLUB REGISTRATIONS

Reputable breeders have an affix which is held at their national Kennel Club. The kennel affix is similar to a trademark in the fashion industry. Some famous affixes are also a mark of quality St. Bernards, but not all. Just because a kennel has an affix, or trademark, it does not necessarily mean they breed quality St. Bernards; so do some

research by enquiring at the Kennel Club or Breed Clubs.

When the litter are a few days old, the Kennel Club Registration form needs to be completed. The stud dog owner will have signed the blue form verifying the date of mating and the name of the stud dog, with KC registration number or studbook number. Ensure you fill the form in correctly. If you do not have an affix, then think of an applicable name for each puppy. The names of puppies must not exceed 24 letters, which includes the affix. If the name has been entered into the KC Stud book, that name will not be used within the breed again. On the back of the registration form are all the guidelines you require, so do ensure you read them carefully. It saves a lot of time and trouble later, should the form have to be returned due to being incorrectly completed.

9 *SHOWING YOUR ST. BERNARD*

So you think your St. Bernard has been well reared, and is beginning to mature into a quality Saint and you really fancy having a go at showing? Assuming that you purchased the Saint from a reputable breeder who has been successful in breeding and exhibiting and making up Champions, then it would be advisable to go back to that breeder, seek their opinion and guidance, and ask them to assess the potential of your Saint. You should be prepared for the breeder to be honest with you. If the breeder really feels that the Saint has not acquired enough quality to fulfil the Breed Standard and to become a prize winner, you should accept that fact and enjoy your St. Bernard as a companion dog. However, if the breeder feels the puppy has a lot of the attributes required to meet the Breed Standard to some level of success in the ring then, with encouragement, do have a go.

You really must be prepared to listen and learn from the years of experience, knowledge, awareness, insight and helpful hints acquired by seasoned campaigners and breeders. Do not be tempted to listen to the "wannabes" who think they know it all. Remember, God gave us all two ears, two eyes but only one mouth. Observe what ringcraft is, see that it is about how to show and get the best out of a St. Bernard, ask appropriate questions, listen to experienced exhibitors and you will learn a lot.

BASIC SHOW TRAINING
If you intend to enter dog shows, remember that these are beauty competitions, they are not testing out brains, so do not include the "sit" command when stopping. No show dog is expected to perform the sit on command in the showring. Show training should be fun. If the dog is an extrovert this can be a big help.

Begin when the puppy is about 12 weeks old. Get the Saint to stand for a few moments only. It does not matter how he is standing, as long as he stands still for those few moments. To encourage the puppy, repeat the word "stand" and gently stroke the puppy under his tummy and groin. When he has done this without moving, give the puppy lots of praise and an edible reward. This is a positive reinforcer for the required behaviour. Gradually increase the time, but do not overdo it or the St. Bernard will become bored.

After the formal session, it is good to spend a little time playing with the puppy in a relaxing way, to strengthen the bond of attachment between dog and man. If there is a loving relationship, the puppy will be keen to please and willing to co-operate, enjoying the extra attention – provided encouragement, praise and a food reward are given.

TEACHING THE STANCE
Once the puppy has understood the principle that he has to stand still, the next requirement is to teach the puppy the show pose, or stance. The forelegs should be totally perpendicular, and parallel with each other. The hind legs should be extended until the hock is also at right angles, to

In the first instance, you must be confident that your St. Bernard has show potential. This smooth-haired puppy is 16 weeks old.

A rough-coated puppy, also aged 16 weeks, learning the show stance.

show the gentle angulation of the stifle. This should create a balanced picture: the dog's head should be raised by holding it under the chin, stroking it gently. The other hand should be run gently under the abdomen, with you saying "stand", "good puppy". Once the puppy has co-operated and held the show pose for a few moments, reward him with a treat. St. Bernards are greedy dogs who generally love their food, so they will quickly respond for the food treats.

After several days of stacking your Saint, as this show pose is called, try a slightly different method. Using a soft rope or leather leash, stack the puppy as before but, instead of holding him under the chin, lift his head up with the leash, gently enough so as not to choke him but sufficient so that the reach of neck can be seen. Let him have some treats to encourage him to remain standing still, with plenty of verbal rewards when he is achieving the desired goal. Do not be too enthusiastic and make him stand still in the show stance for too long a period as he, once again, will become bored. In time, as they become more mature, St. Bernards trained in this way will stand steadily, without manual assistance, in a natural stance.

EMPHASISING THE GOOD POINTS

In the United States, dog judges tend to have all the St. Bernards facing the same way in the line-up. However, in Britain and Europe, judges usually judge the Saints as the handlers choose to set them up. A good tip is to practise setting the dog up in front of a large mirror to ascertain which, if any, is the more pleasing side. Prop the mirror up in the garage, or out-building, and be constructively critical with your handling. Then you will really learn by your mistakes, in a non-threatening way, about which handling technique is best for that particular Saint, before the two of you enter the ring.

If your Saint is a splash-back, instead of self-coloured with equal markings on both sides, he or she can look different on the left side from the right side. It is sensible to show your Saint with the better markings visible to the judge, rather than concealed against the handler. Why not ask a fellow exhibitor to stand your Saint so you can take a "judge's eye view" and assess the Saint from a distance. It can be beneficial to see your Saint from the "other side of the fence", so to speak. View the dog in a holistic way, by taking into account the complete picture. Look at all the quality attributes, rather than focus on the faults. Be mindful of those weaknesses and faults but they have to be considered in relation to the whole dog, not as separate entities. Remember to be honest with

The skill of the handler is to show off the dog to best advantage. This is Ch. Burnswark Alicia.

yourself when you are emotionally involved with an affectionate, adoring Saint. Sometimes it is difficult to be objective and you will forgive some glaring faults due to wishful thinking, rather than being constructive.

If you cannot find and acknowledge the faults in your own Saint – and this does not mean that you have to broadcast these weaknesses to everyone else – then you should not criticise fellow exhibitors' Saints. Kennel blindness is a trend which can be detrimental to breeding for the improvement of the breed. Sometimes it leads to hereditary faults being perpetuated, instead of being considered undesirable and consideration given to how best to eradicate them.

MOVEMENT

When considering movement, it is worthwhile getting someone else to move the dog at an early stage in his development in an effort to gauge the dog's optimum pace. The KC Standard in the UK requires a St. Bernard to have "easy extension, unhurried or smooth, movement capable of

covering difficult terrain". It does not mean you go around the ring as fast as you can go – showing is certainly not a race. The judge needs to be able to ascertain if the Saint has easy extension on the move, if the dog has an unhurried gait, whether the Saint uses drive from the hindquarters, using first and second thigh muscles, has good kinetic balance or looks out of proportion when in full locomotion. When moving directly away from the judge, does your Saint move in a straight line or is the Saint cow-hocked, toes turning out, hocks almost touching each other? With the help of a friend, you will be able to judge which pace best suits your dog.

VIDEO HELP

Enlist the help of a video fanatic. In this fast-moving world of technology, the videotape of you and your dog will hold evidence of positive qualities, as well as areas for future development. Make sure you do learn by your mistakes; we all make them from time to time, even the most experienced of handlers. Study the film, slow it down and consider where improvements can be made. What were the best standing shots of the dog? Ask yourself why, what can be done to reproduce this look in the ring, then aim to achieve this result.

There is a lot more to showing a dog than just standing holding a St. Bernard by a slack leash. The exhibitor who has put a lot of work in beforehand, and who is confident, will reap the rewards of their efforts as their dog stands quietly in the stance position, oozing with quality and tip-top condition and presentation, and then moving with drive, and will have an advantage over a less meticulous handler and exhibit.

HOW TO SHOW

Although you might be feeling nervous inwardly, you need to give the outward appearance that you are full of confidence. A St. Bernard will quickly pick up on your body language if you are nervous and act inappropriately, no matter how temporary this is. Demonstrating confidence will help inspire your St. Bernard – along with being prepared.

Most St. Bernard exhibitors stack their dogs, while a few encourage 'free-standing'. Unfortunately, unlike a lot of other breeds such as

THE SHOW STANCE
Photos: Steph Holbrook.

The front legs are moved into position.

The back legs are now positioned.

The St. Bernard is now standing four-square and balanced, with his attention focused on the handler.

Rottweilers or Beagles, which seem to free-stand on command, St. Bernards do not follow this natural stance and tend to be set up formally.

To encourage your Saint to free-stand, use treats and practise a great deal when he is a puppy. If your Saint does have the ability and aptitude to free-stand, then build on this to your advantage. There is nothing that looks more impressive than walking into a ring with a powerful, majestic Saint proudly holding his head up – one who is well-balanced, with that air of confidence, "challenging" metaphorically speaking, other Saints to beat him after proudly walking into the stance naturally.

The response to free-showing depends very much on the mental attitude of the St. Bernard concerned. From observations over numerous years, I feel that male St. Bernards do tend to have a more arrogant look about them and will free-show better than bitches, especially if they are used at stud. I m certain it is all to do with their ego and testosterone. It is all in the mind of the confident St. Bernard. They really do enjoy showing and, more importantly, winning.

If a Saint has an eager, inquisitive nature, it is much easier to encourage that natural look. This can be encouraged at home by placing a leash on your Saint. Walk around then stop if the dog is free-standing correctly, then reward him with a treat. In other words, bait the dog. If the St. Bernard is not quite right, encourage the leg or foot which may be out of place to move that small amount so that the dog is standing four-square, which means like a square table with a leg in each corner.

It is much better to allow Saints to develop a natural stance if possible; however, this breed is extremely stubborn, and if they become bored or just decide they do not want to do something, they are not the easiest of dogs to move, due to their physical size. Try to make showing fun. Encourage the correct pose, then reward with a treat.

The Saint who dislikes showing intensely will demonstrate this by his body language, and will stand like a sack of potatoes. It can be so frustrating trying to encourage him to smarten up – at home the dog can look so majestic in familiar surroundings, yet in the ring becomes a wilting violet.

TRAINING FOR THE SHOWRING

Having discussed showring training in general terms, we will endeavour to be more specific for the novice exhibitor. Remember, training for the showring should be fun for the puppy, with the end result being to get the Saint to stand still for a few moments in the show pose. On the ground, with smaller breeds, it is possible gently to lift the dog at the front, under the chest, letting the front legs drop perpendicular and parallel. This same stance is the desired goal, without having to "drop" the Saint into the stance, as they are far too heavy to pick up. We have found that, by *lifting* one leg at a time from the elbow and under the chest when the Saint is relaxed, it is possible to *move* one leg at a time. From our experience, if you just try to move one paw at a time, the Saint will move the paw back just as quickly as you have placed it; however, by lifting one leg at a time, they do seem not to move this as quickly.

Coatham Smooth Liaison is a real nightmare to show, as she is such a fidget. At home, Sophie, as she is called, will stand for ages in the show pose, with her food treat as a reward. In the showring, if something attracts her curiosity, she is fine. However, in the all-important line-up, while the judge is concentrating prior to making his or her final decision after endeavouring to assess the Saint with the most required attributes to fulfil the Breed Standard, Sophie can just flop into "turn off" position. Which is precisely what can happen. Despite years of practice and experience, we have not found any real cures for St. Bernards who just do not enjoy showing and who switch off. Stringing them up and getting annoyed makes the task worse. If Sophie is in the correct frame of mind to show she can be marvellous, as her two Challenge Certificates and several Best in Show at club shows verify. However, this unpredictable Saint knows exactly how to wind us up. Regardless of this, we love her deeply as she is such a character.

DISGUISING FAULTS

If your Saint has a constructional fault at the front, you will have to endeavour to discreetly realign the forelegs. Having achieved the desired effect at the front, gently run your hand down along the back line, lift the hind leg and slightly move back or forward until the Saint is square. The hocks should

MOVING THE ST. BERNARD
Photos: Steph Holbrook.

Moving the dog away from the judge.

Towards the judge.

Movement is assessed in profile.

be perpendicular to the ground, parallel with each other. Raise the head by placing your hand under the jaw and gently tickle your Saint under the chin. The muzzle should be parallel to the ground, not pointing up or down. This angle should show the reach of neck off to the best advantage. There should be a gentle turn of the stifle on your Saint Bernard. If the dog is too straight in the stifle, this is emphasised when the hind legs are stretched too far back. Shorten the rear stance and it will not look as bad. However, a good judge will still be able to assess the fault when going over your St. Bernard. Try not to advertise glaring faults.

It can be helpful to ask another handler to set your St. Bernard up in a show pose, then you stand at a distance, critically viewing the overall picture. Hopefully, if you are honest and objective, it should be possible to see, from the stance of your Saint, where improvements can be made, unless there are too many constructional faults.

At least in our breed, we do not need to concern ourselves about holding the tail, as happens in some Gundog breeds, hounds such as Beagles and in some Terriers. The tail should not be held over the back like an Akita or Pug, as this is a fault. Should your Saint persist in doing this when standing, push the tail down between the legs, saying "tail, tail". When the Saint understands that his tail should be kept down, then give the dog lots of verbal praise. If the tail begins to rise again, sharply say the words "No, tail". When it goes down, once again, lots of verbal praise. Remember the old proverb "practice makes perfect"!

TRAINING AND SHOW LEADS
For training and control, the best aid is a choker chain with leather leash. We prefer leather as it does not burn or damage the skin if the dog pulls, whereas some rope or nylon leashes do. An important tool we humans have is an awareness of psychology. From the St. Bernard arriving at your home at about eight weeks old, it is vital that you are accepted as pack leader. If the puppy thinks you are stronger and more powerful than him or her, then there is a built-in instinct to respect and conform. It is essential to reinforce this message when the St. Bernard is small. Should the puppy pull on the leash, a quick, short, sharp jerk on the choker chain shows that walking to heel, not

pulling, is the required behaviour. The large, fully-grown St. Bernard dog or bitch may well be much heavier than you but if the St. Bernard *thinks* you are stronger and more powerful, he or she will respond appropriately.

It is most important to be consistent in your approach so that the St. Bernard does not receive confusing messages about what is right and acceptable behaviour and which behaviours are wrong and will not be tolerated. You must not wait until your Saint is acting up and getting out of control at about nine or ten months old, as he will then be aware that if he pulls and takes off, he is stronger, and you will be unable to prevent him from going his own way. Reinforcing control and boundaries is much harder when the Saint can weigh well over 10 stone – so be warned.

Once you have convinced the Saint that you are boss, then, when he responds well to a choker chain, a fine-leather, slip-type leash can be used to show the dog. This lighter leash gives you control, as well as being unobtrusive. It can be lifted up behind the ears of your dog to encourage a more alert expression. The St. Bernard should be on your left side with the slip chain put on in such a way that, when the chain is pulled, the ring attached to the lead pulls upwards. Many people do not know that there is a correct, as well as an incorrect way of using a slip chain.

GROOMING FOR THE RING
As previously stated, showing requires the dog to look its best; this entails making certain the dog is clean and the coat is thoroughly brushed, whether the Saint Bernard is long-haired or the shorter-coated variety. Some trimming may be necessary but this needs to be carried out carefully, not done in a rush, otherwise the finished results will not look professional. Every effort should be made to get the dog to look as smart as possible.

Conditioning the St. Bernard is not just about giving the dog a bath. It involves planning and plenty of exercise, along with quality food to maintain both condition and energy levels. As previously stated, a St. Bernard should have the minimal amount of free exercise before it is twelve months old. Once the St. Bernard has reached his first birthday and you are serious about showing, then he requires a regime of controlled exercise to develop and maintain optimum muscle condition. If your St. Bernard has a loose front, this is partly due, we have to say, to construction. However, regular exercise will tighten and tone up the front and forequarters.

THE GROOMING TABLE
From an early age, it is a good idea to encourage the Saint to get up on to a large box or table, about the height of the benches at Championship shows, for grooming purposes. About two days before the show, encourage the dog to get up on to the box or table to appraise his condition, and to ascertain what needs to be undertaken to tidy him up prior to exhibition. Give the dog a thorough groom with a short-toothed brush, getting all the under-coat out, regardless of whether the Saint is rough-haired or short-haired.

It may be necessary to use a pair of thinning scissors around the neck or through the flanks and feathering. The type of scissors we recommend is a pair with one side serrated, the other blade solid. Using the serrated blade of the thinning scissors, with the whole scissors opened out as wide as possible, pull the blade through all the body coat. Starting at the neck, work down the back, over the sides and hindquarters; also up the underside of the tail and under the abdomen. This brings out all the dead hair. You will be surprised at how much hair comes out. The tail-end should be discreetly tidied up, especially on the short-haired or smooth-coated dogs. It just gives the dog the edge over the competitors as it looks finished off. A standard type of stripping knife can also be used.

NAILS
Adequate exercise on hard surfaces will ensure that the nails on your St. Bernard are kept short. If, for any reason, the dog has rather long nails, they should be cut back with the guillotine clippers suitable for giant breeds. Providing these are sharp it is a relatively quick job, once you have successfully secured that elusive paw! If you do accidentally catch the quick, the St. Bernard paw will be sensitive for a few days, so never risk leaving the toenails until the day before the show, just in case of accidents. St. Bernards are really great big softies and can totally over-react to a small amount of blood from a cut toenail. They can sulk and be

unfriendly towards you all day, as this accident is taken so personally. Sometimes, as soon as they see the clippers, they can take off. It is amazing how small a Saint can become when wishing to escape under a table to avoid toenail trimming. Always remember to reward the St. Bernard with a special treat when completing the last toenail; it helps to encourage co-operation next time if the dog thinks it will receive a reward for the appropriate behaviour.

If the Saint freaks out and will not lie still to have his nails clipped, use a large metal file and gently file away at each toenail. Try this when the dog is in a deep sleep so that in time, he will come to accept that this does not hurt. I think it is the noise of the clippers which some Saints dislike so intensely. Cutting off the white part of the nail does not hurt; it is psychological with a lot of St. Bernards, who are proper cowards.

WHISKERS
"To be or not to be, that is the question". Personally, we do not trim the whiskers off the muzzle of our St. Bernards. This area has important senses which send messages to the dog's brain, so we leave the whiskers alone. However, other exhibitors and breeders do trim the whiskers off in the belief that it enhances the muzzle, foreface and cheeks. Our comment would be that this is a matter of personal preference. We do not believe any of our Saints have been put down to a lower place because their whiskers were not removed, nor do we believe that removing the whiskers enhances the appearance of the St. Bernard.

FACE, FEET AND TAIL
When preparing the St. Bernard's face, make certain the ears are cleaned out and free of brown wax. Details of how to do this have been discussed earlier in the book. The olive oil can be used as an aid to loosen some of the stubborn wax. Ensure the eyes are clean from any dry mucus in the corners and that the eye itself looks healthy. Remove any wispy hair from the ears, both around the ear canal and externally on the ear flaps. Use finger and thumb to pluck the hair or a stripping knife. Carefully examine all the feet, checking in between the toes for dried mud and foreign bodies such as grass seeds or hair which has become matted or

tangled. Check to make certain the Saint has no eczema starting up in between the toes, as this can become very sore, causing lameness.

Take one paw at a time and groom the hair, lifting the excess up from between each toe. Working with the conventional scissors, trim this hair. Always point the scissors the same way as the growth of the hair as this leaves a much smarter line and does not have the appearance of a step. Placing the paw flat on the box or table, trim the hair around the paw until it resembles a cat-foot. Be careful not to cut the hair too far back so that all the nails protrude. On the back of the front legs above the toes, usually before the feathery hair begins to appear longer, is an appendage similar to a rubber "stopper"; this is the heel pad. The hair at the back of the pastern below this stop can be neatly trimmed down, using a sharp pair of scissors, thus encouraging a judge's eye to focus on the clean lines on your St. Bernard.

Return to the hair on the back of the hocks and comb thoroughly, then take a sharp pair of scissors and go down the hock, trimming carefully the surplus hair, again aiming for clean lines. Stand back and examine your Saint. If the hair on the abdomen is long and untidy looking, take the scissors and just trim the feathery ends to give the Bernard a tidier appearance.

Check the tail. On the long hair, comb the hair thoroughly, then hold the tip of the tail out and carefully trim along the feathery hair just to tidy the tail up. The end of the tail needs "rounding" off slightly. Be careful not to take too much off or it spoils the lines.

BATHING

If the St. Bernard has been to a few shows, he may not require an all-over bath, so just wash the face, feet, tail and undercarriage, leaving the back and sides. Check the anal glands. If they require emptying this can be done in the bath, then dry the dog. Once the dog is thoroughly dry, any hair which is inappropriately sticking up on the feet should be trimmed off as described. Put the St. Bernard back on the box or table, brush through again and assess the overall picture. A spray of mink oil will just bring the coat up with that extra gloss. Your Saint should now be ready to take on the challenge of the dog show.

YOUR FIRST SHOW

I would really advise anyone who is thinking of showing to make an effort to attend a Breed Club show or a Championship show and observe the specific breeds you are interested in, including St. Bernards, to get a feel of the classes. Observe the dogs and handlers to familiarise yourself with ring culture and procedure. A fun day, match or exemption show is a relaxing way to gain experience and to learn the ropes in a non-threatening, less intense way. Some novice exhibitors do become extremely nervous and this can affect your dog, especially if they exhibit at a Championship show. Assuming you have taken this advice, at a match or exemption show your Saint Bernard will be expected to stand in a line, along with other breeds in a traditional show stance and then move when requested by the judge. If you have observed what other exhibitors have done, as well as listened to the instructions from the judge, remain calm and move your St. Bernard, following the judge's instructions.

SHOW EQUIPMENT

Large, suitable bag to carry all the "doggy" gear.
Large water vessel for your Saint Bernard – to have a drink of water, not to bath the dog again!
Large towel to dry the dog in case it is wet.
Blanket or small rug for your Saint to lie on, which helps the dog to settle.
The show lead .
Benching chain as there may be an appropriate place to fasten the dog.
Leather collar to attach to the benching chain.
(*Never* bench any dog, especially a St. Bernard, on a choker chain).
Tempting titbits to reward your Saint for good or appropriate behaviour. Do not give treats or rewards if the St. Bernard will not get on to the bench. This is rewarding the dog for something he has not done.
Suitable brushes and comb, possibly dry shampoo. Do not used talcum powder as this is against UK Kennel Club rules.
A spare pair of shoes for yourself in case it is wet.
A pen to write down the winners in the catalogue or to take notes.

Most dog shows do have refreshments. The cost of these can vary from reasonable to very expensive.

Also, the refreshments could be some distance from where the dogs are. You may decide to prepare some refreshments and take them along to the show for your own comfort. Take some small change for the telephone and for emergencies. Do not take too much cash. Unfortunately, dog shows do attract opportunist thieves who pounce when the exhibitor is in the ring, so do take care.

ON THE DAY

Make certain you get to the show in plenty of time before the class is due, so that you can find the venue. Allow your dog to exercise and relieve him or herself. Make sure you clean up any faeces – there will be plenty of bins around. Allow the dog to sniff around, becoming accustomed to the surroundings.

When your class is called, if you are inexperienced, stand toward the latter end of the line-up. This will give you opportunity to observe the proceedings and how the other exhibitors show their dogs.

Once the class is assembled, endeavour to stand your Saint correctly, facing the same way as the other St. Bernards in the class. The judge will be glancing down the line for a quick look at the overall quality of the Saints in the class, to see if any are outstanding and catch the eye. First impressions are terribly important and should never be underestimated. If your Saint is presented really well (which includes appropriate handling) and catches the judge's interest, this will encourage a more in-depth examination when all the St. Bernards are examined in more detail as the judge focuses on the assessment.

The judge will probably ask everyone in the class to move round the ring at a steady pace. This does not require the first exhibitor in the class to set off at breakneck pace; it is not a race. What the judge is looking for, as the Saints move round the ring, is kinetic balance. Does the Saint move with flowing movement or is he ungainly and pacing, which makes the dog have a crab-like action?

Once the dogs have been moved around the ring, giving them the opportunity to loosen up, the judge will ask each exhibitor in turn to stand their Saint. While this process takes place, allow your own dog to relax. Do not keep him standing in the show pose all the time, otherwise he will become

bored. Make sure you concentrate on what the judge is doing, so that you know what type of judge this is. Some judges can be extremely rough, especially with puppies and juniors, so you need to be ready to gently talk to your Saint in an encouraging way, so that he stands correctly for the physical examination. Make use of this time to see what other exhibitors are doing, the exact place where the judge would like you to stand and so on. As the dogs in front of you are moving on you will be coming nearer to the assessment of your own St. Bernard. Remain calm, be confident, think positive. Do not rush in, panic and have him standing like a sack of potatoes. Try to get the best from your Saint by placing him in the show stance, feet placed correctly apart, what some breeders refer to as "four-square". Ensure he is relaxed with his or her head up, demonstrating that there is a good reach of neck. Talk to your Saint in an unobtrusive way to encourage him to stand still. Make sure you know the age of your dog. The judge will not want to know the exact age, but requires information as to whether the dog is 18 months, 22 months, 2, 3 or 4 years old, etc.

Listen to what the judge says carefully, then follow the instructions and move your Saint, probably in a triangle. It is amazing how many exhibitors do not understand how to trot with their Saint in a triangle.

THE TRIANGLE

If you are asked to do a triangle, then try to achieve this. Do not do an arc, or a square. What the judge is hoping to see is a clear view of hind movement from your Saint as you move away, the dog in profile as you cross the top of the triangle, then the dog's front movement as you come back towards the judge. A correctly executed triangle allows the judge to see all aspects of the Saint's movement in a relatively short period of time. The triangle has the advantage that the judge can remain more or less stationary in the desired position for optimum assessment on movement. Remember, do not try and engage the judge in any conversation; simply answer the question which the judge may ask regarding the dog's age.

On returning from the completed triangle, you may be expected to allow your Saint to stand as naturally as possible, or to move him up and down in a straight line, then stop. If a hind leg is not exactly in the desired position, gently place it where it should be in as unobtrusive a way as possible, to create a balanced St. Bernard. Once the judge has stood back and had another glance then you, when asked or signalled to move back into line, will do so, keeping an eye on the last dog to be moved.

THE FINAL ASSESSMENT

When the dogs have all been seen, ensure you have your Saint standing on a level piece of ground in the show stance. Keep careful observation on the judge, as well as your Saint. The judge may well look at all the Saints from a distance, or may move each exhibit once again. This usually does not consist of another triangle, just moving in a straight line, so the judge can assess hind and front action again. If this happens to be a large class, the judge may pull out several Saints for further appraisal before placing any exhibits, so try to encourage your Saint to remain in the show pose. If you are fortunate enough to be selected, ensure that you listen to the judge, and keep your dog in the show pose, as well as observing what the judge is doing.

In the UK the judge will usually bring his first place winner out and ask the exhibitor to stand the dog, then return to the remaining line-up for second, third, reserve and very highly commended placings. Some judges may take yet another look at the dogs in these placings to ensure that the Saints are in order of merit. Occasionally, the judge may move the placings. This can be disappointing for exhibitors who think they have won first place, only to find the dog moved down to a lower placing. Once the judge has written the numbers down in the judging book, your place is secured. Do not immediately rush out of the ring; wait until the prize cards and, sometimes, rosettes have been presented, usually by the stewards. If you were fortunate to be in the first two placings, wait until the judge has taken some notes on your Saint Bernard, then you can leave the ring. It is customary to offer brief congratulations to the winner of the class out of courtesy.

In Europe, the judging is different in that the judge or judges (sometimes there can be two judges, such as at the World Union of St.

Bernards) eliminate the Saints with the least number of required attributes to the FCI Standard. The Saints are then placed in reverse order, with fifth, fourth, third, second, and finally first.

It is well worth visiting other shows in Europe, USA, Australia and so on, as the opportunity to assess other Saints and observe ring procedures helps broaden your knowledge and experience. Do try to be objective in your opinions, being able to appreciate the virtues in other exhibitors' Saints. This is essential if you are going to enjoy the dog shows. Remember, showing should be fun; it is a hobby. If you go for a day out and win, then obviously it is extra special. However, if you do not win, then you have still had a day away from the usual routine, even though you may feel disappointed that your Saint was not among the prize winners on that particular day.

If your dog is beaten, do not be tempted to go off home. Return the Saint to the benches, give the dog a drink, then follow the rest of the judging. You should be trying to learn as much as you can about St. Bernards and the intricacies of judging.

THE DON'TS OF SHOWING

The following is a list of twenty recommendations from a booklet given to potential St. Bernard exhibitors by Joseph H. Fleishli, who was President of the St. Bernard Club of America and had the Edelweiss Kennels (1954).

- DON'T wear your hat in the ring – it is there figuratively only.

- DON'T smoke in the ring.

- DON'T pay so much attention to one part of the dog that you overlook other important parts.

- DON'T call the judge's notice to a fault by trying too eagerly to conceal or minimise it.

- DON'T call your dog by its registered name (or any other name).

- DON'T converse unnecessarily with the judge or the steward or other exhibitors and certainly not at all with the ringside.

IN THE RING

Photos: Munro.

The handlers prepare their dogs for the judge at the St. Bernard Club of America National.

The judge, Carol Otto Mastrup assesses the exhibits. They are (left to right): Am. Ch. Raphael Van Rijn, Am. Ch. Sweetholm's Gad About, and Stoan Firenze Of Miyou.

About turn: The hindquarters come under the judge's scrutiny.

Be calm and related when showing your dog.

- DON'T tell the judge about your dog, his pedigree, or his wins at some other show.

- DON'T argue with the judge as you leave the ring if you don't agree with his placings. Ask him after he has finished all his work, to explain his reasons, if he feels so inclined.

- DON'T get too close or permit another exhibitors to get too close to you or to your dog.

- DON'T have the jitters. Be calm and collected; if you are nervous, you transmit your lack of control to the dog.

- DON'T let the dog boss you; keep both the dog and yourself under control.

- DON'T punish or scold your dog in the ring; it shows poor training and lack of control.

- DON'T fuss with your dog if he is showing well.

- DON'T pose your dog facing a strong light or in the sun; nor place him in a dark part of the ring.

- DON'T let the judge's hand come close to the mouth of a biting dog.

- DON'T get between the dog and the judge at any time.

- DON'T loaf in the ring before, during or after your class is judged.

- DON'T mope around, stand idly or gaze absentmindedly; keep your mind and your eyes on your dog, with a side glance at the judge every second until the ribbons are handed out.

- DON'T get too close to another dog or person purposely or not purposely. The other fellow may be a bigger bully than you.

- DON'T try to draw attention to yourself; the dog is on show, not you.

10 *JUDGING THE ST. BERNARD*

The judge has an important role to play and this should not be undertaken lightly. Through their decisions, judges can influence a breed. St. Bernards which are consistent top winners tend to be an obvious choice when it comes to breeding. A St. Bernard which has several CCs and Best of Breed to his credit will often have a number of enthusiasts wishing to take their bitches to him for stud. If judges go for a certain "look", a trend can be set. Would-be breeders try to reproduce the current style, hoping they can sell their progeny for top-rate prices. As we have observed over the years, it is not always the top winners who produce the best progeny. Some dedicated breeders will not be influenced by fashion or current trends; they will continue to produce their own lines, deriving satisfaction from doing their own thing.

A lot of exhibitors want to win at all costs and they will be mindful of what type of dog is appealing to the majority of judges. For this reason, it is of vital importance for all those who presume to judge our lovely breed that they should be fully aware and understand the St. Bernard's essential characteristics and its original purpose, and should have a thorough knowledge of the Breed Standard for the country where they are judging. Judges who are conversant with the UK Kennel Club Breed Standard, who accept judging appointments in Europe, must ensure they familiarise themselves with the FCI Breed Standard on St. Bernards.

Most people who judge St. Bernards have read the Breed Standards carefully; however, how they perceive, understand and interpret this information and then formulate a mental picture of the 'perfect' St. Bernard, may well be different from some other recognised judges. This is why there is diversity of opinion among specialist judges, who state they are judging the attributes of St. Bernards in accordance with Breed Standards.

I firmly believe that judging is focusing on the positive qualities of a St. Bernard, not focusing on one or two faults. Certainly faults need to be assessed and taken into account; however, these need to be measured against the dog as a whole. The holistic approach considers the whole St. Bernard. Is the dog balanced? Does it fit into the frame? Are the majority of the required attributes as stated in the Breed Standard present? Can the dog move? Is it capable of being a working dog? Sadly, I have judged St. Bernards in the past which could not move comfortably for a few paces, never mind be capable of climbing a mountain!

THE CHANGING FACE OF DOG SHOWING

Over many years the whole culture of dog showing has changed considerably. Gone are the large kennels owned by wealthy landowners who could employ numerous personnel to care for their estates, and kennel staff to meet the needs of their beloved Saints. Changing economy and market forces throughout the world, not just in the UK, have brought about vast social changes in society. People now have much more leisure time and dog showing has become a hobby for many dog fanciers.

Not too long ago the majority of judges tended to be people with a thorough knowledge of livestock in general. These judges were true stockmen who often judged cattle, horses, fur and feather, as well as dogs. Their knowledge may not have been as thorough as true breed specialists, but these judges had an eye for balance, conformation, quality, soundness of mind and body, and then judged accordingly. These were the great "all-rounders" of the past. Breed specialist judges did officiate at major shows but these tended to be well-established breeders who could demonstrate their knowledge and who had not just a kennel, but established bloodlines. These were real specialists worthy of the title, who had probably served an 'apprenticeship', learning from experienced breeders and other judges for several years.

When obtaining my first St. Bernard, my own apprenticeship was served under the guidance of Kath and Ken Gaunt, with much encouragement being given by Miss Marjorie Hindes from Burtonswood St. Bernards. Enid Muggleton provided early background history on the breed and shared her vast knowledge on pedigrees. The presentation of Saint Bernards left a lot to be desired in the sixties, although Burtonswood Saints were all turned out to perfection. In those 'good old days', people who showed dogs did not automatically presume to become judges in a short period of time.

After serving a lengthy apprenticeship – which included lots of listening and careful observation, as well as asking questions – when some of the breed elders felt it was appropriate you might be invited to judge a few classes of the breed at a small show. The performance of the potential judge was carefully monitored. Those who could demonstrate an understanding of the breed characteristics as well as attributes of the KC Breed Standard, were encouraged to go on; those who were considered to have shown no basic understanding were soon discouraged from ever judging again.

Today everything is different. Exhibitors who have shown their first dog with modest success feel they have the right to jump onto the judging bandwagon. The KC have recognised this and now require breed clubs to be far more discerning about

Ch. Meadowmead Helena with top British judge Pamela Cross Stern.
Photo: Carol Ann Johnson.

who can be placed upon the club's judging lists. Potential judges are now being asked to provide evidence of their basic understanding, knowledge and awareness of breed characteristics, and the required attributes of the breed as set out by the recognised Standards. The breed clubs are asking for evidence of stewarding, wins at shows and what attempts have been made to improve a person's knowledge by attending Breed Club seminars, teach-ins and so on, before the name can be considered for inclusion on any judging list.

UNDERSTANDING JUDGING LISTS
There are various categories of judges. The KC states that a registered Breed Society must produce a list of judges on an annual basis. The purpose of this list is to indicate, to interested parties, which people the Club would support to judge at different levels.

List A: This includes the names, addresses and telephone numbers of those whom the Breed Club would support to issue Challenge Certificates in the breed. These people will have already judged at Championship level. The breed club need not include the names of all the judges who award CCs in the breed, only those it considers fit to undertake the task. The KC expects breed clubs to review their judging lists annually. It is not a case that a previous judge has had their name removed from the list, more a case that for whatever reason, it has not been included for the current year.

List B: This list indicates the judges who may have undertaken several Open Show appointments, possibly including a Breed Club Show. The judge may be ready for awarding CCs so would move up to the A list when the list is reviewed the following year. Others on the B list may have only judged a couple of Open shows but due to their evidence and level of competence, the breed club feels the B list is appropriate. Some judges on this list may have undertaken the Canine Studies Institute's Judging Diploma, having successfully passed after months of study. Those supported by the club have their names, addresses and telephone numbers included on this list.

List C: This includes the names, addresses and telephone numbers of people who have written to the breed club requesting to be placed upon the list, giving details of their experience and providing evidence of membership, stewarding, breeding and so on. It may be that they have judged at an Exemption Show or matches, possibly a few breed classes or Open shows.

Different breed clubs may have additional rules for inclusion on the lists. The breed club does not have to give an explanation as to why a person is not considered appropriate for inclusion on the list. Other clubs may expect potential judges to undergo some form of assessment or undertake an examination.

Currently the Kennel Club is considering new rules and regulations appertaining to judging, and to seminars and learning opportunities for people wishing to judge. More emphasis is going to be placed upon assessments and examinations and the Canine Studies Institute's Judging Diploma will be more widely recognised. The FCI have a different system, in that trainee judges can accompany an experienced judge to learn the art of ring procedure, and judges also have to take examinations. In America a potential St. Bernard judge has to judge three Sweepstakes before being considered as a specialist judge. A knowledge of the breed, together with experience as a breeder and exhibitor, must be demonstrated. Saint enthusiasts who would like to learn the finer points of judging must also attend seminars run by the SB Club of America.

UNDERSTANDING JUDGING

These observations about the art of judging are applicable in every country in which dogs are shown. Judging, in my opinion, is not about going on an ego trip. It offers a wonderful challenge to assess a collection of dogs – but being armed with knowledge of the breed and an 'eye' for a St. Bernard, is the best preparation. Obviously other people 'judging' from the ringside will no doubt disagree. However, this is acceptable, as exhibitors may well have their own ideas.

The real thrill of judging is the anticipation that something truly special may turn up, perhaps an unheard-of youngster, or perhaps an unknown Saint suddenly shows to its full potential in the Post Graduate class. This can make the hairs on the back of your neck stand up or send a tingle through the nerve endings. A real incentive to continue judging is the prospect of discovering a real star. This does not happen very often; however, finding a quality puppy or junior with all the required breed attributes, along with charisma and that extra magnetism which draws your attention, is a marvellous feeling. It is extremely rewarding, and it is difficult to describe the thrill of assessing that extra-special St. Bernard, the one I would dearly love to take home.

Judging should never be undertaken lightly. Firstly, it is vital that you understand the St. Bernard fully; this means detailed study. I strongly urge anyone wishing to judge to read as much as you can about the origin, history and development of this breed. It is really fascinating. Try to appreciate that feeling of tradition which is so much part of any breed but particularly of the St. Bernard. Imagine the hostile conditions, the wind-chill factors, the blizzard sweeping across the mountains, the difficult terrain which early St. Bernards encountered when endeavouring to trace stranded travellers in the snow.

Having thought about the hard reality of these large dogs living in difficult conditions, and focused on how fit the dogs must have been, with plenty of sturdy muscles to support their bone, it is a good idea to study the Breed Standard. Read and re-read it, try to understand it fully. Knowing the words of the Standard parrot-fashion is quite a different matter from truly understanding it. Ask yourself questions. As the Standard suggests that a St. Bernard should have "broad shoulders, sloping well up at the withers", ask why? The strength of dogs is in the forequarters; to undertake working in mountains, over uneven ground. St. Bernards would require tremendous strength.

Remember that all Breed Standards were originally drawn up around "form and function" by the founding fathers of the breed. There has to be a reason for everything; no requirement of any Standard was invented on a whim or for purely cosmetic reasons.

Studying the Standard in isolation will only tell you so much. I have to say that Standards can be quite vague, with wide parameters for interpretation. You will only make sense and appreciate the Standard by studying it in conjunction with top-quality dogs. When I was in the formative years, I observed the best St.

Bernards in the breed when they were in the ring, then endeavoured to relate their good points to the relevant part of the Breed Standard. This helped me develop an 'eye' for the dogs. Another tip is to try and study 'type' in the ring. This can be more difficult with current trends, as there are what I consider to be several 'types' around.

No matter how many examinations are set for judges in the future, it is my belief that if a person does not have the ability to have an 'eye' for a quality dog, it cannot be taught – it is a gift. Joe Braddon, a larger-than-life judge from the past, stated that in his opinion good judges are born and not made. While it is possible to learn about a breed, you will only become an outstanding judge if you have an instinct for finding quality, harmony, balance and temperament.

CORRECT MENTAL ATTITUDES

Think positive! A vital requirement in a dog judge is to have the correct mental attitude, which has to be totally positive. Judging dogs is about putting the good ones up because of their virtues, not putting the bad ones down because of their faults. Every St. Bernard may have some shortcomings; however, a successful judge will appreciate a dog with outstanding virtues, seeing minor faults in perspective. Far too many judges, in my opinion, fault-judge; novice judges tend to be the worst offenders in this respect. To give an example, they

The honour of judging at Crufts is highly sought-after Ch. Mountside Movie Star, Best of Breed (left) and Ch. Whaplode Be Our Williams. Photo: Munro.

may look at an exceptional Saint and notice it has a light eye, instead of assessing the Saint holistically. All they see is the light eye and, instead of measuring quality attributes, fault-judging occurs. Exactly the same thing happens with a quality Saint who is more than capable of undertaking the job he was bred for, yet it has a "gay tail" which is undesirable. The novice judge forgets about all the required attributes and puts the Saint down for its gay tail. Novice judges can focus on what are obvious, sometimes cosmetic, faults, so much so that they cannot see the wood for the trees. Unless a positive attitude towards judging is developed, you will never contribute anything to the breed. A judge's brief should be to promote excellence, to help improve the breed. Try and look at the Saints in the ring and endeavour to find out what is good about each one.

Like other experienced judges and breeders of our breed, I have overheard ringside exhibitors rubbishing excellent Saints because they are not quite perfect. The perfect St. Bernard has not been bred yet – in any country. Unless you are able to see beyond what is wrong and appreciate what is right, you should not consider judging. Sometimes exhibitors make comments that the dog only won because a well-known handler or exhibitor was "at the other end of the leash". Why not focus on the attributes of the Saint? You may learn something, instead of being a poor loser. Dog showing should be fun.

Given that you have studied the breed, been successful in the ring with quality dogs, have bred typical stock yourself and wish to judge, it is better not to ask direct for an appointment. This will be resented by many. If you have been seen showing quality Saints and have been consistently breeding good specimens of the breed, then sooner or later you will be invited to have your name put forward on a club judging list or possibly be offered a judging appointment at a smaller show. Show societies are on the lookout for new judges as they hope that person will draw a good entry, based upon the "unknown quantity" theory.

STEWARDING
Prior to accepting your first appointment, I strongly recommend stewarding for experienced judges at several shows. George and I have stewarded a great deal; it is extremely worthwhile as you learn such a lot about different breeds. Not only will you get used to standing in the middle of the ring, exercising assistance to the judge, but it will acquaint you with the official judges' book and relevant paperwork. During the judging you can take the opportunity to observe the technique of this specific judge, as he or she goes over and assesses each dog in turn. Most judges appreciate genuine enthusiasm and will be happy to discuss their placings with you afterwards if there is a decision which you would like clarifying. However, do not interfere with the judging by being too obtrusive.

If you would like to steward at a Breed Club show under the wing of an established steward, it would be an idea to write to the secretary of the society. This could then go before the committee for their consideration. The secretary should write back, informing you of the committee's decision. If agreement has been reached that it is acceptable for you to steward, you will be given written instructions as to your duties. Should the committee feel you may need more experience before undertaking stewarding at a Breed Club show, where there are generally a lot more classes, you would be notified. Do not be too disappointed if initially you are rejected. If you are determined to gain experience in stewarding, keep on asking other societies to give you the opportunity. Once you have had these opportunities, Breed Clubs will be more favourable to your application to steward and will generally give you a chance to prove yourself.

THE TEMPERAMENT OF A JUDGE
Well, you have decided to commence judging. Are you really ready for this experience? The centre of the ring can feel like the loneliest place in the world. Quite often, prior to a judging appointment, you will find you have more friends than you ever imagined. After completing the judging appointment, you will have a handful of friends who will still talk to you! Far too many exhibitors take it as a personal slight if their Saint Bernard does not win on the day. It is imperative to be objective and honest with yourself when it comes to evaluating judging. To some exhibitors, their dog or dogs are an extension of their own persona; if you as the judge do not like their dogs, they really

take it as a personal insult. This is true of many exhibitors in all breeds, not just St. Bernards. Generally speaking, the serious breeders will appreciate honest, knowledgeable and considered judgement, win or lose. It helps to have a thick skin if you are contemplating judging. This must be accompanied by integrity.

The breed ring can be a challenging place. Many of the exhibitors showing under you may well be judging your own Saints in the near future. It takes strength of character to ignore this fact, but to be an honest judge you have to forget about who is judging where and concentrate on the dogs on the day. If you are a regular exhibitor or breeder, you will also be aware of which dogs are winning and may have knowledge of their pedigrees. These extraneous factors have to be pushed to the back of your mind and you must concentrate on each dog in the class, valuing each one in turn. You will gain respect and have success as a judge if you can demonstrate fairness, honesty and integrity; it is not easy. Judges are human, but endeavour to do your best. Never settle old scores in the ring. This is discrimination and totally unjust to a quality St. Bernard.

Various respected judges have given me helpful advice over the years. Ken Gaunt felt it was appropriate to judge St. Bernards in the order in which you would like to take the dogs back to your own home, having taken into account the relevant Breed Standard. Andrew Brace, a well-respected, all-rounder judge, suggests the following advice:

when you judge and you find a dog that you really like, imagine this dog with your worst enemy. Now, do you still like the dog as much? Similarly, if you discover a dog that you really dislike, imagine your best friend is showing the dog. Is the dog still really that bad?

This exercise can help focus the concentration and thought pattern while evaluating the dogs in the line-up. You really need to discipline yourself as well as develop a knack of looking at a dog with confidence and a professional attitude when judging, oblivious of all the irrelevancies, which can sometimes cloud one's judgement.

DEVELOPING JUDGING TECHNIQUE
It is no use accepting even a small show held under Kennel Club licence if you have had no experience handling or "going over" dogs. You need to familiarise yourself with the structure and conformation of the dog, then develop your own technique. When judging, it is important to remain consistent in your approach, treating each dog the same. Remember that exhibitors have sent in an entry and have paid for their dog to be assessed and require your opinion of this exhibit on the day. If you do not value or respect the judge, then do not send an entry to the show. There are a few judges whose opinions we would not wish to have even for free, so we certainly would not pay for their opinion. Thankfully, these are a minority of people who have set themselves up as "instant experts" with no in-depth knowledge of breeding, structure,

The line-up at the WUSB show in San Diego, California. The judge comes under considerable pressure and must have the temperament to remain calm and collected. Photo: Munro.

soundness or balance. From our observations, they seem to progress by doing a lot more talking rather than listening and learning.

People judging in Britain do place importance on "hands-on" aspects of judging, whereas in Europe, there appears to be less hands-on and more observation going on. Andrew Brace describes some of the "hands-on" judges as a new generation of "faith healers", especially the multi-breed judges who seem to manhandle every square inch of the dog's surface area in a misguided attempt to display thoroughness, while neglecting lengthy study of movement.

Personally, I do love to get my hands on a quality Saint to have it confirmed that structurally, everything is in the right place. On a short-haired or smooth St. Bernard, it is far easier to visually assess, especially the muscle tone of first and second thighs. However, to actually feel the firm muscles is wonderful. Another point that is important is that sometimes looks can be deceptive. It is only when you get your hands on a Saint that what can look pleasing from a distance may in fact be disappointing to the hands.

When judging I like the Saints to move round the ring twice to enable them to move with fluidity without braking for a tight triangle. If there is a large entry in a particular class, the dogs should be split, otherwise no exhibitor has the chance to move with their Saint. St. Bernards are large dogs and need to get into their stride. Sometimes a Saint sets off with a high-stepping action which is undesirable, but can, however, move correctly by the time the second appraisal round the ring occurs. It is important for the Saint judge to really analyse movement. Kinetic balance, as well as the structure of the locomotion, should be taken into account.

TYPES OF JUDGING

When a Saint enters the ring, regardless of what type of show it is, a quality Saint should have an intensity of type – the essential breed characteristics and attributes which make it immediately recognisable as a Saint, otherwise it becomes just another dog. This quality will make a breed specialist, as well as an all-rounder, keen to make a more in-depth appraisal of this exhibit.

So let us discuss ring procedure, assuming that you are about to judge your first Match or Open show. Have a look at the hall or area for judging

Terry Munro judging in Denmark. Pictured (left to right) Int. Ch. Bernegardens Winchester and Zirino-Vsuuri vd Roja-Horst.

and plan how you will move the dogs, line them up, etc. If it is a Match, it should be relatively easy as this is a knockout competition; if it is an Open show with a large number of entries, you will need to devise a strategy. If there is insufficient room, then it is inappropriate to move the dogs in a triangle; you will have to make do with straight up and down. Take all these points into consideration prior to judging so that you adopt a consistent approach.

In the advanced dog showing world there are two types of judging: dogs being judged against other dogs in competition, and judging in two stages, as in the countries which follow the rules of the Fédération Cynologique Internationale (FCI).

Open competition is followed in Britain, the United States of America, Canada and Australasia. In Europe, where the FCI format is followed, the competition consists of two stages. Firstly, each individual dog is assessed against the appropriate Breed Standard, given a written critique and graded as Excellent, Very Good, Good or First, Second, Third and so on, based upon the dog's merit relative to the Standard. Then, only the dogs who have achieved an Excellent or First (depending upon in which country one is judging) return to compete with others who have the same or similar grading. Further evaluation and assessment occurs, then the dogs are placed from fifth, fourth, third, second and finally, first. This is a more lengthy and complex system; however, it does have advantages for both exhibitor and judge. Whichever process or method is used, the objective remains the same – to find the best St. Bernard.

TAKING YOUR FIRST CLASS
This could be a puppy class or veteran, depending what and where the show is. Assuming it is a puppy class, you will have inexperienced youngsters as well as, possibly, inexperienced exhibitors, so do be patient. Make allowances for youngsters and the novice exhibitors; do not be too rough when examining teeth as this can deter a Saint from wanting anyone else to examine their teeth and mouth. As the class are lining up, look along the line from where you are standing and take a brief look to see if anything special appeals to you. First impressions are very important when judging dogs. Invariably, the Saint which catches your eye has the all-important attributes, charisma and "feel good" factor – which may prove to be the best, all other things being equal.

Before you are in the centre of the ring, quickly observe the handlers setting up their dogs. Believe me, exhibitors can be extremely helpful in unwittingly helping the judge focus on some faults. You can guarantee if a St. Bernard has a suspect topline the exhibitor will be fussing about, tapping the dog under his belly or sometimes stringing the dog up, which can make it worse! A less than perfect front will receive maximum attention. Rest assured the exhibitor will be determined to almost screw the front legs into place before you even get to see the Saint. Remember to think positive, be mindful of these faults and take them into account when judging, but the qualities will hopefully outweigh the negatives.

Once the steward has informed you the class is ready, look at the dogs from a distance to gain an overall picture of the Saints and try to gauge the quality. You will be constantly seeking for that special one who will give you that buzz, a slight sense of relief that, thank goodness, there is probably something in the class worthy of a closer evaluation. It is really disappointing when nothing catches the eye and the class lacks type and quality altogether. Never mind, carry on regardless.

Ask the exhibitors to move around at a steady pace. Some exhibitors wish to set off as though competing in the Olympics. This is not helpful to a puppy, as they tune into this non-verbal communication and decide to outdo their owner. It sounds amusing, but it does happen. The judge is in charge of the proceedings so, if necessary, stop the class going around and remind the exhibitors to go round again at a steady or quick hacking pace. Hopefully, this will provide exhibitors and their dogs with the opportunity to acclimatise themselves to the ring procedure.

As the dogs are going round, study the dogs' carriage, kinetic balance, reach and drive of movement. Is there anything which stands out? Then begin the individual assessment of each St. Bernard in turn. Do remember to pay equal attention to the specimens which really do not come up to Breed Standard. Always be polite and courteous to owners and handlers; this way, even if their dogs do not win, they cannot feel aggrieved

The judges line up in Holland with Best In Show winner Dk. Ch. Asbjorn.

that the judge was rude and unpleasant. There is no need to be discourteous to people; this may be their first experience of showing a dog and it helps if the memory is a pleasant one.

Ask the handler to position the St. Bernard where you feel you have some level ground, where it is possible to obtain the best assessment of the dogs. Give the exhibitor the chance to set their dog up. Stand well back – you will never obtain a good appraisal if you stand over the top of the exhibit. What you are looking for is a general overall picture. Imagine that the St. Bernard is painted black or in silhouette; this will help focus on the picture in your mind. This is of paramount importance, regardless of breed. Forget the points of the Standard for a few moments – such as is the dog the correct size, is the dog in proportion as regards height to length, or is the Saint straight in the stifle or over-angulated – savour the overall outline of the St. Bernard.

JUDGING PUPPIES

Approach the puppy from the front; some may be a little unsure of things, so do make allowances; be gentle and speak to the puppy in a soft voice. Do not go verbally over the top and make the Saint puppy get out of control; use some common sense. If necessary, come down to the pup's size, do not tower over him if you are tall, as this can feel intimidating for a novice exhibit. However, be confident. Commence with the head, look and study the expression, analyse the ear set, the shape of the eye, stop, depth of muzzle, balance of the head, the nose, depth of flews, which should not be too pendulous. Allowance should be made in puppies, as some required attributes may need time for further development. It is difficult judging puppies. This is where a knowledge of development is essential. Breeder judges, who have an awareness and insight into the various stages of growth and where certain points will change with age, have an advantage over an all-rounder judge. For example, a St. Bernard puppy with a sloppy front may well tighten up. An outline where the St. Bernard is "high at the rear" at six or seven months of age will settle into a level topline by twelve months. A head which appears somewhat plain and lacking in stop will invariably "break" and finish with an ideal stop and balanced head.

A dilemma about judging puppies is whether to judge them "on the day" against the Breed Standard which is based on a mature adult. Usually judges with expert knowledge of breed development will make allowances for the deficiency of youth. This could be something of a "Catch 22" situation, however, as the secret is knowing what a St. Bernard puppy should look like at a certain age, and that different lines can develop at a different rate to others. In any event, it is hoped that you are sufficiently experienced to realise which allowances can be made in the name of maturity.

HANDS-ON JUDGING

Having assessed general appearance of the head and expression, handle the head gently to check teeth and mouth. Lift the upper lips carefully to examine the bite; this should be a perfect scissor bite even in

117

English judge Pat Muggleton at the WUSB in Portugal, 1999. Her winner is Ivon De Estepona.

puppies. Check the ears for texture, cleanliness, length and where the ears are set on. Move down the St. Bernard's neck, checking for excessive loose skin at the throat, remembering that puppies may have some loose skin into which they will eventually grow.

Feel the forechest – this should be well-filled, not hollow; then check the bone of the forelegs for strength, roundness and length. Short forelegs are undesirable and are beginning to become the "norm" in certain lines. This needs to be addressed now, otherwise St. Bernards will experience problems later in their development, having large heads, sturdy body, but with short upper arm and short legs which may be unable to support the large bodies.

Lift the forefeet to feel for strong and serviceable pads. When the foot is back on the floor, consider if it is well knuckled up and tight like a cat foot. Far too many Saints have flat open feet, an undesirable fault which detracts from the overall picture. Flat feet do not improve with age, so allowances should not be given for these poor feet. The forelegs should drop parallel, provided the chest is correct. The forequarters in a Saint should be strong.

Having dealt with the forehand, run your hands down the neck to confirm that the neck is clean. Your hands should continue down the neck to the withers, where you can check the huge scapula and shoulders. The shoulders should be laid back, not too upright and set well apart. Upright shoulders go with short upper arms which prevents flowing action when the St. Bernard is on the move. Run your hand along the contours of the forechest in profile, to confirm that the dog has a forechest.

With both hands spanning the body, check spring of rib, depth of chest and ascertain how far back the ribs extend. Several Saints look long in the back, being too long in the loin, and this makes the Saint look unbalanced. Remember the proportions as outlined earlier in this book.

In handling the body, draw your hands from front to rear, making sure the body is not too tucked up with an exaggerated underline. Feel the set of the tail by laying your hands flat over the loin. Remember to feel the thickness of the tail, going right to the end, ensuring that there is no kink at the tip. Move onto the hindquarters, which should be sturdy. There should be quality muscle tone on both upper and lower thigh. St. Bernards should have a good turn of stifle, but not over-angulated like a German Shepherd dog. The Saint should also have strong hocks, not too long, with well-rounded cat feet, with plenty of cushioning on the pads. Having completed the "hands-on" examination, stand well back and again look at the overall picture.

POSITIVE JUDGING

As previously stated, positive judging by focusing on the virtues of the Saint are part of the whole philosophy of judging. Any idiot can spot straight stifles, cow-hocks and gay tails; however, it takes a connoisseur to appreciate type, balance and quality. It is important to recognise excellence; this is not achieved by studying mediocrity. This applies to judging St. Bernards. Good judges need to be constantly exposed to quality. It amazes me that so many novices leave the show before the top awards are given out, yet these are often the very people who push themselves forward to judge. A Breed Judge should be influenced by the best specimen of the breed that they have ever seen. How can one possibly be in a position to evaluate other people's dogs without ever taking the time and trouble to study the best available?

EVALUATING MOVEMENT

Having examined the St. Bernard, you now have to evaluate movement. Try to move the dog in a triangle, then straight up and down. The dog should move freely, driving from the hocks, which should be parallel at a steady pace. Some St. Bernards are very close behind and do not move with drive; others may be too wide behind. Either action is indicative of constructional failure.

When the St. Bernard comes towards you, the dog should be moving freely with elbows neat against the chest, not sticking out spoiling the line, and the forelegs should be reaching over the ground with easy extension. As the speed increases, the forefeet may move closer together. This, if it is only slight, is deemed to be acceptable; however, if it is acute, it is referred to as "pinning". Several Saints do have problems with overloaded fronts and poor front action. There can be unnecessary play at the elbow, which can be due to under-developed muscles or badly angulated shoulders, or short upper arms. Occasionally, the elbows seem quite tight and there is still a perplexing "sloppiness" of the forelegs where the St. Bernard appears to be pushing his forefeet out to the side, "flipping" its feet. This is poor and uneconomic movement, a waste of energy.

Another undesirable trait which we have observed are narrow fronts where the legs appear to come out of the same joint. This is more like a terrier front. The chest is totally undeveloped and not typical of a St. Bernard. The Breed Standard requires the general appearance to be "well proportioned and of great substance" worthy of a large-sized, mountain-rescue dog, not a weak, narrow-chested, hound-like dog.

Few judges spend sufficient time evaluating profile gait in St. Bernards. Movement is vitally important in a working dog, which should be built for stamina. In profile the St. Bernard should display a degree of forward reach where the foreleg is stretched fully forward without undue lift. The dog should cover the ground effortlessly. The locomotion should be fully co-ordinated with a rear assembly which is equally strong, showing flexion of the hindquarters, with good drive from the hocks. As with the front, there should be no unnecessary lift. A hackney action is not appropriate in this breed. The St. Bernard's action should be strong, with easy extension, unhurried or smooth and capable of covering difficult terrain.

A positive reason for paying more attention to side action, rather than moving the Saint "up and down" is the fact that, when studying the profile, you observe the whole dog. This provides an overall picture, again, where you can study kinetic balance, topline, length of back, tailset and length of neck when the Saint is moving naturally. A good handler can lengthen necks, straighten toplines and increase angulation when the dog is static. However, when the dog moves out, it is much more difficult, almost impossible, to disguise these faults from the discerning eye.

A good tip is to stop the handler and dog, requesting that the dog be allowed to stand naturally. Not all Saints can stand automatically into a show stance when they come to rest. Taking a moment to glance over the natural stance can be very revealing and remarkably constructive from a judge's point of view. Repeat this process with each individual Saint. Having seen all the dogs again together, it is time for selecting your choice.

MAKING YOUR CHOICE

The whole judging process is subjective. It is not an exact science, and there are so many fascinating anomalies. Remember, it is your opinion that matters, and how you have interpreted the Breed Standard – it is this which the exhibitors are paying for. You will no doubt have your own personal list of priorities. The old proverb "One man's meat is another man's poison" is so applicable to judging Saints. Some judges tolerate light, staring eyes but dislike flat, splay feet. Others turn a blind eye to flat feet but will not accept light, almost yellow eyes. This is what makes dog shows unpredictable – the diversity of opinion.

While there are certain fundamentals which should remain constant and not be subject to dispute, other decisions come down to personal preferences and taste. These preferences can be influenced by becoming an established breeder. For example, if you have experienced problems breeding out straight stifles or incorrect shoulders, as a judge you may be more critical of these points; whereas you are more likely to be lenient with faults which you as a breeder have not experienced during your breeding programme.

Hopefully you will conduct yourself in a professional manner and carry out an honest appraisal of the Saints, being mindful that owners and handlers have paid a lot of money for your honest opinion. If exhibitors feel this was "face" judging as opposed to dog judging, many will not enter under you again.

THE DOGS' TEMPERAMENTS

A puppy can be forgiven for feeling overawed, sometime nervous; however, adult St. Bernards should have been socialised to ring procedures. Any Saint which demonstrates aggression should be excluded from the ring. Dogs of this size should not try to bite anyone, as they can do a lot of damage with such powerful jaws. Poor temperament should not be tolerated, no matter how beautiful the Saint may look. No matter how many wonderful virtues the Saint has, if the temperament is suspect these virtues mean nothing. This breed should be benevolent and steady, not aggressive and waiting to attack an unsuspecting judge.

One can accept the Saint being territorial on home premises or in the car or transport vehicle, where a protective instinct can take over; however, in the ring their behaviour should be exemplary.

WRITING CRITIQUES

Most important when judging is to find the best St. Bernard with the most desirable attributes of the breed as stated in the Breed Standard. Ask yourself what each dog may do for the breed.

While decisions should not be rushed, judges should be decisive, not dithering about, apparently unable to make up their minds. The dogs should be placed in the centre of the ring on your left, from first down to fifth place. Mark up your judging book and if a critique is required, jot down the notes that will form the basis for the critique which will be included in the dog press, as is customary in the UK.

Judges who officiate in FCI countries will have to undertake a detailed critique on every entered dog, on the spot. Different judges have a variety of styles for correlating the information for critiques. In Scandinavia the type of critique required is one where the major virtues are highlighted, as well as comment on the dog's shortcomings, where improvement may occur. I would agree with Andrew Brace and other all-rounder judges such as Ann Arch and Fevelin Somerfield that this is not damning the Saint, but demonstrates that you have considered the dog to be a worthy winner by virtue of merit which overshadowed the shortcomings.

Eventually it will be time for your most important decision, the Best of Breed. Be confident and judge according to the Breed Standard of the country you are judging in and remain courteous and professional.

Do not judge politically; this is not honest judging. Take some advice from Andrew Brace: "When you judge, judge as if you will never judge again. Judge as if this is your last appointment and the appointment you wish to be remembered for." This will help you focus on the task in hand. It is rewarding when an exhibitor informs you that although their dog did not win on the day, they enjoyed observing you judge and learned something. This makes it feel worthwhile.

11 YOUR ST. BERNARD'S HEALTH

St. Bernards are healthy dogs if cared for properly; however, the breed does have some hereditary problems which will be discussed later in this chapter.

St. Bernards, like several other breeds, are very greedy, so do not be tempted to overfeed, as this causes a lot of problems, especially in later life. Use treats for training purposes only and keep any leftover food or vegetables to accompany the dog's main meal. St. Bernards will soon pile weight on if given the opportunity to overindulge, so be warned.

The temperature for a normal, healthy St. Bernard is around 38.6C (101.5F) to 39.2C (102.5F).

VACCINATIONS

There are a variety of canine diseases which can affect all breeds, some are viral diseases such as distemper and parvovirus. As these two specific diseases are so unpleasant for the dog, it is better to have the puppy vaccinated. Your vet will be able to advise you regarding combination inoculations which cover other diseases such as leptospirosis, as well as distemper, or hard pad, and parvovirus. As the UK is currently rabies-free, dogs do not have to be vaccinated against rabies unless they are being exported to countries which stipulate that this must be done. However, under proposed new legislation, when 'dog passports' will be issued, exhibitors wishing to exhibit dogs in Europe will need to have their stock vaccinated against rabies. Anyone taking

a holiday abroad and wishing to take their dog with them may be able to do this once 'dog passports' and rabies vaccinations come into force, together with micro-chipping the dogs for identification purposes. Currently, you can take your dog on holiday abroad; however, he or she would then have to spend six months in quarantine on return to the UK – until the new legislation comes into force.

COMMON AILMENTS AND FIRST AID TREATMENT

ABSCESS: This is when a collection of pus occurs in any part of the body as a consequence of bacteria forming. Some St. Bernards can be susceptible to abscesses forming in between their toes, especially in winter months. Symptoms are: pain and heat in the infected area, followed by swelling. Sometimes the dog can have a rise in temperature. It is better to wait until the abscess has ripened, then administer treatment after it has burst. When facilitating drainage, remember to be gentle, as this area will be painful. Often when an abscess bursts, it can have a foul smell. Clean or bathe with warm water and antiseptic solution such as Savlon, or a solution of coarse sea-salt crystals and boiled water. Consult a vet in serious or persistent problems for a course of antibiotics.

ANAL GLANDS: In the dog, there are two small anal glands situated one on either side of the

With the correct care, your St. Bernard should stay fit and healthy.

opening and inside ring of the anus. These scent glands secrete a musky substance and smell. When the dog's faeces are firm, anal glands normally excrete their fluid in a spontaneous way. Under certain circumstances, such as when the food is incorrect and soft motions are passed, these ducts can become occluded and the secretion does not escape. The glands become swollen, sometimes inflamed, causing discomfort to the St. Bernard.

Symptoms are: dragging themselves along the ground, frequently licking the anus, suddenly looking round and tucking the tail in as if something were prickling it. Sometimes the Saints will bite themselves at the base of their rump towards the tail as if they have acquired a flea. In severe cases of accumulation, there can be an unpleasant odour and an abscess may occur. Some St. Bernards can have extremely foul breath when their anal glands need evacuating. Several breeders and dog enthusiasts are able gently to squeeze these glands, enabling the secretion to be discharged. With some Saints, their glands can be difficult to express, so it requires a visit to the vet. The process does not take very long and it enables the Saint to feel more comfortable. Unless there is an abscess, the only pain is to the St. Bernard's dignity and pride!

ARTHRITIS: This is inflammation of a joint or joints, more strictly articular inflammation. The chief forms are traumatic, rheumatic or specific, and all occur either as acute or chronic. Symptoms are a swollen joint which is very painful, the dog becomes lame, in some cases being unable to put his paw to the ground. During acute inflammation rest and warmth are necessary, and soothing remedies should be applied, for example, a piece of lint, large enough to cover and go round the joint with hot or cold fomentations. In serious cases, veterinary treatment should be sought and anti-inflammatory drugs administered to ease the pain.

BACKACHE: Owners become accustomed to their own dog, so are aware of their St. Bernard's body language and communication skills. If we are familiar with a healthy St. Bernard, then we are more likely to be aware when the dog is ill. If the Saint arches his back or is reluctant to turn around or go up and down any steps, this may be due to pain in his back. This could be caused by a kidney infection or muscular arthritis. It is a good idea to obtain a morning sample of urine from the dog, placing it in a small container and taking it for analysis when visiting the vet. A test of the urine will be able to support the diagnosis. It may be appropriate for the dog to have an X-ray.

BED SORES: St. Bernards can develop bedsores, not due to improper care and attention, but due to the fact that they "flop down" very heavily onto their bed or floor. Sometimes they can develop large, unhealthy-looking wounds or ulcers on their hips, points of the elbow, buttocks, and sometimes shoulders or other parts. The sores can be cleansed with warm water containing Fuller's earth. When dry, zinc and castor oil cream can be rubbed gently onto the damaged area. Prevention in kennel dogs is difficult. House dogs can be given softer bedding and encouraged to lie on this rather than on tiled or linoleum flooring. However, St. Bernards much prefer to lie in a draughty or cold area. They can be stubborn and do not like to be deterred from "flopping down" in their favourite spot.

BITES: Should your St. Bernard be bitten by another dog or kennel mate, the severity of the wound should be assessed. The difficulty with dog bites is that all teeth have bacteria around their base and, as dog bites are invariably puncture wounds,

infection and bacteria are transferred from the teeth to wound.

After the bleeding has stopped, it is important to clean the wound as thoroughly as possible. This can be achieved by using boiled water mixed with coarse salt crystals. This is a natural antiseptic. Use one level tablespoon of coarse salt crystals to half a pint of boiled water; the crystals should dissolve in the hot water. Allow this solution to cool, then bathe the wound with cotton wool (cotton). When the area is dry, apply a coating of wound powder. Obviously, if there is a deep wound and bleeding is copious, visit the vet as soon as possible. Remember that a lot of damage can be caused internally without any external signs being visible. Some St. Bernards can go into deep shock after a dog fight, so observe their behaviour.

BLOAT: This is an extremely unpleasant, painful and, in severe cases, life-threatening experience for a St. Bernard. The precise cause of bloat or gastric torsion remains a subject of debate between veterinary medicine and scientific research. Symptoms are an abnormal swelling and hardening of the abdomen. The stomach or bowel actually twists, preventing the passage of food and this allows gases to accumulate and inflate the tract. This places pressure and exertion upon the diaphragm, sometimes causing the dog to try to be sick, bringing up froth. Owing to the pain, the St. Bernard begins to breathe quickly and the heart rate rapidly increases. Unless immediate treatment can be administered by the vet, the dog can die from asphyxia or shock.

As there are so many theories regarding the cause, it is difficult to prevent. One theory is that it can occur after the dog has eaten a large dry meal, followed by a great quantity of water. Another is that in certain lines it is felt to be a hereditary condition. Another theory is that if the dog has been chasing around, or had a lot of heavy exercise immediately followed by a large meal, then bloat can occur. Should you experience any of the given symptoms, contact your vet immediately.

Thankfully, we have only experienced bloat once in over thirty years of breeding St. Bernards. This occurred when we were unable to obtain the large green tripe which we fed our dogs, accompanied by biscuit. In 1996, with the concern for CJD in humans, all offal from cattle was withdrawn from the public. We had no alternative but to change the diet for all our dogs. Unfortunately, this did not suit Ch. Mountside Movie Star (Hannah), and she died on Easter Monday that year. The vet operated as soon as we were aware of the problem, but it was too late. The whole family were devastated by the loss of this very special St. Bernard.

BURNS AND SCALDS: Obviously, treatment will depend upon how badly the St. Bernard is burnt or scalded. In severe cases, ALWAYS consult the vet. In minor cases, the following treatment may be helpful. Apply an ice pack to the infected area to reduce the heat. As a substitute, a large packet of frozen peas can be wrapped in a thin towel and applied to the damaged area. Trim the hair from the sides of the affected area. Acriflavine emulsion can be placed on some gauze and the dressing applied to the damaged area. A clean linen or cotton compress soaked in an infusion of cold tea can be applied to the damaged area if no acriflavine is available.

CHOKING: The utmost care is required when giving St. Bernards toys and objects to chew, especially when they are puppies. Chicken, rabbit or small bones should never be fed to a St. Bernard. Sometimes, popular hide chews can become soft and be easily swallowed causing a blockage. Immediate action is required, simply by putting your fingers down the dog's throat to ascertain if the object can be retrieved manually. If possible, pull the offending object out of the mouth or, should it be further down the throat, give the dog a piece of dry bread which he may swallow automatically and then, hopefully, the chew will be gradually digested. When he has calmed down, give the dog a drink of fresh, clean water.

CONSTIPATION: This can be caused by an inappropriate diet or giving the dog too many bones. Since the expulsion of waste products from the digestive system is dependent upon the proper performance of the digestion of food, the obvious cause of constipation is some kind of digestive disturbance. Inadequate exercise can also contribute towards constipation. Symptoms are small or diminished motions. If the condition is serious,

there is pain and straining and the St. Bernard shows signs of being distressed. The abdomen can be swollen, the dog may lose his appetite and vomiting can sometimes occur.

Where no toxins have been absorbed, or the St. Bernard has been constipated for only a short time, the condition is treatable at home. Obstinate cases may need a modern organic compound purgative but, generally, liquid paraffin can be administered with a satisfactory conclusion. One level dessert spoonful twice per day should ease the problem until the motions return to normal. Alternatively, add some corn or olive oil to the dog's normal feed for a short period of time.

COUGHING: What is often referred to as "kennel cough" is a misnomer, as it is often passed on by housedogs and it is not restricted to kennelled St. Bernards. This contagious, airborne virus can be contracted by dogs meeting each other in the local park. The symptoms are a rasping cough, often accompanied by the impression of choking, with the St. Bernard bringing up froth. This can be treated by administering a human expectorant, especially if the dog is more lethargic than normal, or refusing food. A healthy St. Bernard will usually get over kennel cough fairly quickly. This is not the case with young puppies or older dogs, so it is better to consult the vet by telephoning in the first instance. Remember, clinics and veterinary establishments are for ill animals, so a lot of infection and airborne bugs lurk around. A home visit is probably more appropriate for this condition.

CUTS: Depending upon the severity and size, these wounds should be treated as for bites. However, if there is any hanging flesh, stitching will no doubt be necessary, which means a a visit to the vet.

CYSTS: Interdigital: these are small cysts which can be found in between the toes of the St. Bernard. This condition can be caused by irritation from a foreign body such as a grass seed or grit from the roads. Often the St. Bernard will lick and lick the affected area as it is uncomfortable, and sometimes this can get rid of the foreign body. In some cases, an abscess can occur if the area is badly infected. Bathe in boiled water and coarse sea salt. If possible, immerse the paw in the warm water for about 3-5 minutes (easier said than done!). Repeat this process twice a day and the cyst should clear up. With reoccurring or severe problems, consult the vet.

CYSTITIS: Bacteria or irritants in the bladder can cause inflammation. Causes are lying in the cold or wet, or the the the formation of urinary deposits; or sometimes bitches develop cystitis prior to coming into season when their urine can become more acidic. The inflammation set up interferes with the natural resistance of the mucous membrane to bacteria in the urine, and bacillary invasion of the bladder walls occurs. In some cases the bacteria gain entrance from the kidneys by the ureters or from the genital passages by the urethra.

Symptoms in acute cystitis are that the urine is passed frequently, accompanied by a burning sensation; often the vulva in a bitch can feel very hot. Pain is demonstrated by the St. Bernard at each effort of passing urine. The amount of urine deposited is small in quantity, and straining often occurs. Sometimes blood or pus may be visible in the urine, albumen can be present and it smells strongly of ammonia. The St. Bernard can show discomfort when the region of the bladder is palpated. Treatment can be frequent drinks of fresh, cold water or better still, barley water. Something we have found most helpful has been to place cranberry juice in the drinking water. It is easy to obtain the cranberry juice from supermarkets, as it is sold in cartons. Use one full carton per gallon of water. In severe cases, consult the vet for appropriate medication.

DIARRHOEA: It has been found that diarrhoea is caused by several factors such as over-eating, a sudden change in diet or water, bacterial infection or stress. If your adult St. Bernard has very loose motions, food should be withdrawn for 24 hours. Give the dog plenty of water – ideally boiled water which has been allowed to become tepid. Glucose can be added, but this is not necessary in most cases, though useful for an older dog or puppy. It is important that the St. Bernard should not be allowed to become dehydrated. Kaolin and morphine or kaolin and chlorodine suspension can

be given to aid the recovery process. If the problem persists and the dog becomes really ill, consult the vet; it may be appropriate to admit the dog and put him or her on a glucose saline drip to aid recovery.

EAR INFECTIONS: Often the first sign of problems, unless owners are vigilant in examining their dog's ears for excessive amounts of wax, is when the St. Bernard begins shaking his head. Sometimes the dog may hold his head to one side as balance can be affected due to problems in the middle ear.

The most prolific cause is infection from the microscopic acarine mite known as the *otodectes canis*. This can be difficult to treat, as the mites breed exceedingly quickly, causing a staphylococcus which is introduced by the mites to infect the ear tissue. In the early stages, Otodex can be helpful. It is better to seek professional opinion from the vet. When treating an ear which has an excessive amount of wax, we have found that using a solution of one part cider vinegar to two parts water to wash the ear has proved effective. Gently dry the ear by patting dry with cotton wool. Remember to use separate cotton wool for each ear. DO NOT poke into the delicate ear canal. To help prevent infections, remove all unnecessary hair from the inside flap of the St. Bernard's ear and hair just around the base of the ear – externally. This will enable air to circulate more easily around the ear.

ECZEMA: This is a non-contagious skin disease. There is evidence which would suggest that certain lines of St. Bernards are more predisposed to attacks of eczema. It seems that hereditary transmission of an eczematous liability from one generation to another has occurred.

Eczema is a superficial disease of the skin of an inflammatory nature, characterised by a scaly and fissured condition of the surface layers of the skin. There is a watery or a serious discharge accompanied by irritation or itchiness. One cause is certainly an allergy or sensitivity to flea bites. Diet can also be a contributory factor if too much cooked protein or carbohydrate is given. Some complete dog foods do not suit certain St. Bernards either.

When treating eczema, it is advisable to change

the diet. Dogs like St. Bernards are usually greedy dogs and will eat most things, so add chopped raw carrot, cabbage or cauliflower to their meal to provide extra vitamins. The left-over water from cooking vegetables can be used to soak the dog biscuit.

Treatment for eczema: trim the hair around the infected area until the skin looks fresh and normal. Wash the infected area with a solution of one part white spirit to three parts boiled water. Try to avoid using creams as this spreads the infection.

There are two types of eczema. There is dry eczema which can be found inside the thighs, under the armpits of St. Bernards and along the undercarriage of the body. Wet eczema may be located on the face, ear flaps, and on the dog's back and rump. Carry out the treatment two or three times a day initially, reducing to once a day when the skin begins to look healthy again.

FITS: St. Bernards rarely suffer from fits; however, occasionally they may occur. Symptoms are frothing at the mouth and convulsions. Place the dog in a darkened room where he can be quiet, and obtain some bromide tablets from the pharmacist, following the administration instructions carefully. These will help to sedate the St. Bernard. If fitting re-occurs, seek veterinary advice.

FLEAS AND LICE: Fleas and lice are parasites. A parasite, according to the derivation of the word from the Greek, when roughly translated, means "one who eats at another man's table".
Fleas: The flea has a complex life cycle, going through a process from egg, larva, then pupa to insect. The flea lays large white eggs, not on the body of the dog, but deposited by the female on carpets, between the floorboards or in dust collected in the corners of the kennels. From these eggs emanates a small, dirty-white maggot which, as a rule, assumes the pupa stage in a cocoon by the following two weeks. A further fortnight passes and the actual flea emerges. The cycle then begins again.

The flea has no wings; however, it possesses powerful hind legs, which enable it to jump several hundred times its own height. The flea is a parasite which sucks the blood of its host.

In view of the complex life cycle of the flea and the way the eggs are laid, it is useless to attempt to

eradicate the fleas unless the habitat and environment are treated too. Fortunately, there are now excellent products available from vets and pet suppliers to treat the St. Bernard.
Lice: There are two distinct families of lice: the biting lice and the sucking lice. Unfortunately, both families like the St. Bernard. Lice are wingless insects which undergo direct development. The egg is laid on the St. Bernard and glued to a hair. The young louse is just smaller in size than the adult – it does not go through the pupal stage.

Sucking lice belong to the order Siphunculata. These wingless insects have compressed heads and strong claws. The mouthparts are constructed for sucking. These are bluish-grey in colour and suck the blood of the St. Bernard.

Biting lice belong to the order Mallaphaga. Their mouthparts are very different from those of the sucking lice. They cannot suck blood and the mouthparts consist of a pair of mandibles on the ventral side of the blunt head. These lice tend to be more orange in colour.

Both families of lice cause irritation to the St. Bernard. Should puppies become infested with lice, it can cause anaemia if not quickly treated. Adult lice can be exterminated with an appropriate spray from the vet or pet supplier. Another method is to bathe the dog with an insecticidal shampoo.

Remember that the lice may not be killed. They have an incubation period of 8-10 days, so the treatment requires repeating at intervals of 8-10 days. Always read the instructions on the sprays and medication.

HEAT-STROKE: This is a condition associated with great exertion or extremely hot weather. Experts suggest this is due to a raised temperature of the brain cells, rather than to the direct action of the sun, as heat-stroke can occur at night. Symptoms are that the St. Bernard becomes extremely lethargic and may become unable to walk or move. The dog may have a glazed look about his eyes and appear to have a lack of co-ordination.

Treatment: The St. Bernard requires his temperature to be reduced as quickly as possible. Hosing the dog all over with cold water is an appropriate way to do this. If there is no access to a garden hose then the dog could be immersed in a bath of cold water, ideally with ice packs added.

Out in the country, encourage the Saint to lie or stand in a stream. If the dog cannot manage to walk to the stream, endeavour to bring cold water to him in a suitable container, or soak towels, blankets or whatever is available to help reduce the dog's temperature. Try not to let the dog drink too much water.

NEVER leave a Saint Bernard unattended in a car in warm weather for more than a few moments, even with the windows open. It is remarkable how quickly the car becomes hot, even when the windows are left slightly open. The Saint will become extremely distressed, begin panting, possibly have diarrhoea, then go into a state of collapse. Prevention is definitely better for the Saint, so do be mindful of where the car is parked and the potential temperature which the interior of a car can rise to, even on just a warm day.

LAMENESS: Often puppies, especially the giant breeds such as Danes, Newfoundlands, Mastiffs and St. Bernards, have growth problems due to lack of knowledge by novice owners. It cannot be stressed too often that the growth rate in giant breeds is very different to that of smaller breeds. Should a dog lover have owned another, smaller breed or an average-sized dog, then what would have been the acceptable 'norm' for that breed is not the accepted 'norm' in the pattern of growth of a St. Bernard. The St. Bernard puppy MUST NOT be over-exercised.

The growth rate, the development of the bone in St. Bernards, is fairly rapid, whereas the muscles take a longer period to build up and they develop at a different rate to the bone and do not keep pace with the growth of bone mass. A St. Bernard has heavy bone and you can expect the muscles to be coarse in texture, comparatively slow in action, quicker to tire but with relatively more applied strength.

When St. Bernard puppies play, they often bump into things so it is possible for the puppy to sustain a mild injury to the shoulder or thigh muscles. DO NOT PANIC and rush off to a vet, who may try to convince you that your young dog has a dreadful hereditary disease or condition due to 'in-breeding'. The Saint should be rested and given the minimum of exercise until he is sound again.

It could be that the lameness is due to a cut pad or damaged toe. Examine the pads closely. Should a cut be detected, treat as a cut and bathe as described. Should there be a hair-line cut, then bathe and, if it is available, use the product 'New-Skin' which can be painted over the cut and will provide some external protection while it heals. The problem with St. Bernards having cut pads is their weight, because the cut tends to re-open when any weight is put upon the paw.

STINGS: St. Bernards are inquisitive creatures, but not as agile at catching flies as a terrier, hound, or gundog. The problem is that the Saints do not distinguish between flies, wasps and bees, so they can become victims to a sting. Should the St. Bernard be stung, remove the sting as quickly as possible, then apply antiseptic cream such as TCP or Savlon. If the Saint is stung in the mouth or throat, then this can be dangerous if swelling occurs, as the wasp or bee could have stung the mucous membrane of the throat. To prevent the dog having an allergic reaction or suffocating from the swelling, consult the vet as soon as possible. Try to keep yourself and the dog calm.

TICKS: The tick is one of the worst enemies of domestic animals, in particular the dog. These parasites are generally obtained from sheep. The engorging female digs her way into the St. Bernard's skin, sucking the blood and gradually increasing in size. This causes a good deal of irritation, making the St. Bernard scratch. The female tick is blue in colour, the male a brownish colour. DO NOT be tempted to pull the tick off your Saint, as the head could well be embedded in the skin of the dog. Should this occur, an abscess may develop. If you are a smoker, draw on the cigarette then place the cigarette's hot end onto the tick, which will encourage the tick to withdraw its head; then remove the tick from the dog.

Another method is to use white spirit or nail varnish remover by dabbing cotton wool into the spirit then onto the rear of the tick. Once the head has withdrawn, remove the tick and dispose of this parasite carefully so that another dog is not infected.

VOMITING: As a natural way of cleansing, the St. Bernard may often eat grass. This causes the dog to vomit froth, along with undigested grass. This is a process inherited by domestic dogs from their ancestors and is in no way harmful to your St. Bernard. However, if the dog has consumed some kind of poisonous or toxic plants of which there are a great variety, he may vomit and collapse. Make up some strong salt water and pour into his throat and encourage him to vomit. Should the symptoms persist, veterinary assistance is essential. If your St. Bernard has an upset stomach, then milk of magnesia is an excellent aid to recovery. This is also useful when a bitch is in season, as her urine can be acidic and milk of magnesia is alkaline.

WORMS

Heart Worms: This is a common parasite of dogs in Central Europe, the USA, Australia, Asia and Russia. The worm larvae are transmitted by mosquitoes and gnats. The adult worm can reach a length of twelve inches and inhabits the right side of the heart. This causes endocarditis and a variety of symptoms, such as coughing, hind leg weakness, collapse when exercising, laboured breathing, anaemia and emaciation. Diagnosis is by blood sample and by smears taken at different times during the day. These worms are difficult to eradicate, so veterinary treatment is necessary.

Roundworms: These are so-called because they resemble a piece of thick string. They may be present in the stomach and intestines of the St. Bernard, varying in length from one to five inches. The roundworms are pointed at both ends. If abundantly present in puppies, they can cause enteritis, sometimes fits and, in severe infestations, even death. Sometimes, if the roundworms enter the stomach of your puppy, he may even vomit worms. Roundworms prevent a St. Bernard from thriving, so it is important to carry out appropriate medication to rid the Saint of these parasites.

Symptoms and signs: The puppy can display a distended stomach, sometimes to a great extent. In severe cases there can be muscle wastage, irregular bowel motions or sometimes diarrhoea. In some cases, rickets can be a sequel to worms.

Treatment: Puppies should be wormed at four, six and twelve weeks, using one of the formal preparations from the vet. Other treatments can be administered earlier, following instructions from the vet. We advise worming the Saints twice a year

for adult dogs, but seek the advice of your vet. It is most important to keep your dog wormed regularly, as the larvae from the roundworms can transmit disease to humans. Toxacara Canis eggs are sticky and a danger to children.

Tapeworm: Tapeworms belong to the class of parasites known as Cestoda Cestoda. Their life-cycle requires two hosts, sometimes three. The highly resistant eggs are swallowed by a suitable intermediate host, and there hatches from each egg a small ciliated larva. The larva then penetrates the gut walls and forms a cystic stage, the bladder worms.

Tapeworms do not breed inside dogs, but the eggs or larvae pass out of the dog to be swallowed by some other creature, who in turn passes the cyst or bladder worms and the cycle begins again. The tapeworm segments are flat, resembling a melon seed, totally different to the roundworm. These small segments, which look like dried rice, appear under the tail of the St. Bernard, on the dog's bed or in the faeces when the dog has passed a motion. You must treat the dog with appropriate medication from the vet.

SPECIFIC DISORDERS

Eye Conditions and Disorders

Cherry Eye: This condition involves the gland underneath the haw becoming very swollen and inflamed. The gland can actually protrude from the corner of the eye, having enlarged to the size of a pea or black bean. Occasionally this will right itself; however, the condition can re-occur. This gland can be lanced or removed in a simple operation without leaving any side-effects. The concern would be centred more on the fact of the Saint having to have an anaesthetic.

Dry Eye: This is not so familiar in St. Bernards as cherry eye; however, occasionally problems have been identified in this breed. Dry eye (keratocon-junctivitis sicca) is a malfunction of the tear gland, resulting in the cornea being dry. As the dog needs to keep the cornea clean and functioning correctly, dry eye is an extremely painful condition. If left untreated, it can cause blindness. It can be caused by the after-effects of other diseases such as distemper or treatment with some of the sulphonamides.

Treatment consists of eye-drops as a replacement for the missing tear production, combined with cyclosporin therapy as an immuno-suppressant. Therapy is often life-long, however, due to the fact that the amount of tear production can vary with time as the treatment takes effect; it can then be administered periodically. In severe cases, the surgical procedure would be to remove the salivary ducts so that they can drain into the eye. This does not always prove successful in St. Bernards.

Entropion: This tends to be more common among the heavy-headed type of St. Bernard in Britain. It also occurs with a St. Bernard which has a small 'piggy' eye. Entropion means 'turning in' which describes the condition whereby the eyelid turns in and then the eyelashes scratch the cornea, setting up an irritation known as keratitis. This frequently follows inflammatory conditions of the eyelids and cornea and causes a lot of distress to the St. Bernard. This condition can be present in one or both eyes, on the top or the bottom eyelid or both. In order for the St. Bernard to be a healthy Saint, the welfare of the dog must be taken into account and he will require surgery to rectify this painful condition.

The surgery involves the vet removing an appropriate amount of flesh from above or below the eyelid, depending on which lids are affected. This is carried out for health reasons for the dog; however, if too much flesh, or the incorrect shape, is cut then the appearance of the St. Bernard can be affected. It is important after surgery to prevent the dog from endeavouring to remove the stitches. Often Elizabethan collars are recommended; however, these can create more distress to the Saint. Recommendations from other breeders and vets are to keep the dog sedated for a few days. Cotton sports socks can be tied to the St. Bernard's front paws to prevent him from catching the eye with his claws. The dog is more likely to try to remove these articles from his paws, so is temporarily distracted from gaining access to the eyes.

Ectropion: This means turning out of both eyelids, so that the conjunctiva is exposed. St. Bernards with particularly drooping eyelids can be prone to this condition and when it occurs the eye is exposed to infections. This is also treated by surgery. Part of the conjunctiva from within the edge of the lid is removed, instead of part of the skin from outside, as in entropion.

Progressive Retinal Atrophy (PRA.): This is also referred to as 'night-blindness'. The nervous elements of the retina undergo progressive atrophy and the Saint can have impaired vision. The pupil dilates in an attempt to redress the problem, making the dog's expression staring. At night the dog is unable to avoid objects and blunders into them; however, he can see better in daylight.

No treatment can arrest the progressive degeneration and the dog becomes steadily worse. This is an hereditary disease but is not commonly found in St. Bernards, although a few Saints suffering from it have been heard of. A St. Bernard diagnosed as having this disorder should not be used for breeding purposes because of the hereditary factor.

HEART DISEASE: Many diseases specific or otherwise can affect the heart. The heart carries out a considerably arduous task, as this organ never completely rests from the time of its formation prior to birth until death occurs.

Inflammatory Affections: These are divided into pericarditis, endocarditis, and myocarditis according to whether the pericardium (muscular substance) or the endocardium (lining membrane) is affected; myocarditis may be of bacterial origin, or associated with a vitamin deficiency.

Valvular diseases form one of the most important groups, there being eight conditions in this class. Each of the four valves may be 'stenosed', i.e. its opening narrowed, or incompetent – allowing blood to flow through in the wrong direction. Hypertrophy, in which the heart is enlarged and its wall thickened, and dilatation, in which one or more of the cavities is dilated, form another group often associated with valvular diseases.

Degeneration: This is when the heart muscle tissue produces an enfeeblement of the heart's action. This could be due to a 'fatty' change, in which there are globules of fat found in the muscle fibres or between them, or it may be a fibroid change in which fibrous tissue is present in excess.

Functional Changes This is when, without apparent diseased change in the structure of the heart, palpitation, rapidity, slowness or great irregularity may appear. Such conditions may exist in the St. Bernard and yet no symptoms may have been previously displayed until they are accidentally recognised when the heart is being examined as a routine matter by the vet.

A strenuous life in which continual strains are placed upon the heart leads to hypertrophy. This can occur in a St. Bernard who is made to go on forced walks for a considerable distance on a daily basis. When the Saint becomes older and can no longer manage long walks, fatty degeneration or fibroid degeneration or even ossification of the right auricle may occur.

All the febrile diseases, especially those due to or associated with bacteria in the blood stream, have an adverse effect upon the action of the heart. Examples are pneumonia, septic metritis, distemper, sometimes mastitis and tuberculosis. Diseases which are associated with high temperatures also alter the beat of the heart.

Disease of the heart could be set up by pressure from a tumour upon the large arteries, or by pressure from an enlarged lymphatic gland.

Palpitations: This condition, where the heart beats fast and strongly, is due to some nervous disturbance brought about by errors in feeding, sudden frights, unusual and terrifying surroundings or other traumas. St. Bernards are not normally nervous but occasionally something can perturb them.

Cardiac Flutter and Fibrillation: These conditions, presenting irregularity in the pulse, are due to the atria emptying themselves, not by a series of regular waves, but by an irregular series of flutters or twitches instead, which fails to stimulate the ventricles properly.

Cardiomyopathy: This term denotes structural or functional abnormalities of the myocardium. Primary cardiomyopathy excludes diseases resulting from congenital, ischemic, hypertensive, vascular, pulmonary, parenchymal, acquired valvular or other cardiovascular disorders.

Primary Cardiomyopathies: Systolic (i.e. myocardial or pump) failure results when the ventricles fail to generate normal contractile force. This is due to primary (idiopathic) dilated cardiomyopathy or secondary dilated cardiomyopathy resulting from toxins, e.g. parvovirus or inflammation such as bacterial, or physical agents such as hypothermia. Congestive heart failure results from both depressed contractility and failure of neuroendocrine, hepatorenal and peripheral vascular compensatory mechanisms. Systolic dysfunction may range from mild to severe contractile impairment, coupled with heterogeneous structural variations.

Dilated Congestive Cardiomyopathy: This can range from six months of age in a St. Bernard until the dog is much older. The actual clinical signs to look out for are exercise intolerance, coughing, abdominal distension and dyspnoea, which can be acute, becoming noticeable over a three-day period. In other St. Bernards, the signs may be more subtle over five to seven days, and these could be pronounced weight loss, mild to moderate lethargy or poor mucous membranes of the gums.

It is vital to seek veterinary attention for the St. Bernard as soon as possible. On examination, the vet may find abnormalities consistent with low cardial output, left-sided heart failure (e.g. pulmonary oedema), or right-sided heart failure (e.g. pericardial, pleural, abdominal effusions). Biventricular failure may sometimes co-exist. A rapid, irregular heart rate and a gallop rhythm may be present. Muffled heart and lung sounds may be due to diminished contractility or the damping effects of pericardial and pleural effusion. Other symptoms are increased bronchovesicular sounds.

The prognosis for St. Bernards with dilated congestive cardiomyopathy is very poor. Appropriate treatment, where possible, may be given by the vet. In some cases it may be kinder to put the needs of the dog first and deal with one's own emotions later, by having the St. Bernard peacefully put to sleep. A happy Saint is a healthy

Saint; if the dog is miserable or the quality of life extremely poor, then it is a terrible existence for the once majestic Saint.

HEREDITARY CONDITIONS AND DISORDERS

JOINTS: A joint or articulation is formed by the union of two or more bones or cartilages by other tissues. Bone is the chief component of most joints; however, in some instances, it can be a bone and a cartilage, or two cartilages which form a joint.

Joints fall into two great divisions, namely (a) moveable joints and (b) fixed joints. In a moveable joint, there are four main structures.

Firstly, there are the two bones whose junction forms the joint. Secondly, there is a layer of smooth cartilage covering the ends of these bones where they meet. This is known as the 'articular' cartilage. Thirdly, there is a sheath of fibrous tissue known as the 'joint capsule', which is thickened into bands of ligaments which hold the bones together at various points. Lastly, there is a closed bladder of membrane known as the 'synovial membrane', which lines the capsule and produces a synovial fluid to lubricate the movements of the joint.

The bones are kept in position by the various muscles passing over them and by the atmospheric pressure. The stifle joint possesses subsidiary structures such as discs of fibro-cartilage, which adapt the bones more perfectly to one another where they do not quite respond, and allows for freer movement.

The joints between the bodies of the vertebrae form a thick disc between the bones, so that the individual joint is only capable of limited movement.

The region of the neck of the St. Bernard is fairly flexible. Gliding joints is a term used for the bones which have flat surfaces capable of limited movement, such as the bones of the carpus and tarsus.

A hinge joint is the elbow, where movement takes place around one axis only; this is referred to as flexion and extension. In the shoulder, the ball and socket joint has free movement which can occur in any direction.

The larger joints, on account of their exposed position in the body, can be subject to injury, and this, together with the wear the St. Bernard has to withstand, along with the peculiarity of the blood supply, renders these joints liable to some disorders which will be identified in this section.

Hip Dysplasia: This term covers a number of abnormal conditions of the acetabulum and head of the femur. These conditions are believed to be part hereditary, with feeding and environment having an influence on the disorders. Some of these hereditary conditions include:

Subluxation: This is when the head of the femur is no longer firmly seated within the acetabulum. Deformity of the head of the femur gradually develops. In layman's terms, this is a ball and socket joint which does not fit properly into the pelvis. The condition can cause varying degrees of lameness. St. Bernards can be victims of this painful disorder which can present symptoms around fourteen to eighteen months of age. Some of the signs are a reluctance to rise from the sitting position, and a sawing gait rather than the normal St. Bernard action. X-rays need to be undertaken to assess the damage and condition.

In severe cases, surgery is the only way to ease the pain and allow the dog an improved quality of life. The operation can be lengthy as the muscles have to be cut through to explore the damage to the bones. It is now possible to have substitute joints if the wear and damage has been severe. When the muscles heal up, the St. Bernard will feel more comfortable in taking several steps.

St. Bernards suffering from Hip Dysplasia should not be used for breeding purposes.

The British Veterinary Association and The Kennel Club have a hip scoring system. However, a lot of St. Bernard breeders are reluctant to have their dogs hip-scored through the scheme as this involves anaesthetics. Sadly, St. Bernards react badly to anaesthetics and can die. The reluctance to have Saints hip-scored results in difficulties in assessing the number of St. Bernards who are affected by this disorder. Another problem is that even breeding from a dog and bitch with excellent hip scores does not mean that all their progeny will have low scores.

When submitting evidence to the BVA/KC Hip Scoring Scheme, the Saint Bernard must be X-rayed by an approved veterinary surgeon. Each hip will be X-rayed individually and these 'plates' (photographs) are sent off for analysis. There are a total number of 54 points, with 6 points being awarded to nine different areas of the structure on each hip. The aim is to achieve a healthy Bernard with low hip score. When the analysis has been undertaken, a score for each hip is awarded, so the results may be 20:18, which indicates one hip score is slightly higher than the other.

In Germany, Sweden and other countries, St. Bernards must be X-rayed to ascertain an analysis of their hips before they can be bred from. This is compulsory. As far as we are aware, it is not compulsory in the USA.

In Germany, the ratings are as follows:

0	=	Free
1	=	Bordering
2	=	Light
3	=	Average
4	=	Severe

Perthes' Disease: This involves a slight subluxation and rarefaction of the femur. Pain may be pronounced. This condition can improve or disappear between 10 and 12 months of age, unlike hip dysplasia, which does not disappear.

Congenital Dislocation: This is caused when the acetabula are too shallow to retain the heads of the femurs in position. As the St. Bernard develops and grows older, often a 'false' joint forms. This usually means the muscles are supporting the joints.

Osteochondrosis Dissecans: This used to be more prevalent in smaller breeds; however, it has recently been diagnosed in the shoulder or scapula of the growing St. Bernard, or in the point of the elbow. Often a fragment of bone breaks away from the main mass of bone and can affect the muscles which support the bone, so that the Saint walks with some discomfort and lameness. A lot depends upon which joint or bone area has been damaged and how large the splinter of bone is, as to the exact treatment.

In some cases, the dog will develop without any surgery being necessary, and as the dog matures the condition settles down. Other cases will require surgery to remove the fragment of bone, which moves around causing a degree of discomfort and lameness. If surgery is left for too long, then arthritis can occur in the joints. X-rays will not always determine the cause, as some tiny fragments of bone may not be visible on them. Veterinary consultation is necessary to assess what is in the best interest for the dog's well-being and to decide if an operation is necessary.

Cruciate Ligament (Torn): Ligaments are strong bands of fibrous tissue which bind together the bones forming a joint. The cruciate ligaments are two strong ligaments which cross over the stifle joint. Their function is to prevent any over-extension of the joint. St. Bernards who love to run and who suddenly carry out a sharp right or left-hand turn can damage their hind leg when the cruciate ligaments stretch or break. This can be very painful and can immobilise the Saint for several weeks, often leaving a weakness in the joint.

Symptoms are the dog hanging his hind leg with the toes just above or slightly touching the floor, with no weight being placed upon the foot. The St. Bernard will be feeling discomfort, so will look longingly at you to "do something" about it. The vet needs to be contacted to discuss appropriate treatment. There will be X-rays taken to determine whether the ligament is stretched or severed. If the ligament is stretched, some vets recommend nature taking its course and advise restricting the exercise of the dog until the ligament regains its elasticity. Should the ligament be severed, then surgery is required to do the necessary repair. This can be carried out using the dog's own resources, if applicable, or by using carbon fibre.

Some vets will carry out a cruciate ligament operation themselves, others will refer the dog to a recognised orthopaedic expert or to a veterinary college. This is a specialised operation requiring knowledge and skills to repair the damage so that the St. Bernard can resume some quality of life. The size and weight of this breed is often not conducive to a complete recovery. Some Saints have a tendency to slight lameness, whereas others are prone to arthritis occurring.

It is most important to follow the guidance of the vet after the St. Bernard returns from his operation and you are responsible for the after-care. There will be several do's and don'ts to follow to aid the recovery of your faithful friend. The first few weeks are vital to enable the ligaments to return gradually to their prime function without over-exertion.

Although torn cruciate ligaments are not hereditary, some lighter, more agile and active St. Bernards are susceptible to this condition, especially if chasing another Saint.

Slack Pasterns: The pastern is not just one bone, as some may suppose. The pastern, at the lower end of the forearm, is made up of a number of small bones (carpals). Sloping pasterns should not be confused with broken-down pasterns. The slope should not start at the joint itself, but either above or below it, keeping this group of bones in compact harmony. The broken-down pastern finds the carpal assembly awry and askew, not supporting the weight carried by the leg. This condition can be hereditary.

The slope should always be sufficient to bring the heel of the pad under the centre of gravity. In St. Bernards there should be a large blade and long upper arm set at 90 degrees; this requires the slope on the pasterns to be more angled. If the assembly puts the pad in front of the vertical centre, then the pastern should slope enough to get it off direct centre and give it flexibility.

St. Bernards with poor pasterns can have difficulty walking. The condition can be part-hereditary, part-diet, as puppies can become far too fat and put a strain on the carpals which form the pastern.

A calcium supplement can be given under the supervision of a vet. Vitamins A and D help to absorb the calcium in small doses. Too many supplements can cause a lot of problems in the growing St. Bernard.

Gentle exercise is recommended. No forced walks. If your St. Bernard does not come up on his pasterns by the age of 12 months, the condition is not likely to improve, so the quality of life may be affected.

SKIN DISORDERS
Mange (Sarcoptic): This is a highly contagious skin disease. Sometimes sarcoptic mange is referred to as canine scabies and it is caused by the parasitic mite Sarcoptes canis. Mites are microscopic organisms related to spiders. The disease is spread from dog, or fox, to dog by close contact. These mites can survive for a few days off their host (dog) in the surrounding environment. This means that some St. Bernards may be infested from their environment even if they do not come into direct contact with another dog. Events involving large numbers of dogs together, such as dog shows, are ideal locations for the mites to attach themselves to a new host.

Symptoms are extreme itching, so that the St. Bernard becomes very distressed, redness of the skin, crusting and hair loss. The Saints typically scratch their ears, face, trunk and underlegs, sometimes almost continually. Due to this irritation, which must be almost unbearable for the Saint, the dog can become depressed, even uncharacteristically aggressive. Sarcoptic mange is very contagious, so if one Saint has this disease, it will spread very quickly to the rest of the dogs if you have more than one.

The Saint needs to be assessed for a diagnosis as soon as possible to establish if this really is mange. The vet will usually undertake a skin scraping and examine this under a microscope. Recently a blood test has been developed to check for sarcoptic mange and this is proving helpful in diagnosing this distressing condition.

The usual treatment is by repeated washing with an appropriate mite dip. All bedding such as blankets, brushes, combs, etc. could be contaminated and these should be destroyed, or washed and sprayed with the available appropriate sprays now on the market. Insecticidal sprays designed specifically for use in the environment are available.

There are only two dips in the UK which are licensed for this purpose. One contains phosmet, an organophosphate; the other, amitraz, an agent which is used for treating mange in pigs. Amitraz can be toxic and should not be used on St. Bernard puppies; however, it should be suitable for adult Saints. It is probably a good idea to trim the hair on a rough-coated Saint to enable the washing to be more effective.

Although other treatments are probably available over the counter in pet shops, it is unlikely that these have undergone properly controlled scientific trials. The old methods were to bathe the dog in benzyl benzoate or gammexane; however, these are no longer available due to possible links to cancer.

Mange (Follicular): This is a skin disorder associated with puppies and young St. Bernards. It is thought to be carried by the female and transmitted to her progeny, as often the whelps appear to be born with this problem. It appears to be a slow, progressive disease and may start with a single bare patch of varying size on the face, the side of the nose, or possibly the back. This can be greyish in colour and have reddish pimples or elevations of the skin, somewhat larger than those seen in ordinary mange. As time goes by, the original patch increases in size and others form, the pustules break, one running into another, looking sore and unpleasant. When these wounds heal, the skin is dry, almost corrugated in appearance, little excrescences of skin are formed, the hair does not always grow back, or is short and breaks off. The skin in follicular mange sometimes has a 'mousy' smell.

Treatment: This appears to be a most unsatisfactory disease to treat; often, after months of hard work, the dog breaks out with another infection and appears to be no better. Veterinary treatment must be sought as soon as possible.

Some conditions which may be confused with Mange:
Allergy to house dust mites and other environmental substances (atopy).

Flea allergy, as previously described.
Louse infestation, as previously described.
Bacterial skin infection (Pyoderma).
Yeast dermatitis.

THE AGEING ST. BERNARD

There is a widely held belief that a biological clock controls the ageing process. Bruce Fogle, the vet and animal psychologist, suggests that this 'clock' is genetic in origin and influences the hormones in the dog's body. This 'clock' could be located in the hypothalamic area of the brain. It is a known fact that this area controls the growth hormones as well as the activities of many of the hormone-producing glands. Environment also has a dramatic effect upon the ageing process. Environmental influences will speed up or slow down a genetically predetermined life span. By improving the environment, we can help prolong the life for a St. Bernard, but the biological clock associated with death is genetic.

Older dogs have poorer reflexes, along with sensory losses, both of which affect a St. Bernard's behaviour. With age, the blood vessels of the brain become less 'elastic' and the lungs become less efficient. The inefficiency of the blood vessels and lungs means the brain becomes starved of oxygen and this has an effect on memory. Older dogs will

The veteran deserves special consideration. This is Snowranger Magnum aged nine years.

not like being disturbed or their routine disrupted; sometimes the older Saint can be disorientated after sleep. As a caring owner, it is important for you to adjust the exercise and feeding regimes. It is probably a good idea to provide less food, but more often, to help the digestive system.

Unfortunately, St. Bernards do not have as long a life span as other breeds such as Westies, Collies or Poodles. The average life span for a Saint is eight or nine years, although some are known to have lived for longer periods. Ch. Coatham Starshine was almost eleven before she died peacefully. A Rough Collie we had at the time was protective of this Saint's body and became distressed when we tried to bury her.

Back to the physical changes of ageing. Gradually, the St. Bernard's hearing changes, there is no longer the hearing of high-pitched sensitive notes. The eyes change too: old eyes become foggy as the retina becomes disorganised and the lenses lose their elasticity; consequently the Saint cannot see as well as he used to.

Taste is also affected by the ageing process. There are a variety of appropriate complete dog foods available for the older dog, so do give it a try, should your older St. Bernard be having problems with his appetite.

A major problem for all large dogs can be the painful condition of arthritis, not only of the joints, but also occasionally with their ears, which causes deafness. With smaller breeds, owners have gone to great lengths to carry the dog outside to urinate or had wheels made to go under back ends riddled with disease. This is not possible in a St. Bernard. We all hope and pray our Bernards will pass away naturally, and that their quality of life will remain acceptable until the end. We humans do not like the idea of having to make 'that' decision.

Should your Saint become so infirm that their dignity and quality of life has been taken away, then you must consider making that decision, no matter how painful or heartbreaking it is. At least we are able to make this decision. Anyone who has observed a lover, friend or relative die from cancer, or other terminal illness, feels so helpless and powerless, watching that person suffer and being unable to release them from such suffering. With our beloved Saints we can at least make that decision, on their behalf.

There are lots of special crematoriums now for pets, so do make enquiries at your vet's. Appropriate arrangements can be made to have your special faithful friend cremated and to obtain the ashes. It is more expensive but a fitting way to return to "dust and ashes" for the magnificent St. Bernard we shared our life with. Fortunately, the wonderful memories will remain with you for ever.

12
KENNELS IN THE UK

The first official record of Saints coming into Britain was in 1815 when a St Bernard from the hospice was purchased by a Mrs Boode from Birkenhead, near Liverpool. Early writers suggest this dog, who was called Lion, was like a Mastiff. A bitch was also imported, and Lion and the imported bitch are believed to have produced several litters. One of the progeny was named Caesar and was painted by Sir Edwin Landseer in the picture referred to as *The Rescue* (1820).

In 1825, two more smooths were imported from the hospice to Mr John Crabtree of Kirklees Hall in Yorkshire. It is thought they were crossed with the Old English Mastiffs to strengthen the Mastiff breed.

In 1854 a natural history expert on alpine matters, Mr Albert Smith, imported two St Bernards, and also a pair of Chamois deer which attracted a lot of publicity. Apparently, the monks from the hospice sent Diane, a good-quality St Bernard bitch, as a New Year gift to Mr Smith in acknowledgement of the increased amount of visitors to the hospice, due to the encouragement and publicity induced by Mr Smith.

After 1863 there is evidence that St Bernards did begin to become really popular amongst the

Ch. Corngarth Be Grand: A Champion from the 1960s owned by Cath and Ken Gaunt. Note the excellent length of leg compared with many St. Bernard Champions today.

Ch. Burtonswood Be Fine.

wealthy in Britain. The Rev. J. Cumming Macdona MP was a member of the Kennel Club committee and owned kennels in West Kirby in Cheshire. The Rector kept Pointers, Setters, Fox Terriers, and Pugs, as well as St Bernards. Apparently, the St Bernards were taken to the beach, and enjoyed swimming in the sea. Rev. Macdona imported a large rough-coated Saint from Herr Schindler in Berne and exhibited this St Bernard in Britain. The dog was named Tell and proved to be a good stud dog.

Another prominent breeder at this time was Mr J.H. Merchison who also exhibited at shows and was a member of the Kennel Club committee. Mr Merchison arranged for a rough-coated Saint to be purchased from Heinrich Schumacher's kennels. 'Thor' duly arrived in England and was much used at stud. Champions were sired by Thor and these were Ch. Heltor, Ch. The Shah, Ch. Dagmar, and Ch. Abbess II, all from the same litter.

So from small beginnings, the breed went from strength to strength.

In 1896 the Bowden kennels were established by Dr George Inman and Dr Ben Walksley. They were successful in showing, with 12 home-bred Champions. When Dr Inman died, the kennel dogs were distributed throughout the country. In 1912,

The Pride of Sussex, who had 23 CCs, was in fact Best in Show at Crufts.

The Bowden Saints were at the fore of the Pearl kennels of Mr and Mrs J. Redwood, who were one of the few kennels to survive the First World War. This couple had 42 Champions to their credit.

ABBOTSPASS ST BERNARDS
These were founded in 1922 by Mrs K. Staines from Reigate in Surrey. This rich lady, though starting off with Pearl St Bernards, began to develop a line of her own, so she imported stock from Switzerland to increase the gene pool and improve her current stock. One of the famous winners was Ch. Abbotspass Romeo. Mrs Staines did not have her dogs at public stud, so little was done to improve stock in other lines. One dog, Ch. Abbotspass Friar was sold to Mr Mellor who did succeed in breeding this dog with a descendant from the Pearl line. On the death of Mrs Staines, following the instructions in her will, all the Abbotspass Saints in her kennels were destroyed.

BOYSTON SAINTS
Mrs Graydon Bradley of Dover began re-establishing the St Bernard kennels after the Second World War. It was difficult to find one St Bernard

during the war, however a nucleus of dedicated breeders succeeded in keeping some Saints. Mrs Bradley worked jointly with Miss Jean Fyffe from Scotland. The Panbride Saints feature in some lines to this day.

CORNAGARTH

Mrs A.K. Gaunt, along with his wife, Kath, had a post-war Champion, Yew Tree St Christopher. This was the first of 61 full Champions to come from the Cornagarth kennels in Derbyshire. This couple began breeding in the mid-thirties, initially under the affix of Twokays. However, this was changed to Cornagarth. In 1952 Marshall con Zwing Uri was acquired by Ken Gaunt when a returning serviceman came back from Britian with this St Bernard. The Gaunts used other stock from Durrowabbey and Chriscon St Bernards for their bloodlines and 11 Champions carrying the affix Cornagarth-Durrowabbey were made up by Ken Gaunt and Mrs Slazenger.

Both Ken and Kath Gaunt died in the 70s, having been custodians of this fascinating breed for almost 50 years.

Much of our present dog stock comes from these old lines and today we can still see the effects of the 'old style' in some modern stock. How many of us can trace our pedigree to some of these wonderful Saints of Mr Gaunt? (Cornagarth)? The legacy left by Mr Gaunt and Mrs Walker is carried on today, albeit the strength of type has changed. No one breeder controls the breed today and that perhaps is a good thing. Nonetheless, who can deny the type of Saints epitomised by Cornagarth? The strength of this kennel can be seen by comparing the Saints of 1954 with those of 1959. Note the stud fees!

Nothing is so constant as change and in the world of Saint Bernards things are always changing. Cornagarth, Peldartor, Daphnedene and Yew Tree are all gone – in fact, but not in memory.

OLD INFLUENTIAL KENNELS

BURTONSWOOD

We owe a debt of gratitude to Miss Hindes and her Burtonswood Saints. As with Cornagarth, the effect of this kennel can still be seen today. Only just recently we had a stud of a smooth bitch who reminded us so much of Ch. Be Elect Of Burtonswood. We looked at her pedigree and, yes, she was bred through our line back to Ch. Burtonswood Be Elect (17 years on).

Ch. Burtonswood Bossy Boots has an immortal place in history. Best in Show at Crufts in 1974, Wow! Sadly we could never get a bitch in whelp from him, but we were able to produce a line from his brother, Ch. Burtonswood Black Tarquin. In our opinion, we thought that Des was more masculine and taller than his illustrious brother. However, he did not match the record of Boots, who sired 23 champions.

Miss Hindes still shows today and we wish to thank her for her contribution to the modern Saint Bernard. Her legacy, hopefully, will be carried on by the modern owners.

LINDENHALL

The Lindenhall affix of Mr and Mrs Beaver is still well-known. Sadly Richard Beaver died in 1991. Who will ever forget the magnificent Saints of the Lindenhall kennels? And we, in particular, were grateful for Ch. Alpentire On Commission, a son of Ch. Lindenhall High Commissioner. Our bitch line can be traced in direct line to 'Raffles' (Ch. Alpentire On Commission) and we can trace ten Champions from our bitch line and multiple CC winners. A wonderful legacy for our kennel.

Richard and Rachel Beaver had Cornagarth Adelaide, mated her to a German import, Cornagarth Kuno von Birkenkopf, and had a litter of seven puppies, five of which were Champions. Ch. Lindenhall High Commissioner was a group winner at Dumfries in 1974.

PELDARTOR

Owned by Mrs Walker, a feisty old lady as we remember, but she and her son Gilbert had some of the best examples of Saints in the fifties and sixties. Although sometimes overshadowed by Cornagarth and Burtonswood, in our opinion Peldartor Saints were much better on the move than many of the Cornagarths.

MODERN TIMES

On to more modern times and we find that many affixes have come and gone. To mention a few is possible – to mention them all is impossible.

Descendants of Ch. Bernegardens Buckpasser: Ch. Abbotsbury Atlantus, Abbotsbury Crackling Rosie, Ch. Abbotsbury Impression and Abbotsbury Unforgettable.

ABBOTSBURY

This kennel was founded in 1979 by Trevor and Norma Goodwin. Their first Saint was Snowranger Magna, bought in 1974 from Mrs Bradley who had the Snowranger Prefix. Trevor and Norma tried for many years to breed quality Saints. In 1990 they purchased Int. Ch. Bernegardens Buckpasser. They made him up in the UK with five CCs. Buckpasser has sired Ch. Abbotsbury Impression who, in turn, sired Ch. Abbotsbury Ialanthus (Arry).

BAVUSH

This was a small kennel based in Lincolnshire owned by Mr and Mrs Riddings. They were active around the late seventies to the early nineties. The best known was Bavush Classic Lady (8 CCs). This kennel, although not prolific in Champions (3), bred some very strong types which are prevalent in many pedigrees today.

BOBANEVE

Eve Slaymaker (née Cooper) went to her first Crufts at the age of 10 and became determined to own her own Saint. She waited for 10 years and on her 21st birthday she acquired one. She called him Bobby and combined that name with Eve to make 'Bobaneve'.

Bobby, who was Ch. Merridale Bouncer, gained his title in 1988. His best win was the Working Group win at Bath, the first St Bernard for 10 years to do so. Eve's only other Champion is Ch. Bobaneve Finesse who won the bitch CC and BOB at Crufts in 1988. Hannah, as she is known, came from a litter of 11, which was a handful. Well worth the perseverance of Eve and her Mum. Eve is now married and still breeds the Saints with her father, Jack Cooper.

Bobaneve Finesse.
Photo: David Dalton.

BRAYPASS

This kennel is owned by Mr M. Braysher. He started his affix in 1966. His first Saint was Burtonswood Belinda. His first Champion was Ch. Cornagarth Mirrabelle. Since then he has had nine Champions. Braypass has had an effect on some notable dogs such as Ch. Be Elect Of Burtonswood, Ch. Dominant Dominic Of Bernmont and Ch. Cornagarth Black Tarquin. Currently Michael favours the smaller type and has some progeny from Opdykes Santa, who came from America.

BRENIDGE

This kennel was founded in 1983 when Jane and Eddy met by virtue of Eddy's encounter with Jane's Saint. He had left his door open and in walked a "huge Saint". Love blossomed and 16 years later they married and together they are the owners of a small successful kennel – the name is an amalgamation of Jane Cridge and Eddie Brennan. Their first Champion was Ch. Sooty Big Bad Wolf, bred by Mrs Yates in 1988. This was followed by Ch. Flashy Jack By Brenidge, who won BOB at Crufts in 1988, followed by runner-up the Saint Bernard of the Year and a Best in Show at the Southern Saint Club.

From their wide-eyed beginnings with Sooty, Big Bad Wolf, Eddie and Jane have started a kennel, which is still growing. They campaign in Ireland and have had notable success. On the circuit they have enjoyed a group 2 and 3 win and several green

stars. Eddie and Jane both judge and are current committee members of the English Saint Bernard Club. We are sure they will continue to develop as breeders and wish them the best of luck in the future.

CHANDLIMORE

This kennel is owned by Mr Tan Nagrecha and his wife Anne Marie in Lincolnshire. Tan came from Bombay to England in 1987. He had never owned a dog because circumstances would not permit it but he had often dreamed of having his own large dog. He soon met Anne Marie, who was walking her dog in the park and it turned out that she came from a doggie family. The couple became close, then married. They now have three children.

Together they purchased a two-year-old bitch from the Bavush St Bernard kennel of Terry Riddings. This bitch, Bavush Our Betty, was mated to Ch. Swindridge Cassius, which produced Storming Norman, who, in turn, produced Ch, Marquis of Chandlimore. The next Bernard was Frauline Gabrielle out of Bavush Storming Norman. She was mated to Ch. Offenbach Field Marshall. This mating produced Ch. Marquis of Chandlimore. Marquis, as Tan says, "was born 20 years too late, his head was over-exaggerated, but he had huge bone and a gorgeous temperament." A fine example for the breed. Marquis has proved to be the pivot of Tan's kennels, producing top stock, including Ch. Chandlimore Centurian and Ch. Snowshire Ritchies Rich With Chandlimore (bred by Mrs M. Ward). Ritchie has won many honours, and before he was two his total was 12 CCs, with 11 BOB, two Reserve CCs, two Group, three Group 3s and one Group 2, plus the working group at the East of England show. This was crowned by reserve Best in Show at East of England in July 1999. In modern times a superlative record.

COATHAM

My first introduction to a Saint Bernard was a ball of fluff named Heidi, or Cornagarth Marquisite, which Mo had bought for the sum of £45.45 shillings, or 45 guineas, from Mr A. K. Gaunt.

In those days the dog world was just as tough for novices as it is now and we showed Heidi against tough opposition from Cornargarth, Burtonswood et al. We made Heidi up in August 1971 and she was owned by Mo in her own name. Time moved on and various Saints came and went for various reasons. Heidi never gave us a litter. We thought she was barren. We think that with modern technology we could have got a litter from her today. We now believe we were mating her on the wrong days – no blood tests then.

We bred our first litter in 1973 and our first home-bred Champion came from that litter, Champion Coatham Star Shine, known as Stella. She was bred from Ch. Burtonswood Black Tarquin and Northern Star Of Coatham. She won ten Challenge certificates, several best of breeds and she holds the record of winning the CC at Crufts three

Ch. Coatham Suffragette.

years running. Stella also won the first bitch CC to be awarded by the Saint Bernard Club of Scotland, the Saint Bernard Club of England and the United Saint Bernard Club.

I bought our first dog from Mr and Mrs McMurray – Ch. Alpentire On Commission in 1977. Mo would not have a dog but I felt we could not progress until we owned our own stud dog. I made him up – although Mo showed him – in 1981. Since then we have owned or bred over 13 Champions at home and overseas including three Champions in New Zealand and one in Holland.

One of our proudest moments was Mountside Movie Star, who won 22 CCs (bred out of Coatham Britania (two CCs) and Ch. Finetime The Great Bear) winning the BOB at Crufts in 1994. We are a small kennel and our motto is 'Quality not quantity'.

Current representatives of the Coatham kennel: Coatham Heaven Blest (left) and Coatham Smooth Liaison.

Photo: Mike Trafford.

Our kennel has its foundations in the affix granted in 1969 although it was owned by Maureen from 1963 in her own name of Catchpole. Mo started with Rough Collies and she has qualified a dog for Crufts every year since 1966.

Like many others, we decided to use foreign blood to strengthen our blood lines and therefore we used Ch. Abbotsbury Impression, a son of International Champion Bernegardens Buckpasser, to our bitch Coatham Goodness Gracious. From this we produced Coatham Smooth Impression who gained his Junior warrant and two reserve CCs before we retired him. He is producing sound stock with a good temperament and sound movement and our intention is to amalgamate his lines with our successful bloodlines and we have, at the moment, our first smooth-to-smooth puppy Coatham Smooth Dynasty. At present we have several promising youngsters and our smooth bitch Coatham Smooth Liaison is waiting for her third CC to make her our 14th Champion.

DENBOW
Owned by Mr Owen in Bristol and active for a short time, this kennel owned Ch. Coatham Gin 'n' Tonic from which came Ch. Denbow Miss Muffett, the first smooth bitch to amass ten CCs, a record beaten by Ch. Middlepark Lettice with 12 CCs – the current record holder for smooth bitch CCs.

ELEETA
This kennel is included here because of its longevity not in Saints but in Great Danes. Elwyn and Rosalie Cobley served a long apprenticeship in a difficult breed. Why on earth did they then move to a more difficult breed? In fact they went rough instead of smooth!

Novices should serve their apprenticeship and serve it well. The Cobleys have done this and they tell us that I gave them their first at Crufts with a Saint 1993. It was a tough class, lots of good quality bitches, and it was a close call at the line-up. They went on to breed their first Saint Champion, Ch. Eleeta Pretty Woman. Elwyn and Rosalie have sound principles, which match many of our thoughts in this book. We hope they go on to many more English-type champions.

FASTACRE
Fastacre was a racehorse. Those of us who know John Bateman, will know of his love of the turf. John and May Bateman are examples of longevity in dog showing and breeding dogs, having bred Cocker Spaniels in the sixties and John trained Greyhounds in the fifties.

John and May bought their first Saint in 1975 from the Gerunda kennels of Mr Reg James. From their bitch came Fastacre Gentle Maitresse who won 40 first prizes and several reserve CCs, notably at Crufts. Sadly she died at three years old. Very upset, John and May did not keep up an involvement with Saints for the next three years except in committee work with the English Saint Bernard Club. The next Fastacre was out of Knochespoch, Ch. Knochespoch High Line from a Fastacre bitch, Fastacre Royal Empress. High line

Int. Ch. Bernegardens JR Of Fastacre.

142

was not campaigned very much but her title came at just two years old.

Fastacre's next Champion came in the form of Int. Ch. Bernegardens JR of Fastacre, and a grandson of his in New Zealand won Best in Show at the New Zealand Kennel Club Show (our Crufts). JR went on to sire Ch. Fastacre High Society, winner of Bitch CC at Crufts in 1990.

FINETIME
This kennel, owned by Mrs Hazel Thomas, was very successful for many years but, sadly, she disbanded her kennels in the early 90s. Hazel is now back in the ring but with a much reduced stock and she is now trying to regain her former bloodlines. Her old Finetime type was very popular, and Hazel has bred seven Champions from 1985 starting with Ch. Finetime Sardonyx. The Finetime effect can be seen in many lines today and their strength of type was very important.

HEARTLEAPWELL
This kennel was active some time around the eighties, starting with another old name, Ch. Benem Sir Galahad. Mrs Evans bred and owned in total five Champions. Again, though the kennel is no longer active, the progeny can still be seen today.

KNOCHESPOCH
This was another small kennel which did not last long. Perhaps their most famous dog was Roddinghead Agent Chris Of Knochespoch, with ten CCs, owned by Mrs Sue Roberts. From this kennel we bred NZ Ch. Coatham Sporting Chance and Coatham Ripe Harvest who, although never a Champion, sired three Champions himself. Knochespoch went into decline and only bred two Champions, Knochespoch High Time and Knochespoch Berenice. From these came Fastacre Highline and Lucky Chance of Whaplode.

MARLENDER
A kennel owned by Mrs Linda Martin in the South West of England. Linda bought her first Saint in 1974 and registered her affix, Marlender, in 1975. Linda has bred several litters which have been of sound quality. Her first Champion was Ch. Marlender Moonraker out of Kempshott Tia Maria

Ch. Saranbeck Sayra At Marlender.

ex Coppice Bertie. She has had three further Champions in Ch. Bavush Classic Lady, Ch. Saranbeck Sayra At Marlender, with 18 CCs, and Ch. Marlender Bucks Fizz. She has accumulated 54 CCs throughout her career and is currently showing Marlender Scarlett Ohara, with two CCs.

MAURBRY
Owned by Mrs Chapman in Lincolnshire, this kennel was very active for many years but produced only four owner-bred Champions: Cornagarth Minty of Maurbry, Modelman, Messenger, and Minnesota. The fifth Champion, Ch. Footlose Freddy, was owned by Kath and Mick Thorpe It should be noted that several Champions were bred

from Maurbry stock – Ch. Heartleapwell Secret Love, Ch. Heartleapwell Magic Moments and Ch. Coppice Bertie.

MEADOWMEAD

This was owned by the late Mr R.W.F. Byles and Mrs Lesley Byles. Sadly Bob lost a brave fight against cancer and died in 1996. Lesley carries on the Meadowmead flag and is helped by their two children, Drew and Faye.

Bob and Lesley acquired their first Saint in 1980 and quickly realised that they would not get far with her. After many unsuccessful attempts at showing they bought Ch. Lynburn Dennis The Menace Of Meadowmead who has quite easily the most amazing record of any Saint in the UK, with 39 CCs, most of them with BOB, and numerous BIS at Open shows. Dennis was not a prolific stud dog but to his credit he has Ch. Meadowmead Helena and Ch. Meadowmead Empress Queen. Other Champions followed and these were Ch. Meadowmead Juliana, Ir. Ch. Meadowmead Cassandra, Ch. Mountside Mauritania Of Meadowmead and Ir. Ch. Meadowmead Florence. Several other Meadowmead Saints have won varying numbers of CCs and Reserve CCs.

Lesley says that they were lucky to acquire Coatham Mary Rose from us. Perhaps they were. We did not intend to keep a pup out of that litter. Fate dealt us a blow when Ch. Coatham Hermes (the mother) died of bloat before we could mate her again. We do not begrudge them their success –

Pictured (left to right): Ch. Dennis The Menace Of Meadowmead, Meadowmead Rene and Ch. Meadowmead Helena with the late Bob Byles.

Photo: Carol Ann Johnson.

we are proud to have helped towards them.

Luck or not, Bob was one of the most astute men I have ever met. I describe him as highly intelligent and not arrogant, always holding his counsel and never showing annoyance at losing. We are quite sure we spoilt his day when Buster, our Ch. Dragonville Lord Snooty Of Coatham beat Dennis to the first South Of England Saint of the Year contest in 1990 and took the title. Bob, always the sportsman, congratulated us warmly.

MIDDLEPARK
This kennel is owned by Mr John and Mrs Sheila Boulden in Kent. John and Sheila bred their first litter in 1974 from Plutopian Kent von Birkenkoph. They kept two dogs. Their first Champion was Burtonswood Black Duke and then there was a succession of Middlepark Champions.

*Ch. Mountside Movie Star
appearing as a real movie star.*

Their first home-bred Champion was Middlegarth Grand Monarque in 1986. However, before that there was Ch. Lady Prudence of Middlepark. It was not until 1994 that another Middlepark Champion emerged. During the intervening period John and Sheila owned several Saints with one or two CCs.

I had the pleasure of inspecting the litter, which was to become very successful, by Ch. Timeside Mr Sloba Doba and Middlepark Gabriella. I remember picking up Lettice and saying to her "I wonder

*Ch. Middlepark Araminter.
Photo: Carol Ann Johnson.*

Ch. Oringlow Hudson.

ORINGLOW
This kennel was owned by Mr and Mrs Swidlehurst in Morecambe, Lancs. Although they bred consistently good moving dogs their head type needed further development. This was ultimately achieved in 1991 with Ch. Oringlow Hudson, who achieved his crown with four CCs. I had the pleasure of giving him the dog CC and Best of Breed at Crufts in 1993. Shortly after this Hudson suffered a torsion of the stomach (a twisted gut). Although he survived, he was never the same again.

PITTFORTH
This kennel was owned by Mr and Mrs Whitelaws in Musselburgh in Scotland. The Whitelaws were active for many years but, due to ill health, had to retire. Mr Matt Whitelaw was president of the Scottish Saint Bernard Club for many years; always a gentleman, his bluff manner was welcoming to all. Mr and Mrs Whitelaw owned and bred six Champions in their time. Our particular favourites were Ch. Calum, Ch. Pitfforth Catriona, and Ch. Pittforth Angus.

RAVENSBANK
This kennel started with a rough encounter in 1977. Pauline Rogers says of her first encounter with a Saint "what a big smelly creature!". Perhaps this is not the most successful of kennels over the

what Mo would say if I took you home". In that litter were Ch. Middlepark Lettice, 15 CCs, bitch CC at Crufts 1996 (in my opinion she was BOB that day); Ch. Middlepark Meridian, five CCs, Dog CC at Crufts 1995; and Middlepark Friar, two CCs and Top Puppy in 1993. From this very successful line came Ch. Middlepark Araminter, seven CCs, out of Coatham the Campaigner and Ch. Middlepark Friar.

MOUNTSIDE
Much is spoken of this line and here we wish to set the record straight. Mountside was closely bred to our lines and we were closely in discussions with them. Ray and Elaine Stokell were our very good friends and it was a personal sadness for us to see their partnership end. Their line was Mountside but its foundations are in Coatham. However, their decisions were ultimately their own. Their most famous dog was our own Ch. Mountside Movie Star. We bought her as a Champion from Ray Stokell, with three CCs to her credit. We went on to amass a further 19 and her proudest record, BOB at Crufts 1994. We feel sure that, had we campaigned her more, she would have had a record which would have proved hard to beat. Mountside bred five Champions but the effect of this line can be seen in some modern kennels and it is true to say that some still aspire to breed to this type. We ourselves are still trying for another Movie Star.

Ravensbank Simply Soloman Of Sileda.

Sanflax Savanna.

SARANBECK

This kennel is owned by Diane Deuchar-Fawcett at Scarborough in the north of England. Diane's early life, pre-Saint Bernards, included provincial repertoire television and ice-skating. For several years she worked as secretary for the Scarborough branch of the RSPCA. Working with animals made Diane and her two daughters, Sue and Sally, realise that something was missing in their lives. There was a litter of Saints advertised in 1971 and the result was that they purchased a puppy from Mr Bruce Everall of the Ghyllendale Saints. Their first was Saint Bernard was Ghyllendale Gay Light. This bitch was subsequently mated to Ch. Burtonswood Black Tarquin. This mating produced 11 puppies; Diane kept a bitch puppy and another puppy from this litter went to South Africa where he became a South African Champion, Ch. Saranbeck King Of Diamonds.

years but we believe it gives the background of some of the most illustrious Saints, for example Ch. Lynbern Dennis The Menace, 39 CCs, bred out of Ravensbank Simply Solomon Of Sileda. Pauline has bred to a true English type and stands by her beliefs firmly. She considers that the English type is preferable and will continue to breed to it. Who is to say she is wrong? Perhaps those that flew to the Continent for their stock should have looked closer to home.

Pauline did not campaign her stock as much as some others. Had she done so, perhaps the likes of Ravensbank Pass No Comment, Ravensbank Lady Justice, Ravensbank Master Of Passion and Ravensbank Simply Solomen Of Sileda would have all been Champions instead of just CC holders.

SANFLAX

Owned by Miss Susan Lodge in Lancashire, this is not immediately the most famous of kennels. However, Susan's mother started the Sanflax line in 1940. Susan has kept the line going over the years and is dedicated to the breed. She deserves her inclusion because of her work with the Saint Bernard Trust and the Saint Bernard Rescue. She shares her home with a variety of livestock and several Saints. She regularly shows and her stock is currently winning.

Coatham Citizen Smith.
Photo: Carol Ann Johnson.

Diane's next purchase was a smooth bitch puppy out of the famous import King Von St Klara Cluster and Ch. Burtonswood Bossy Bess, sister of the famous Champion Burtonswood Bossy Boots. Through various line breeding exercises Diane produced Ch. Sarenbeck Sweep in 1989. Sweep was subsequently mated to Swindridge Columbus and they in turn produced Ch. Saranbeck Sarah At Marlender. Sarah was mated to the smooth import of Mr Goodwin's Ch. Bernegardens Buckpasser. Diane, through the eighties and into the nineties, had various litters and she subsequently used one of her various outcrossings mated to Ch. Coatham Goodnews Of Wyandra who produced Ch. Saranbeck Smugglers Gold. Another promising youngster, Saranbeck Spruce was hit by cancer and although he was shown in his early years and won several awards his career was curtailed by the illness and his potential would never be realised. Diane's kennels have amassed 22 CCs, she is now in

partnership with Barbara Swaine-Williams and the foundation stock are two rough-coated puppies.

SCHNOZZER

Founded in 1979 by Paul and Josh Girling. Their first Saint was from the Topvalley kennels of Greta Topping. She was Topvalley Anne Karlisa, a smooth coat. They successfully bought another Saint, Olympic Princess. Greta Topping asked them to take in Topvalley J.R. and so it began. They produced Ch. Schnozzer Huggy Bear who, along with Swindridge Laura, gained their titles. These were followed by Schnozzer Dark Golden and Schnozzer Latest Edition, both of whom were made up. Ch. Schnozzer. Huggy Bear was BOB at Crufts and was actually never beaten. He was being awarded the BOB while the Best in Show was being judged, so did not have the opportunity to take this dog into the Challenge for the working group.

SWINDRIDGE

This kennel was formed by Ann and Michael Wensley. They lived at Sandy in Bedfordshire for many years. Ann and Michael have bred consistent champions for many years and were top breeders in 1983 and 1984. Their first Champion was Ch. Benem Lady Guinevere in 1977, followed by several others including with Ch. Swindridge Catherine out of the famous Klara Koster kennels. This is a fine smooth kennel which still influences our smooth Saints today. Swindridge have bred and owned 12 Champions. Our particular favourites were Ch. Swindridge Sirdorian and Ch. Swindrridge Madeline. Currently Michael and Ann are in partnership with Pat Muggleton.

TIMESIDE

Owned by Tony and Pearl Davis, this kennel was formed in the early 1990s. Tony and Pearl have striven to achieve a distinctive type. They purchased Mountside Solitaire who was bred by Ch. Dragonville Lord Snooty of Coatham out of Mountside Melody.

Tony and Pearl continued with the Mountside connection and purchased a puppy bitch out of Mountside Movie Star. Solitaire produced Timeside Mr Slobba Dobba, a dog with a proud record – winning 12 BBs, 22 RCCs, two Group 3s, and one

Swindridge Cassius.
Photo: Neil Franklin.

Ch. Timeside Mr Slobba Dobba.

Photo: Hartley.

Best in Show at the working breed show. He was top dog in 1995 and 1996 and top Sire in 1995 and 1996 and also had six Open Show Best in Shows. The cherry on the cake was Best of Breed at Crufts in 1999 when he was seven-and-a-half years old, out of Veteran. A true ambassador for our breed, Oliver is a real Saint and has proved his worth by siring three Champions – Ch. Middlepark Lettice, Ch. Middlepark Meridian and Timeside Brothers In Arms At Essjay.

TOPVALLEY
Owned by Mrs Greta Topping and her late husband Eric, this kennel was prominent in the late seventies to the late eighties. Sadly it went into decline but the legacy lives on through several breed lines including our own kennels and the Whaplode and Schnozzer kennels. The most famous of this line was Ch. Topvalley Wogans Winner, 19 CCs, sired by Ch. Burtonswood Bossy Boots.

WARDANA
This kennel is owned by Mrs Mary-Ellen Collis in Hampshire. Mary purchased her first Saint in 1974 from the Whaplode kennels of Mr John Harpham. Wardana was registered in the late 1970s and the first litter was registered in the early eighties. Mary,

Mary-Ellen Collis with three of the Wardana imports.

in spite of being a keen enthusiast, did little breeding or showing. Her preferences lie in the type favoured in America and the Continent – so much so that she has imported from the Continent a total of four dogs to use as her foundation stock.

So far Wardana has had some success in the show ring with Wardana Raggamffyn who has two CCs and four RCCs. Wardana Run Em Ragged has achieved a junior warrant, as has Wardana Ambassadors Daughter. The former competed at the Kennel Club's junior warrant winner contest.

Mary-Ellen Collis plans to mix the blood types to try and achieve the best balance of the English and Continental types. She says that only time will tell. We think that this has been achieved already, as there are many fine examples around of successful crossings.

WHAPLODE
John and Mary Harpham have owned Saints since 1954. Their first litter was in 1957. They had their first CC in 1957 at the LKA and their first Champion came in 1958. Unfortunately, John then became ill and it would not be until 1976 that their next Champion came – Ch. Whaplode Desdemona. Since then they have bred 15 Champions. Three of these were breed record holders and 10 were Top Dog of the year. They have expanded widely and have several Champions overseas.

Their best dog is Ch. Whaplode Be Our William. Mary Pearl (nee Harpham, daughter of John and Mary Harpham) reckons I started him off at Crufts in 1993 with a Reserve CC, out of Postgraduate class. He has an outstanding record – 43 CCs, 22 Reserve CCs, 33 BOB and four Champion children.

Mary and John have judged extensively over the years. John has judged at Crufts twice. As a footnote, John's best puppy at Crufts 1992 was Oringlow Hudson. I made Ch. Oringlow Hudson BOB at Crufts 1993 – who says judges do not agree?

The Whaplode type is much sought after. Many kennels can trace their progeny back to the Whaplode type. Many try to emulate the type, but often fail. We have to say, that of all the kennels in the UK, Whaplode is one of the few kennels who have stamped a true type on to their stock.

Pictured (left to right): Ch. Whaplode Beyond Valour, Ch. Whaplode Be Our William, Ch. Whaplode Be Smart and Ch. Whaplode Beyond Pardon.

Ch. Coatham Good News For Wyandra (left) and Coatham Saxon Monarch Of Wyandra. Photo: BSW.

Currently, John is retired from active showing, but his canny wisdom is still in evidence at home. Mary Pearl, his daughter, shows and campaigns the stock. In the words of Mary: "We are a team: dad pays the bills, I show the dogs, and mum does all the work."

WYANDRA

This is the kennel owned by Miss Barbara Swaine Williams in North Wales. Barbara showed German Shepherds for many years; she registered her affix in 1960 but was showing as early as 1953.

Barbara is now a retired schoolteacher, having had a tough fight with cancer. She is a formidable lady and her strength of character brought her through many hard times during the struggle. She bought her first Saint as a present for her mum. He was Jamie Of Burtonswood. A fine dog, he was campaigned in Ireland and won Green Stars (equivalent to the UK's CCs). Barbara went on to purchase Middlepark High Hopes For Wyandra who did well for her but did not get his title.

Barbara says her breakthrough came with "the best dog she has ever owned", Ch. Coatham Good News For Wyandra, known as Harvey. He became a junior warrant winner in eight months, amassing 48 points in total. Harvey went on to gain a formidable record of seven CCs, nine Reserve CCs, two Best in Shows, and quarter finalist at the Welsh Contest of Champions. Harvey was a fine dog and one we were proud to breed. Barbara

went on to purchase Burnsware Senator of Wyandra who won 2 CCs. Barbara has not campaigned him further due to ligament problems.

Barbara has campaigned Harvey's grandchildren with some success. She has in the wings a grandson of Harvey Lanleaddanes Exclusive To Wyandra out of Ch. Timeside Brothers In Arms Essjay. In addition she is now in partnership with Diane Deuchar-Fawcett under the title Barandi. They have imported stock from the Continent. We wish them luck in their venture together.

SCOTLAND AND IRELAND

Both countries are relatively small but both have a long history of St. Bernards. Scottish owners can be traced to the early part of the century and a famous dog called Lord Montgomery which was owned by a Mr George Sinclair who lived at Stevenston, Ayrshire. A quote from *Our Dogs,* dated December 5th 1906 about Ch. Lord Montgomery by Ch. Tannhausser ex Duchess of Sutherland states that "his head is a perfect study and his type cannot be surpassed. He moves about like a terrier and his action cannot be improved upon, his legs and feet being perfection." How many of us would like a write-up like this today? Today's Scottish Saints are varied in type. No one breeder can claim to have stamped a type. The modern kennels can best be described as small and of good quality.

SCOTLAND

ALPENTIRE
This kennel is owned by Mr and Mrs McMurray in Kilmarnock, Ayrshire. The McMurrays were active in the late sixties and are active to a limited extent today. Their first Champion was Ch. Snowranger Cascade. This dog won the Working group at Crufts in 1975, the year following Bossy Boots' famous win in 1974. He won a total of seven CCs but was unfortunate never to sire a litter.

The McMurrays travelled extensively in Europe, visiting many of the then famous kennels in an effort to gain knowledge of the breed, and went on to breed a further three Champions, Ch. Alpentire Paters Princess, Ch. Alpentire Paters Promise and our own Ch. Alpentire On Commission. Unfortunately due to business pressures in the late seventies their active involvement came to a temporary halt. However, their interest was rekindled in 1991 when they purchased Mountside Starlight and made her up. She was called Lucy and was a daughter of our Ch. Mountside Movie Star (ex Coatham Britania) and gained nine CCs. She died of bloat before she could produce a litter; such is fate. The McMurrays still have an interest in the breed but business interests now keep them very busy. Judy McMurray has judged extensively, including at Crufts twice.

ASPENHILL
From this small kennel based in Cupar, Fife, Mr and Mrs Simpson have campaigned two Saints to their titles, gaining seven CCs and ten RCCs in ten years – an achievement based on hard work and dedication. Their Champions are Ch. Mountside Secret Of Campsie out of Ch. Mountside Movie Star and Ch. Finetime Brother Gabriele and Ch. Burnswark Alicia At Aspenhill by Ch. Coatham Good News For Wyandra. The Simpsons are active on the committee of the Scottish Saint Bernard Club.

BIRKENBUSH
This small kennel was established in 1989 with sound beginnings – Burnswark Samantha At Birkenbush ex Coatham Good News For Wyandra and Burnswark Duchess Hall Debutante, who won her first CC at the Eastern Championship Show in October 1998.

BURNSWARK
A kennel owned by Miss Ann Druce in Lockerbie, Scotland, who bought her first Saint in 1988. Her first litter came in 1990 when she mated her bitch to Ch. Dragonville Lord Snooty Of Coatham. There were 14 pups in that litter but only one was alive, Douglasshall Debutante. The affix was named after the area called Burnswark, an ancient Roman arena in the Lockerbie district.

Douglasshall Debutante, 'Bron', produced a litter to Ch. Coatham Good News For Wyandra on two occasions. Both litters have produced top winning stock: Burnswark Amber Gambler Burnswark Louisa, Burnswark Senator Of Wyandra and Burnswark Samantha At Birkenbush. All three gained their junior warrants and all three went on to CCs and reserve CCs. This kennel's first win came in 1999 from Burnswark Alicia At Aspenhill, owned by Mr and Mrs Simpson.

In Scotland there are several smaller kennels who, though not top winners, have been faithful members of the Saint community. Mr and Mrs McClauchlin, of Culrain, have owned a Champion. Mr Zandor McClauchlin is the current president of the Scottish Saint Bernard club, Mr McMenemy, Friarshall, and Mr and Mrs Coyle, Doocroft, have all bred and owned top-quality dogs. We do not have enough room to list them all but they are enthusiastic keepers of our breed.

IRELAND

Ireland, like Scotland, is a small country with a dedicated group of fanciers and breeders. The Irish Saint Bernard club was formed in 1972. Built on high ideals, the Irish club, like the American club, has a code of ethics. There are about 100 active members and there is a number of small kennels and one or two active breeding kennels.

In the early sixties Mr Walter Berry was active in Northern Ireland under the affix Walnel. He now judges the breed, mostly in Ireland but occasionally in England. A prominent affix until recently was that of Mrs Marie Maxwell, who lost a long fight against cancer early in this year. The Montaryie dogs were very sound and some Champions came from this establishment, notably Ch. Montaryie Fandango, Ch. Fernet Branca and Ch. Gaelstorm. Gaelstorm, owned by the Longdoyles, took the CC at Crufts in 1988. Killin was another affix prominent in the 70s and 80s and some Killin dogs took many honours over this period. Breeding is now mainly the province of three affixs, Barnahely, Longsdoyle and Oatfield.

BARNAHELY
Owned by Mr and Mrs Barry in Cork, in the south of the country, this kennel has been successful over the years. In recent times they have bred a number of Champions including Barnahely Begonia, Buckingham, Brendan, Buckfast and Bow Woo Woo.

LONGSDOYLE
Anne and Austin Longsdoyle, whose kennel is at Greystones near Dublin, bought their first Saint in 1978 and have had an impressive record since then. Their stock includes Ir. Ch. Meadowmead Cassandra (ex Coatham Mary Rose). This bitch held the title of Top Saint in Ireland in 1993, 1995 and 1997. Cassy went on to win the title of Champion of Champions in 1995 in the competition organized by the Irish Kennel Club. Currently they are campaigning Longsdoyle Grand Prix, three green stars and a best in breed at 16 months. Anne and Austin are active members of the Irish Saint club and Austin represents the club at the Irish Kennel Club.

OATFIELD
This kennel near Dublin is owned by Mr Seamus Oates who has been active in Saints for over thirty years. He had his first Saint from Peldartor. He has had close links with Miss Hindes and her Burtonswoods. The main winner from this liaison was UK Ir. Ch. Oatfield Nero. Seamus is also known as an excellent handler and he campaigned Mr and Mrs Carey's Ch. Burtonswood Black Domino to many wins, including several Best in Shows all-breeds in Ireland. Seamus Oates is an international judge of reknown.

13 THE ST. BERNARD IN AMERICA

There is speculation about whether a famous dog known as Plinlimmon was the first St. Bernard to be imported to the United States of America. In any event, it is known that an American actor named Mr Emmet proudly took Plinlimmon, who had been imported from England, around a number of theatres in America cities in the 1880s. This was probably a good marketing strategy as Emmet was given a lot of publicity for himself and Plinlimmon. This Saint was bred by F. Smith from Ch. Pilgrim out of Bessie II. The publicity no doubt generated an interest in the large brown and white giant dog which is a St. Bernard.

Other early imports were Loc Bute who, it is believed, was purchased for 4,000 dollars, and Madam Bedivere for 3,000 dollars. These two Saints were owned by Knowles Croskey of Philadelphia. Another early Saint in America was Sir Bedivere who was purchased for the princely sum of 7,000 dollars.

In 1886, at the prestigious Westminster show, there were St. Bernard classes scheduled. Best of Breed was Merchant Prince owned by E.H. Moore of Melrose, Massachusetts. This dog had won a variety of cups and trophies in England prior to being exported to America and he sired many winners in the USA.

Saints in America have developed from the early dogs of Beatrice Knight with her famous Sanctuary Woods Kennels, who followed on from the Alpine Plateau stock. Many top-winning Saints exhibited during the 1990s can trace their heritage back to the Sanctuary Woods influence. Mrs Knight bred over a hundred Champions, having obtained her affix in 1948. Such was Mrs Knight's influence that the SBCA catalogue for their Centenary Show had the following inscription: "The St. Bernard Club of America proudly dedicates this centennial celebration to Mrs Beatrice Knight of Sanctuary Woods Kennels for her contribution and dedication to the St. Bernard." Mrs Knight remained an enthusiast for the breed, encouraging novices and attending dog shows, well into her late eighties.

THE ST. BERNARD CLUB OF AMERICA

The St. Bernard Club of America was founded in 1888 by a group of St. Bernard enthusiasts, several of whom had imported dogs from England. There is in existence an early stud book recording important information. Several St. Bernards were registered with the club, including Chief, who was born in 1879 in New York.

The SBCA is one of the oldest clubs recognised by the American Kennel Club. Since its formation in 1888 there have been several reorganisations. The first National Specialty show was held in May 1935 with Ch. Rasko v.d. Reppisch winning Best in Show. In 1974 this club held its first Obedience Trials and added Sweepstake classes for Saints from 6 months to 18 months as well as Working classes and events at their annual show. The SBCA Board of Governors has done much to provide members with relevant information and promote the welfare

Am. Ch. Vieledanke Tiramisu: The St Bernard is well established in the American show ring. Photo: Kitten.

of the St. Bernard. The National Specialty week now includes all these events, as well as many educational seminars to help novices, breeders, exhibitors and potential future judges learn more about the breed. Gloria Wallin, along with her husband Jerry, did much to raise the knowledge and awareness of Saint fanciers throughout the US. The educational programme of the SBCA is informative and up-to-date.

The SBCA Rescue Foundation endeavours to find appropriate homes for those Saints who otherwise would be put down. Each region has persons responsible for co-ordinating the rescue services, so anyone wishing to be a "Saint" and take on an unwanted St. Bernard should obtain an up-to-date list of co-ordinators from the SBCA.

Although the popularity of the St. Bernard has diminished since the 1970s, the SBCA endeavours to raise the awareness of St. Bernard fanciers about the fascinating heritage of this beloved breed. The club promotes the welfare of St. Bernards and is attempting to ensure that the breed has a healthy, realistic future.

So, whether you wish to realise a long ambition to own one Saint, to become an exhibitor and show the dog, or are just keen to learn more about the

breed, do remember that the SBCA is there to help.

Most people in America will have heard of the famous all-breed Westminster Kennel Club Show in New York which includes classes for St. Bernards. There are, of course, many other St. Bernard Specialty Shows organised by the regional Clubs so, hopefully, you may feel inspired to find out more information about them. Like many St Bernard enthusiasts in the USA, we have shared our lives with this amazing breed in the UK and continue to learn more facts and true stories about their courage, strength, faithfulness and loyalty. Perhaps these gentle giants are the right breed for you too. Before taking on such a responsibility, find out as much as you can about the St. Bernard and its welfare and care.

DIVERGENCE IN TYPE
Imports came to America from Switzerland between 1860 and 1870 through a prominent breeder named Schumacher, who apparently kept his own studbook. By 1930 a total of 263 Saints were registered with the AKC. Gradually two types of St. Bernard ermeged in America – the English type and the Swiss type.

It became apparent that the St. Bernard in

155

England had evolved differently from the Saint in Switzerland. In fact, the Swiss St. Bernard Club, along with the Swiss Kennel Club, issued a Breed Standard in 1884. The first recognised St. Bernard Standard set out by the Kennel Club in England was not formalised until 1887.

There appears to have been consternation among the St. Bernard exhibitors of English stock when that Breed Standard was issued by the Swiss St. Bernard Club. According to records and information available, there followed three years of conflict regarding which Standard should be accepted in America. An International Congress took place in Brussels in 1886 to debate whether England or Switzerland should be the breed authority. This matter could not be resolved then, so another International Congress took place in Zurich in 1887, where all the countries except England accepted the Swiss Standard as the recognised Standard.

We feel the British Kennel Club are still unwilling to accept a lot of FCI Standards, not just in St. Bernards but in other breeds. As the KC is the governing body of the breed clubs in the UK it is difficult to instigate changes. We know that when judges from the UK judge abroad they are aware of the relevant Breed Standards and judge accordingly.

BREEDERS' GUIDLINES
The St. Bernard Club of America have a code of conduct for breeders and assume that members will conform to these guidelines.

GUIDELINES AND STATEMENT OF POLICY
Saint Bernard Club of America, Inc.

The basic reason for breeding and exhibiting St. Bernards is the improvement of each generation of the Breed over the previous generations. All Breeding and exhibiting activities should be viewed in this light. In keeping with this aim, the following practices are suggested.
1 Breeders shall strive for the perfection of the St. Bernard in accordance with the Official Standards set by the American Kennel Club. In this regard they shall:
A Maintain high standards of health, care, safety and humane treatment of their dogs.
B Remember that only a very small percentage of St. Bernards are of breeding quality.
C Use only physically sound and temperamentally sound stock, free from severe hip dysplasia, eye malformations, and poor temperaments. St. Bernard with outstanding defects should be spayed or neutered.
D Refuse stud service to any bitch that is unregisterable or shows the above or other obvious defects.
E Study and learn the good and bad points of their own

stock, never doubling up on a known or visible fault or faults represented in the pedigree of the dogs concerned.
F *Ideally, X-ray for evidence of hip dysplasia at the age of one year or older, treating the mild cases as they would any other fault and excluding from breeding programs dogs with more severe evidence of hip dysplasia. X-rays should be read by recognized authorities on the disorder. Not every veterinarian is competent to take or pass judgement upon such X-rays.*
G *Refrain from breeding the bitch until her second season, preferably waiting until at least 18 months of age. A bitch shall be bred no more than two out of three seasons, depending upon the size of the litter whelped and her condition. It is suggested that in most cases a period of one year lapse between litters.*

2 *Breeders shall not sell stock or offer stud services without true representation to the public, nor use misleading or untruthful statements verbally, in writing or advertising.*

3 *No member shall buy or sell St. Bernards through commercial pet outlets, nor buy or sell in litter lots, nor sell to persons whose activities tend to degrade the Breed.*

4 *The buyer shall be supplied with a truthful four-generation pedigree, written instructions concerning the care, feeding and training of the dog purchased, a written statement as to the inoculations and other veterinary care, and a Bill of Sale in accordance with AKC requirements.*

5 *Purchasers shall be urged to spay or neuter St. Bernards not suitable for breeding.*

6 *Registration papers shall be supplied without extra charge with every AKC-registered dog. If the dog is not for breeding, this may be agreed to in a written contract between buyer and seller.*

7 *A breeder shall guarantee the health of his stock subject to a veterinarian's examination within 48 hours of the sale.*

8 *Breeders shall price their dogs in accordance with local rates for quality St. Bernards. Undercutting the price of Saints eventually will make it impossible to breed good dogs for the return which can be anticipated.*

9 *A breeder shall try to keep in touch with the progress of this breeding in order to better analyze his own programs.*

10 *Breeders shall exhibit at dog shows where feasible. In so doing, they shall show a spirit of good sportsmanship and behave and dress so as to enhance public opinion of the Breed.*

11 *Members shall not degrade any other kennel or member. It is the obligation of all to give advice and assistance to less experienced fanciers in a spirit of kindness and courtesy.*

In applying for membership in the Saint Bernard Club of America, I agree to comply with all rules and regulations of the American Kennel Club and with the rules and by-laws as set forth in the Constitution of the Saint Bernard Club of America Inc. I understand that serious infractions of the above Statement of Policy, where they are deemed detrimental to the Breed or the individual dog, will result in expulsion from the Club, as outlined in the Constitution in Article VI (I).

Reproduced by kind permission of The Saint Bernard Club of America.

SHOWING AND EXHIBITING
The show scene in America is largely regional, as the distances between the show sites preclude the owner/handler from extending the exhibition of his or her Saint at major Specialty shows on a regular basis. However, some owners are able to achieve a high level of involvement. I think it is difficult for St. Bernard enthusiasts in England and Europe to appreciate the vastness of America and that a lot of American citizens hop on a plane to commute

Am. Ch. Belyn's Quartermaster.
Photo: Munro.

between cities, whereas Europeans tend to use their cars or trains.

In America a lot of owners do not exhibit their own dogs but pay a professional handler for showing the dog. Some professional handlers undertake this work as a full-time occupation. Lots of regions have their own St. Bernard Clubs and Specialty shows. The SBCA has Specialty Shows which are the equivalent of the Breed Club Championship shows in the UK.

ST. BERNARD RESCUE

Like most countries, the USA has a National St. Bernard Rescue, organised by the SBCA. It is sad when, through no fault of their own, St. Bernards, like children, can become unwanted. Obviously, before purchasing a Saint, it is most important to raise your awareness regarding the advantages as well as the disadvantages of looking after a giant dog to ensure that you can care for the dog appropriately. As discussed in the section on socialisation in a previous chapter, a well-behaved, responsive St. Bernard is a joy to own; a St. Bernard who is out of control is, however, a liability.

Breeders, whichever country they are from, have a duty and responsibility to ensure that the St. Bernard puppies which they have bred go to the best possible homes. In our opinion prospective buyers should be challenged as to why they want a St. Bernard. People considering purchasing a Saint Bernard should be informed of possible hereditary defects such as hip and elbow dysplasia, entropion, heart defects and bad temperament.

The SBCA has taken a lot of trouble to produce information in well laid out, easy to read booklets for prospective owners. Titles of these information documents include *Owning a St. Bernard*, which gives guidelines for buying a puppy, suggestions about visiting kennels, questions you may wish to ask the breeder, information about the training and discipline of the St. Bernard, and veterinary care for the dog.

Another booklet is *The Resource Booklet*, which gives useful information including names, addresses and websites of officers of the SBCA, the relevant addresses for the secretaries of the thirty-one regional clubs, as well as the local St. Bernard Breed Clubs and the Rescue Centres or officers

responsible for the regional rescues.

If you are considering a Saint, but do not necessarily want to train a puppy, then it may be worth considering a Saint who is awaiting an appropriate, kind, loving person or family who is willing to take an adult on. Consider all the positives but also the negatives, including the fact that the dog may have some habits which need to be discouraged such as pulling on the leash and getting onto the furniture. A lot of unwanted Saints do make excellent, faithful pets, so do think about this option. This is a real opportunity for you to be a Saint!

The following is a list of points from the SBCA which potential St. Bernard owners are asked to consider in order to prevent Saints ending up on the rescue in the first place.

FACTS
1 Puppy buyers should visit as many breeders as possible and ask to see the parents of the puppies.
2 ALL Saints should be friendly and outgoing.
3 Puppies should be kept in a clean environment and be socialized by the breeder.
4 Puppies should not leave the kennel or their littermates until a minimum of seven weeks.
5 Breeders should be happy to give you references.
6 Responsible breeders provide AKC registration papers with each dog unless reasons such as spay/neuter are provided.
7 The average life expectancy of a Saint Bernard should be 8-10 years.
8 Saints do DROOL – there is no such thing as a dry mouth.
9 All Saints shed.
10 Saints are NOT guard dogs.
11 Breeders should be responsible for the dogs they have bred and be willing to find new homes for the occasional dog who needs it.
12 High prices do not determine quality.

KENNELS OF NOTE
The United States has a variety of St. Bernard fanciers, far too many to include in this book. A sample of breeders has been selected, some of whom are longstanding members of clubs, and others are comparatively new members who have made Champion St. Bernards and have bred dogs of note.

ARIZONA

CHADWICK SAINTS
Jack and Carol Terrio have been breeding Saints for eighteen years, being members of the St. Bernard Club of America (SBCA) for twenty years. This couple have bred 22 Champions, two of whom were Ch. Chad's Katarina and Ch. Chad's Navazo Brave. The Terrios do not have more than one litter per year so do not 'flood' the market.

WAUGHMAR ST. BERNARDS
Pamela Waugh has been breeding St. Bernards for over 23 years. Pamela has bred 13 AKC Champions including Ch. Waughmar's Kodachrome von Fair and Ch. Waughmar's Zenith von Woodcress. The Waughmar Saints have one or two litters per year. Pamela does some reporting for the *Saint Fanciers* magazine.

MICKEY'S ST. BERNARDS
Mike and Honey Gardner, from the Phoenix area of Arizona, have been involved with Saints for over 25 years. Their policy is only to have one or two litters per year. At the time of going to print they had bred 12 AKC Champions, including Ch. Mickey's Matterhorns Enforcer and Ch. Mickey's Instant Replay. In the 1999 *Saint Fanciers* magazines another four AKC Champions were included, which Ch. Silvercrown's Rocky Road had sired. In 1999 Mike and Honey received an award for Brood Bitch of the Year, for producing four Champions from Ch. Mickey's Cupcake.

KEEPSAKE SAINTS
Lynn is busy as editor of the *Saint Fanciers* magazine of the SBCA. Lynn and Larry Jech have been involved with Saints for nine years and with the SBCA for over ten years. They have bred four Champions, including Ch. Keepsake's Duncan Idaho and Ch. Keepsake's Dream Comes True. As a means of improving their knowledge of the breed they have attended several SBCA seminars, as well as being leaders of seminars on subjects such as getting your dog ready for draft work, showing harnesses, discussing early training and so on. Larry is involved with the activities of the St. Bernard as a working dog and is chairman and secretary of the draft section.

ARKANSAS

SUNSHINE SAINTS
If you live in the state of Arkansas and fancy a Saint Bernard then the person to help you may be Faye M. Heath of the Sunshine Saints. Faye has been a member of the SBCA for 11 years. Two special Champions are Ch. Sunshine's Sugar von Mont d'Or and Ch. Soapstone's Zara. Faye states in the Breeder directory that she only has one litter per year.

CALIFORNIA
The SB Club of California is popular, being organised with support from the Buells of Sandstorm, and Sandra Rodrigo of the Subira Kennels. The San Diego Club is organised by Minnie and Ray Horlings along with Michael Sharman. Ray Horlings is the SBCA delegate and representative to the World Union of St. Bernards.

SANDSTORM
Sondra Buell has been involved with Saints for 29 years, actually breeding for 23 years and making up 27 AKC Champions. Two of the Champions listed are Ch. Subira's Benny and Ch. Sandstorm's Shirley U Jest. Sondra is a member of the San Diego St. Bernard Club as well as the SB Club of Southern California, the SB Club of the Pacific Coast and the SB Club of Greater San Jose. This demonstrates the variety of Clubs for Saint Bernard enthusiasts in the USA – and these are just a few of them!

DILETTANTE'S
For 25 years Patricia G. Serresseque has been a member of the SBCA and she has been breeding Saints for 24 years. There has been a series of over 23 Champions including Ch. Dilettante's Gotaheart and Ch. Dilettante's Homespun. Patricia is also a member of the SB Club of Greater San Jose.

SKY MEADOWS SAINTS
Jack and Delores Langraf have been members of the SBCA for 24 years and have bred St Bernards for 26 years. The couple have bred 17 Champions. Two which they have specifically identified are Ch. Sky Meadows' Frosty Knight and Sky Meadows Renegade. Jack and Delores take an interest in the seminars and exhibitors.

BEAU MAR

Joyce Simmons is another long-standing breeder and member who has been breeding Saints for 24 years and kept up membership of the SBCA for 27 years. Joyce has bred over twelve Champions. Worthy of special mention are Ch. Beau Mar's Benefactor von Zip and Ch. Beau Mar's McDuff von Dreamer. Joyce has between one and two litters per year.

CONNECTICUT

SHAGG-BARK SAINTS

Betty Roberts-Nelson has been breeding Saints for 47 years and for 45 years has maintained membership of the SBCA. There are well over 30 Champions bearing the Shagg-Bark affix, two of which are Ch. Shagg-Bark's Ali Bubba and Am. Can. Ch. Bowser Waller. The New England St. Bernard Club also takes up a lot of the time of Betty Roberts-Nelson.

GEORGIA

EXCALIBUR ST. BERNARDS

Barry and Judy Roland have been members of the SBCA for 22 years and breeding Saints for 19 years. The couple have bred four Champions including Ch. Excalibur Anastasia UD and Ch. Excalibur's Enchantress CD. They, like other breeders, attend breed seminars.

LA CASA SAINTS

Janet Frick Ansfield from Stone Mountain has been a member of SBCA for 28 years and has bred 16 Champions, two of which were Ch. La Casa's Fabio von Stoan and Ch. La Casa's Herriot. Janet is an Eastern Governor of the SBCA.

MOUNTAIN SPIRITS ST. BERNARDS

Tanya Bryan has been a member of SBCA for six years but has been breeding Saints for 20 years. Ch. Mountain Spirits' Big Boozer was the Champion which she bred and made up. Tanya is also a member of the Greater Atlanta SB Club, as is Janet Frick.

ILLINOIS

KRYSKARA SAINTS

Carole and Kenn Wilson have been members of the SBCA for 28 years and breeding Saints for 27 years. Another club close to their hearts is the SB Club of Greater St Louis. The couple have bred 23 Champions including Ch. Kryskara Cherry's Jubilee and Ch. Canicula Kryskara Instant Replay.

LONGMEADOW SAINTS

Rita Rynder has been a member of the SBCA for over 17 years. Rita has bred St. Bernards for over 22 years, having a litter once a year, and successfully bred eight Champions. Two of her Champions are Ch. Longmeadow's Break The Bank and Ch. Longmeadow's Avalanche. Rita is also a member of the Greater Cincinnati SB Club and the SB Club of Greater St Louis.

KANSAS

CROWNEPOINT KENNELS

Robert and Kit Bostrom have been members of the SBCA for 20 years and have been breeding St. Bernards for 22 years. Robert and Kit are also involved with the Heart of America SB Club. This couple have bred 15 AKC Champions. Two particular Champions with a special place in their hearts are Ch. Crownepoint's Grand Jury and Am. Can. Ch. Crownepoint's Legal Eagle. Bob Bostrom is Governor of the SBCA for the Central States.

MISSOURI

CANICULA SAINTS

Lonnie and Colette Weishaar are relatively new enthusiasts, having been members for only five years and breeding Saints for five years. However, this couple have been successful in their breeding programme, having made up four Champions including Ch. Canicula Classic and Ch. Canicula Kryskara Instant Replay. Lonnie and Collette are also members of the SB Club of Greater St. Louis.

NEW YORK

HIGH CHATEAU KENNELS

Horst and Winnie Vogel have been breeding Saints

High Chateau's Zima v. Morgan.
Photo: Munro.

since 1966. The couple are honest and modestly admit that their first St. Bernard was not particularly good as far as Breed Standards went; however, this meant they could learn what was wrong and what was right about their Saint. Winnie states that this learning process is still on-going. Even after 34 years, having bred well over sixty Champions, this couple are keen to absorb more information, experience and knowledge about this fascinating breed.

An old English proverb is "Reading maketh a full man": with so much modern technology available, younger people are tending to look at websites for information rather than read books, unlike Horst Vogel who has read and owns many early books on St. Bernards from Germany and Switzerland.

The couples first litter was born in 1969 using a Mallen St. Bernard with Sanctuary Woods mating. This produced their first Champion, Ch. High Chateau's Tobi. A famous Saint in the USA was Ch. High Chateau's Gero. Currently Ch. High Chateau's Yuri is having an influence on the breed with 10 Specialty Shows to his credit. Horst became a judge in 1977 and Winnie has written many articles on the breed. The couple are now retired so have more time to spend with their beloved Saints.

Am. Ch. High Chateau's Tobi.

Am. Ch. Slaton's Justin Credible.
Photo: Munro.

Opdyke's Abbey.
Photo: Munro.

BERIC KENNELS

Dick and Beverley Nosiglia have been members of the SBCA for 27 years and been breeding for over 25 years. As well as being members of the National Club they are also involved with the St. Bernard Club of the Finger Lakes. The Beric Kennels have produced over thirty Champions. Two which have a special place in the hearts of Dick and Bev are Ch. Beric's Ishmael and Ch. Beric's Lucina Lee.

In 1999 Bev was given the honour of judging St. Bernards at the World Union of St. Bernards Specialty Show in Portugal. Bev was part of a team of eight judges from all over the world who officiated at this marvellous show in Porto. If you have the opportunity to attend a WUSB event, especially the World Show, it is a most interesting experience.

ALPINE SAINTS

Donna Tuttle-Perkins has been a member of the SBCA for 13 years and has bred Saints for 15 years. Donna has one litter in a year. Two Champions of note are Ch. Vonnies Lady Chelsee and Ch. Nakeea von Beric. Donna supports and attends the seminars organised by the SBCA on various aspects of health, reproduction, fertility, conformation and working aspects of the Saints.

OHIO

RUSH'S ROYAL RETREAT

Georgia Rush has been a member of the SBCA for 27 years and been breeding for 25 years. Georgia has been successful, having produced 22 Champions, two of whom are Ch. Rush's Royal Retreat Super Samson and Ch. Rush's Royal Retreat Bear Bryant. Georgia is also a member of the Greater Cincinnati SB Club.

SAUNDALIN SAINTS

John and Saundra Nadolin from London, Ohio have been members of the SBCA for 27 years and have been breeding Saints for 24 years. The couple have bred four Champions, two of them being Ch. Saundalin's Giovanni and Ch. Saundalin's Set The Style HH. This couple are involved with the Ohio SB Club and the Greater Cincinnati SB Club.

SLATON'S SAINTS
Shirley and Joe Wolf, along with Linda Bullicz, have been members of the SBA for 16 years but breeding Saints for 24 years. The Slaton Saints have been extremely successful in the showring, making up over fifty Champions. Two of their Champions are Ch. Slaton's Piece Of The Action, CD, HF, PE, and Am. Can. Ch. Slaton's Lite Weight He Aint. With over 50 Champions to its credit the Slaton affix is known in different States as well as Ohio. The Wolfs and Linda are also involved with the Ohio, Cincinnati and the SB Club of Western Pennsylvania.

OPDYKE KENNELS
Glenn Radcliffe and Carolyn Vanderhoof have been members of the SBCA for 28 years and have been breeding Saints for the same length of time. The Opdyke Kennels are known world-wide. Several Opdyke Saints have been exported to the UK. There is a wonderful collection of Champions from these kennels, well over a hundred. This record has to speak for itself. Two of the Champions are Ch. Opdyke's Lancaster and Ch. Opdyke's Stetson. Glenn Radcliff has judged at the WUSB show in the past. They also are involved with the Maumee SB Club.

OREGON

REVILO ST. BERNARDS
Bill and Diane Oliver have been breeding Saints for 28 years, having between two and three litters per year. The couple have been members of the SBCA for 30 years. These kennels have been successful in the American show scene, making up 20 Champions. The following two are Saints from these kennels: Ch. Revilo's Bogart v. Holly HF(2), PE, and Ch. Revilo's Houston v. Dolly CD, CGC, HF(2). As well as being members of the SBA, this couple are involved with the SB Club of Puget Sound and Willamette Valley SB Club.

STAR'S SAINTS
Carol Varner-Beck has been a member of the SBCA for 24 years and has been breeding St. Bernards for 23 years. Carol has one or two litters per year and has been fairly successful, breeding 15 Champions. Two of these Champions are Ch. Star's

Revilo's Quincy.
Photo: Munro.

Shenendoah and Ch. Star's Simply Sioux. Carol is also a member of the SB Club of Greater Phoenix, and attends several appropriate seminars.

PENNSYLVANIA

RIDGEWOOD ST. BERNARDS
John and Jennifer Risser have been breeding Saints for 23 years and been members of the SBCA for 26 years. This couple have between two and four litters per year. The kennels have been successful, breeding 25 Champions. Two for special mention are Ch. Ridgewood's Magnum and Ch. Ridgewood's Poetry In Motion.

TENNESSEE

SNOWLAND ST. BERNARDS
Byron L. Smith has been breeding for 25 years and been a member of the SBCA for 17 years. Byron has one litter a year and has produced six Champions, two of which are Ch. Snowland's Deacon and Ch. Snowland's Just In Time. Byron is a keen participant at seminars, having attended 25; he is also a member of the SB Club of Greater Atlanta.

SEBASTIAN SAINTS
Janet and David Maxwell have been members of the SBCA for 10 years and breeders for seven years. So far they have been reasonably successful, with seven Champions, including Ch. Sebastian's Bare Necessity and Ch. Sebastian's Cara v. Fabia Falls. Janice and David are members of the SB Club of Greater Atlanta.

BIB N TUCKER

Karen and Ivan Tucker have been members of the SBCA for eight years as well as breeding Saints for eight years. The couple have a litter once a year and have bred two Champions, Ch. Tucker's Empty Pockets and Ch. Tucker's Blocker v. Morris. This couple support another two SB Clubs, the Greater Atlanta and Greater Cincinnati SB Clubs.

UTAH

STORY BOOK ST. BERNARDS

Although Dan Wheeler has been breeding Saints for 22 years he has only been a member of the SBCA for 13 years. Dan has between one and two litters per year. The following Champions have been made up by Dan: Ch. Story Book Legend v. Sand Creek TD, CGC and Ch. Sand Creek's Once Upon A Time. Dan is also a member of Great Salt Lake SB Club.

CACHE RETREAT KENNELS

Ivan Palmblad is known for the many Champions he has bred, 115 so far over a 25-year period. Ivan has been a member of the SBCA for 28 years. Two

Cache Retreat Bodacious.
Photo: Munro.

of his Champions are Ch. Cache Retreat On A Clear Day and Ch. Cache Retreat Academy. Ivan is President of the American St. Bernard Cub and is also a member of the Great Salt Lake SB Club. There are between five and six litters bred in a year at Cache Retreat Kennels.

VIRGINIA

BRANDY STATION ST. BERNARDS

Mary E. Varela has been a member of the SBCA for 24 years and has been breeding for 18 years. Mary usually just has one litter per year. Over the years she has bred eight Champions, two of whom are Ch. Brandy Stations Jeremy and Ch. Brandy Stations Celebration. Mary is also a member and active with the Greater Washington SB Club.

WASHINGTON

MORRIS ST BERNARDS

Ladd and June Morris have been breeding Saints for 27 years as well as being members of and supporting the SBCA for 27 years. Ladd and June have between one and two litters per year. Over the years the Morrises have bred 95 AKC St. Bernard Champions. Two of the dogs are Ch. Morris Hawkeye and Ch. Morris Garth. The couple attend

Ch. Cache Retreat On A Clear Day.
Photo: Munro.

seminars put on by the SBCA and are active in the SB Club of Puget Sound.

STOAN'S ST BERNARD

Stan and Joan Zielinski from Kent, Washington have been breeding Saints for 33 years and been members of the SBCA for 31 years. In total over this period of time they have bred over 60 Champions. Two of them are WD Ch. & BREW Ch. Stoan's Dudley Do Right Of Jay U, CDX, DD. WPX, and Ch. Stoan's Valiant Bart Of Mica. Stan and Joan are also involved with the SB Club of Puget Sound. Stan has recently put his thirty years of experience and knowledge into print by writing a book on St. Bernards which is sold in the USA.

Am. Ch. Vieledanke Luis Miguel.

VIELEDANKE SAINTS

Carmelo and Cheryl Zappola of Seattle, Washington took over the Vieledanke kennel name in the early 1970s from Tom and Pearl Thank. The Thanks had founded the kennel in the early 60s with their foundation stock, the brood bitch being Des Neiges Eternelles Kati Did, of early Sauliant breeding. Their foundation stud dog was Ch. Vieledanke Gombu sired by Sanctuary Woods Gulliver.

Both Kati Did and Gombu, along with their immediate progeny, produced many top-winning Champions. In the mid-70s one of these was Ch. Zappala's Vontare Vieledanke. Vontare was the sire of Ch. Vieledanke Ali d'Ranchet, a top-winning Saint in the early 80s.

In the late 80s and the 90s, the Vieledanke line combined with Opdyke stock. Special wins for Carmelo and Cheryl included winning with Ch. Opdykes's Madonna under the late Dr Antonio Morsiane of Italy and Carl Otto Mastrup of Denmark at the large California Specialty Shows.

Other breeding stock came from top European lines such as Int. Ch. Sanky Card's Anton (Denmark), who was mated to Hanaethorp Ruby (Holland). Other winners were Vieledanke Luis Miquel (Longhair) and Vieledanke Jagger (Shorthair). Both have had impressive wins under noted American and European Specialty judges.

Ch. Stoan's Neil of Nelba.
Photo: Steven Russ.

14 THE ST. BERNARD WORLDWIDE

AUSTRALIA

The records of Walter Beilby state in *The Dog in Australia*, published in 1897, that a Captain Clark imported St. Bernards in 1880; however, the dogs did not establish themselves. One, Maplecroft Belle, died without leaving any progeny. Beilby records that the first person to introduce and exhibit Saints in Australia was Mr E. F. Stephen of Sydney who owned Monargue III, and Minerva who went on the win many prizes. Beilby records that between

1883 and 1887 the St. Bernard in Australia did not make much progress.

In 1891 Captain Clark imported Baron of Greystoke who unfortunately died shortly after his release from quarantine. However, a few St. Bernard bitches had been taken to Baron for breeding purposes. Then tragedy was to strike again. Nervelstone Patch, a winning bitch at that time, described as "a fine animal excelling in legs and feet", was a daughter of Baron. Sadly she, along with most of her puppies, died shortly after whelping. It is believed another of Baron's daughters, Lady Lucia, went on to breed some puppies.

In 1896 there were forty-one entries of St. Bernards at the Royal Easter Show; however, in 1900 it was down to seventeen. It was not until the 1960s that there was an increase in St. Bernards, with a surge of imports from the UK. Mr Kennedy of Sydney imported Cornagarth Gareth from A. K. Gaunt's Cornagarth kennels in Ripley, Derbyshire. Mr Mullane, also of Sydney, imported Cornagarth Bonnie and Fernebrandon Corvette.

St. Bernards are first recorded as being in Tasmania in the late 1800s. The dogs were often shown at agricultural shows. However, it was not until the 1970s that the breed became firmly established in the island. The first Saints were mostly from English stock, with a few exports from America and New Zealand.

The St Bernard is thriving in Australia. This is Sylvenus Yankee Magic.

DALE END KENNELS

Dorothy and Gwen Chisman of New South Wales imported Saints in 1964. St. Rae Of Dale End was exhibited, along with St. Francis Of Dale End who began his show career in 1968. Ch. Vanessa Of Dale End was an Australian Champion in 1969. In 1975 Dale End purchased Cornagarth Chiquita who had done a lot of winning in England, having two Challenge Certificates prior to her export. This lovely bitch had been mated to the famous Ch. Burtonswood Bossy Boots, so she went out to Australia in whelp. She produced two Champions in her first litter and five Champions in her second litter.

Some of the Champions from Dale End have been Ch. Dale End St. Ramon and Ch. Dale End St. Angella, who were brother and sister. Ch. Dale End St. Nicholas and Ch. Dale End St. Moira won the Dog and Bitch Challenge at the Sydney Royal and Spring Fair. At the Victorian Kennel Club Dog of the Year in 1980, Ch. Dale End St. Anthony was the winner.

SNOWSAINT ST BERNARDS

Mrs L. Briggs exported Aus. Ch. Karl Of Cornagarth (Kuno von Birkenkopf ex Ch. Burtonswood Big Time) in 1972. Aus. Ch. Karl Of Cornagarth was sire of seventeen Champions and is featured in many of the pedigrees of current winning St. Bernards in Australia today.

PAXIS ST. BERNARDS

Mr and Mrs Ormsby owned the Paxis Kennels and one of their dogs was Ch. Daneeal Targus, bred by Mrs Lawrence. The sire was Ch. Karl of Cornagarth and a US import, Karacsonya Dee Dee Of Pal Mal, the dam. Ch. Daneeal Targus won many CCs, going Best in Show at the St. Bernard Club of Australia in 1980. The Ormsbys also owned a daughter of Ch. Daneeal Targus, Ch. Zebedee Alpine Melody. This bitch was put to a German import, Aramis von Der Kurstadt, and produced Ch. Paxis Amos.

MERRIBUFF KENNELS

Miss Dowsey and Miss Bridges own Merribuff, a well-known kennel in Victoria which imported Whaplode Great Expectations who became an Australian Champion and was responsible for siring several top winning Saints. Merribuff Bernadina CD did extremely well competing in Obedience competitions. The Merribuff Saints are still active in Australia, with young progeny making their presence felt in the showring.

STINIYASU KENNELS

The Stiniyasu Kennel of Matina and John Butcher was established in the mid-80s with the importation of two bitches and a dog from Cache Retreat Kennels in the USA. The dog became the first Australian and American Champion, Cache Retreat Encore v. New Era. These three were joined in later years by Aust. Ch. Bernedagardens Nothing But Trouble (Imp. Swe.) and Am. Aust. NZ Ch. Stoan's Disney v. Valinta (Imp. USA). The kennel has produced numerous Champions and winners of note, developing the breed in many areas formerly more influenced by English stock.

METHUSELA KENNELS

Aust. Grand Ch. Boroniahil Daytona, known as Stollie, made his place in breed history in 1998 by becoming the first NSW-owned, and the first Tasmanian-bred Saint to gain the status of Grand Champion. During the course of his show career, he was twice Dog of the Year (SBCNSW), was a semi-finalist in the Pal Puppy of the Year competition in 1995, won a Best in Show, a Runner Up Best in Show, and numerous Best Exhibit in Group awards. He is proudly owned by Liane Bruton of Methusela Kennels.

CASPER'S COVE KENNELS

The kennel of Tracy and Jamie Clapham in New South Wales has enjoyed considerable success. Their first top winner was a dog bred by Judy Peka-Rawhira from the first litter of Saints produced with frozen semen. The dog was Aust. Ch. Arohatenui Bernes Pride (AI), whelped in 1992 and still winning at seven years of age. He has been joined over the years by several NZ imports, most significantly Aust. Grand Champion and NZ Ch. Bernedale Britt Maritt. Brittany has won at every level and with great consistency over a long period of time. Other well-performed Saints from this kennel include Ch. Casper's Cove Oops A Daisy, Ch. Casper's Cove Gentle Jolie, and Ch. Casper's Cove Sudden Impact (AI).

URSIDAE KENNELS
Aust. Ch. Seanlisaint Rheannan was a major performer within the breed and in all-breed competition during the early to mid-90s. Rheannan also produced a number of Champion progeny for owners Wayne and Karen Slender.

SEAFERN KENNELS
Sharon Andrews started her kennel during the early 80s, and introduced a new line and direction for Seafern in the 90s with the importation of Bernedale Just in Case (Imp. NZ). This shorthair dog has sired a number of Champions and winners of note over the years. Ch. Seafern Just Call Me Chloe was a top winning bitch for the kennel.

LYMPNE KENNELS
Sue and Allan Johnson began their Kennel in Tasmania, based upon English imports. One of their early winners was Aust. Ch. Whaplode My Explorer (Imp. UK) who, tragically, was lost too young to see his true potential. Aust. Ch. Lympne Pandora was the first Saint Bitch to take Best Exhibit in Show in Tasmania. The kennel has continued to feature since its move to Queensland, with dogs such as Aust. Ch. Tai Yuan Proto Type (Imp. NZ) and Aust. Ch. Tai Yuan Top Notch (Imp. NZ). Sue and Allan have also titled several NZ-owned Saints, including Aust. NZ Ch. Fastacre Cotton Duke (Imp. UK), and Aust. NZ Ch. Tai Yuan Man About Town (Imp. NZ).

BRONBASHEI KENNELS
After having Saints for many years, John and Debbi Egglestone imported Bernedale Secret Image (Imp. NZ, longhair bitch) in 1994, and then in 1996 imported litter brother and sister, the longhair dog Bernedale Call Me Beau, and the shorthair bitch Bernedale Call Me Angel.

Aust. NZ Ch. Bernedale Call Me Angel, at her second show, and at just age 6 months, took Reserve Challenge Bitch at Melbourne Royal from an entry in excess of 30 bitches. Angel was awarded her Australian Champion Title at under 12 months of age, and went on to receive Multiple Best Exhibit in Group and Runner Up in Group awards. At two years of age she returned to New Zealand, achieved her New Zealand title in only six weeks and, in addition, received two Runner Up to Best

Aust. Ch. Berndale Call Me Beau.

Exhibit In Group wins. Angel returned to Australia in whelp and produced 10 beautiful puppies.

Aust. Ch. Bernedale Call Me Beau was as a puppy shown very rarely, and did not consistently enter the showring until he became a Junior. Beau received his three Best In Shows in his home state, but has also been awarded BOB at Adelaide Royal, Brisbane Royal, Darwin Royal, Sydney Royal, and Toowoomba Royal – the only Saint to have achieved BOB in five of the seven states of Australia.

PORTWAY SAINT BERNARDS
Portway began in 1990 as a merger of two other kennels upon the marriage of Phillipa and Ian Clark. A 1992 litter – the last to be sired by Ch.

Hollylodge Zoltan – produced three Champions and four In Group winners, most notably Ch. Portway Man Of Colours. Following the move of the kennel to Victoria in 1996, Ch. Bernabby Piano Man (Imp. NZ) made his home at Portway as a two-year-old.

BORONIAHIL KENNELS
John, Judy and Susan Teniswood started with their first Saint in 1977, a Victorian-bred bitch, Ch. Elkeef Cutencuddly. In 1983 Ch. Tremel Distant Saint arrived from the UK and made breed history by becoming the first Saint to win Best in Show all-breeds in Tasmania and went on to win the Tasmanian Contest of Champions in 1988. He sired five litters. In 1991 Aust. and NZ Ch. Chenalette Golden Rule arrived from New Zealand and many of his progeny have become top winners at all levels. His son Grand Champion Boroniahil Daytona in NSW is the first Tasmanian-bred Saint to become a Grand Champion.

ACTONGOLD KENNELS
The Actongold Kennels of Madge and Vicki Burn was established in 1985. The kennel imported Aust. Ch. Tremel Faraway Lady (Imp. UK) who produced just four puppies. One of these became Aust. Ch. Actongold St. Columb. In the mid-90s Aust. Ch. Bernedale Call Me Cassie (Imp. NZ) joined the Burn family and has been a consistent winner of Best of Breeds and In Show awards.

SOUTHERTON KENNELS
The Saints of Julie and Wayne Bald have enjoyed great success, with numerous Best in Show awards at all-breeds level. In recent times, brothers Ch. Southerton Show BIS and Ch. Southerton Touch of Class have performed well, and Ch. Southerton Katarina won Best in Show at Royal Launceston Show.

SYLVENUS KENNELS
Ch. Sylvenus Casey, a shorthair bitch, won Challenge at Melbourne Royal Show in 1990 and 1991. Her daughter Ch. Sylvenus Lylla (Hunter) won Reserve Challenge at Perth Royal in 1991, Challenge in 1992 and Best of Breed in 1993. Her granddaughter Ch. Sylvenus Oh So Smooth won Group and in-show awards at all-breeds level.

Aust. Ch. Portway Man Of Colours.

Aust. Ch. Tremel Distant Saint.

Aust. Ch. Actongold St. Columb.

Sylvenus Kennels imported Bernegarden's Navigator and Bernegarden's Odessa from Sweden in the early 90s, and in 1999 have brought in the shorthair dog Stoan's Oh Brother at Victory (Imp. USA). This kennel also produced the first frozen-semen litter from American semen in Australia – 10 pups out of Sylvenus Catch The Wind, sired by Am. Ch. Opdyke's Anthony.

RAALEPPO KENNELS
Owned by Mrs Ann Oppelaar, this kennel has produced a series of good winning Champions. Aust. Ch. Raaleppo Torn Amber dominated the scene locally during the mid-90s, with multi Group awards and Best of Breed at Perth Royal in 1994. Aust. Ch. Raaleppo Kalgurli Sir (Shaw) was also a consistent winner. This kennel introduced new bloodlines by importing Swedish lines from Bernedale Kennels in New Zealand.

KOOLANDRA KENNELS
Owned by Sue Mail, Ch. Stiniyasu Kickboxer is a

Runner-up Best in Show winner and multi Best in Group winner. He won Best of Breed at Perth Royal in 1995 and then Runner-up Best in Show at the NSW SBC Championship Specialty, being beaten for Best in Show by his two-year old daughter, Ch. Koolandra Wild Eyed Dream, who gained her title with this win.

CHRYSTLEPARK KENNELS
Ch. Chrystlepark Trans Am, owned and bred by Val Schroder, won Best of Breed at Perth Royal in 1990, 1991 and 1992, including a Runner-up Best in Group.

SUGARMOON KENNELS
The kennel owns Ch. Ursidae UR Grand Vjoker who won Best in Group at the prestigious West Classic in 1997. The kennel imported Clareline Ushana from Belgium and has produced winning pups from the combination.

NEW ZEALAND
During the 1970s several Saints were imported from the Jonjersi Kennels of the late Audrey French. Ch. Jonjersi Toynbee sired over thirty-six puppies, several of whom became Champions. Ch. Jonjersi St. Royale was also made up in NZ after being exported from the UK. Miss Hindes from Burtonswood exported Burtonswood Famous Boots who also became a Champion. Maurbry Most Southern Star was another import, as was NZ Ch. Coatham Star Attraction.

In the 80s Coatham Sporting Chance was imported and Tony Calvert made up Ch. Leo The Lionheart Of Coatham. Other exports were Coatham Agent Bruno and Coatham Lady Cleo. Both have produced quality puppies.

More recently dogs and bitches have been exported from Scandinavia. Jim and Joy Harvey of the Bernedale kennels imported Bernegardens Lachelis from Britt Maritt Halvorsen, now based in Belgium.

The Tai Yuan kennels are owned by Clyde Rogers and Cath Tippett. Their Saints are well known in NZ with well over 40 Champions. In 1984 they were successful in artificially inseminating their NZ Ch. Tai Yuan Claudia with sperm from Ch. Whaplode My Lord in the UK. In 1993 they imported NZ Aus. Ch. Fastacre

Cotton Duke (sire Int. Ch. Benegardens JR of Fastacre ex Fastacre High Society who proved his worth as a stud dog.

Other notable kennels include Sanctum Grove, Tony and Vicky Hill, and the Neuchalet Saints of Karen Fuller where there has been some success with frozen sperm from the US. Charmaine Kendrick of Le Baricant Saints has bred 11 Champions, including NZ Ch. Le Baricant Emerald Isle. Allan and Sue Stretton, Snowpeak Saints, have a litter brother and sister who have done well – NZ Ch. Snowpeak Alpine Lad and Ch. Snowpeak Alpine Lass. The Top Saint Bernard for 1999 was NZ Ch. Trevlac Caesar's Chariot, dam Coatham Lady Cleo, owned by Michelle MacDonely Timaru.

THE SAINT IN EUROPE

Europe has been a closed shop to British exhibitors for many years due to quarantine regulations. However, these are due to be lifted if and when the new pet passport is introduced. Perhaps in the near future British Saints may well compete against our neighbours on the Continent. If we do, we in the UK will need to ensure that our stock is more matched to the FCI Standard.

Albert De La Rie was the architect of the World Union of Saint Bernards and, since the 1970s, shows have been held all over Europe with the exception of Britain. Since the fall of the Wall and the relaxation in former closed countries, it is now possible for Saints to be shown in countries such as Russia and Hungary.

NZ Ch. Bernegardens Khedive (left) and Aust. NZ Ch. Bernedale Incredible.

SWITZERLAND

The Swiss Saints have been recognized as the foundation of the breed and The Swiss Club was formed in 1884, making it the Senior club – and rightly so. The first St. Bernards show was held in Berne in 1871. There followed, over the years, much indiscriminate breeding and the type went into decline. This was reflected in the gradings given in various shows during the period up to the First World War.

Many lines in all parts of the world can trace their origins to Swiss Saints, particularly many lines in the UK – Cornagarth, Snowranger and Bernmont, to name three. The influence of the Swiss type can be seen in the descendants of Cargo von Leberberg, a notable import of the 50s. Pehaps it could be said that the type in the UK reached its greatest height in the dog Snowranger Cascade (Crufts Working Group 1975), a direct descendant of the some of the Swiss type. Over the last century the Swiss, together with many other Europeans, struggled to maintain standards, particularly during the war years. By the fifties things had started to improve and registrations have steadily increased.

SPAIN

A small group of enthusiasts formed the Spanish Saint Bernard club in 1983. Saints in Spain have largely been imported from Germany. However, some kennels, such as Estepona owned by Kari Augustad, and Estisager owned by Lisa Estisager, have imported from the Scandinavian countries. From these imports a number of Champions have emerged. There are now a number of breeders in Spain who are very caring and who are in the process of adopting the principles of the WUSB.

SCANDINAVIA

The Scandinavian clubs in recent years have shown the way in excellent type breeding. Their foundation stock came from Germany and America. However, there are some British influences in the early breeding and the overall result has been the improvement of type and temperament. The Scandinavian clubs are affiliated to the WUSB and a Danish dog, Int. Ch. Hanaethorp Ruben went BIS at the WUSB show in 1990.

Particular kennels doing well include Deinhards, who has bred several Champions founded on UK and US stock and later crossed with the best of Europe. A vibrant and exciting kennel with huge potential for the future is owned by Karin Byrevik, and there is Bernegardens owned by Britt Maritt Halvorsen who has produced over 97 champions. St. Zambas is owned by Ruth Borger. The Borgers

Sp. Ch. Amalia De Estisager.

Nor. Sw. Dk Ch. St Woods Busybody, based in Norway.

Int. Ch. Deinhard's Kreamer On The Rocks, S Ch. Deinhard's Countryside Beauty, S Ch, Deinhard's After Me and Int. Ch. Quimbra.

live about 70k from Oslo and believe in letting their dogs run free. They have had several Champions which is not surprising as their stock favours the Dienhard type. The Sankt Cardis kennels, owned by Lause and Karen Nielsen have been established for 25 years and have produced over 50 Champions, including Int. Ch. Sankt Cardis IB, a rough coat, and Int. Ch. Gerhardt.

Another leading kennel is St. Woods, owned by Katerina Heiberg, who has bred some nice dogs that she is proud of. The first St. Bernard born and bred in Norway who got the International Champion title was Sisu, a tall, shorthair male, who was born in 1981. He was very sound compared to many other dogs at that time. His sire was Olaf v. Rigihang, a Swiss dog.

THE NETHERLANDS

The senior club of the Low Countries is the Dutch Saint Bernard Club which is one of the founder members of the WUSB. It was founded in 1926 by the late Mr Albert de la Rie and is one of the largest clubs in the world. Their membership is around 700. In the 70s and 80s it was double this. However, today's quality is better than in the past. Market forces create puppy farmers and, as we all know, this creates poor breeding. We think this is happening in the UK today. There are people, quite frankly, who are not fit to breed dogs. .

The Dutch type is prevalent in many countries, with much success. In the UK this type has not been too successful apart from one or two exceptions, notably Saranbeck Spuffington, out of Dutch import Esther v. Irsteanjo At Saranbek, who has won many honours. Miss P.H.Muggleton has also imported several Dutch stock whose lines are prevalent in her dogs.

The Belgian club was formed in 1972 and hosted the WUSB show in 1982 and 1989. Because of its geographical position Belgium hosts many international shows.

HUNGARY

Dog breeders and owners in Hungary have always been interested in large breeds. Their first St. Bernards were imported from Switzerland. For many years the Saint Bernards were grouped with other large breeds, but since 1993 there has been a separate club and the WUSB have accepted it as a member. It is the Hunnia Szentbernathegyi Klub. Since the eighties breeders in Hungary have been striving to improve their stock and have imported widely from Switzerland, Holland, Germany, Italy and Norway. The programme seems to be working, as in 1996 a Hungarian bitch, Szent Bernat Hagoi Orchidea, won the WUSB show. At present the Hunnia Szentbernathegyi Klub has about 170 members and is growing. In the year 2002 the Klub will organize the WUSB show.

ITALY

The Italian St. Bernard world has been dominated by the famous Soccorso Kennels of the late Dr Antonio Morsiani, his wife Maria Leda and their two sons, Giovanni and Luigi. Dr Morsianni devoted a lifetime of experience to the breed he found so fascinating and built up his kennels at the Villa Morsiani, near Bagnera di Romagna. He had bloodlines from Switzerland and Germany and had a preference for large dogs.

His first St. Bernard was Emir v. d. Lueg and a great favourite was Ch. Anton v. Hofli, who is said to have stood 34 inches tall and to have weighed 215lbs. Dr Morsiani died in March 1995, since when Giovanni and Luigi have maintained the kennels' Saints. Giovanni is involved with the Italian Club and also the WUSB. The WUSB Millennium show is being held in Italy in June 2000 at Bagnera. The Morsiani family are currently working with the International Morsiani Foundation to help raise awareness about the origins of the breed

There are far too many Soccorso Champions to name individually as the list would be over a hundred, but a few to mention are Int. Ch. Zio Del Soccorso and his litter sister Ch. Zedz Del Soccorso; Ch. Saturno Del Soccorso, who was owned by Richard Steinberger and Glenn Radcliffe of the Opdyke kennels in the USA, and Int. Ch. Fedor Del Soccorso and Ch. Vittorio Del Soccorso.

GERMANY

As the greatest collection of St. Bernard breeders during the late 1890s was in the Bavaria region it was an enthusiastic group of people there who formed the St. Bernard Club in 1891. The Club, however, gathered memberships from the whole country over a period of time. In 1982 the SB Club of Germany established the Zuchtbuch to retain all the records of the St. Bernards in the country, along with relevant pedigrees. In May 1991 the Club celebrated its centenary and held a Jubilee weekend in Leverkussen attended by thousands of people and with over 300 St. Bernards entered in the show. The Best in Show was Sando v. Geutenreuth, owned by Werner and Edith Moses.

The Wolfsmuhle Saints were owned by Prince Albrecht in the nineteenth century and his St. Bernards were considered to be the largest on the Continent. His first import was Courage, a large male who won at the 1878 Berlin show. This dog was believed to be thirty-five inches tall weighing 140 pounds. In comparison to present-day St. Bernards this does not seem particularly heavy; however, Saints of the 1800s were much finer-boned and did not have the substance of current St. Bernards. As quarantine had not been introduced into the UK Courage was exhibited in England where he won some first prizes, and also in Holland. Prince Albrecht used Courage at stud, and the dog sired a few litters. Courage II was produced and, when used at stud with Hedwig, produced Courage III.

Prince Albrecht also owned Gessler and imported two bitches from Switzerland, Bernina II and Hospice. Courage II was mated to Berna II producing an excellent litter with large heads and good conformation. Some of the Wolfsmuhle males were exported to Switzerland, as a lot of the quality male dogs from Switzerland had been exported to England and Russia at exorbitant prices.

Herr Harkenstein of the Plavia kennels imported Swiss St. Bernards, one of whom, called Prinz of Burgdorf, had an influence on the breed in Germany.

Herr G. Schmitbauer of Munich had several quality St. Bernards. Herakles was from Switzerland but Ch. Munichia Lord, Ch.

Munichia Pierette, Munichia Ivor, Munichia Rival and Sparta formed part of the foundation stock, back to which a lot of the current St. Bernards in Germany can trace their heritage.

In 1894 there were 301 Saints registered in the Stud Book held by the Klub, 175 short-haired and 126 long or rough haired St. Bernards. At that time the St. Bernard was the most popular dog in Germany.

Mr Kempel of the Urach Saints felt temperament was most important and tried to breed for dogs with steady personalities. Some of the current German St. Bernards are descendants of his dogs.

In 1956 at the World Show in Dortmund, the winners were Astor von Heldenhof and Bella v. Werdenfels. Two years later Otto Jacob started his St. Klara Kloster kennels. This was a strong line of steady, balanced dogs, well-marked, who moved with drive and correct hind action. These kennels exported Saints to England in 1969.

The Birkenkopf kennels were established in 1959 and produced quality St. Bernards. In 1969 a bitch from Germany, Gundi von Birkenkopf, was sent to England having been mated to Alex von Pava. This produced a well-known litter, including Kuno von Birkenkopf who was the sire of Ch. Burtonswood Bossy Boots, Best in Show at Crufts in 1974. The owner of Daphedene St. Bernards took on other males who were litter brothers of Kuno and had a lot of success with Ch. Karro von Birkenkopf and Ch. King von Birkenkopf.

In 1982 Pat Muggleton imported Pankraz von den Drei Helman, whom she made up in 1985. This dog was bred by Wolfgang Schreiber out of Herma von den Drei Helman, sired by Casar von Holdersberg. The von den Drei Helman Saints are still active in Germany, producing quality, sturdy dogs which are consistent winners in Germany.

BIBLIOGRAPHY
AND REFERENCES

American Kennel Club Information on the Saint Bernard Breed Standard.

Baynes, E.H. (1927) *The Book of Dogs*
The National Geographic Society.

Beaver, R. & R. (1980) *All About the Saint Bernard*
Pelham Books.

Beaver, R. (1997) *All About the Saint Bernard*
Kingdom Books.

Brace, A. H. (1997) *Beagles Today*
Ringpress Books.

Brown, C.M. (1986) *Dog Locomotion and Gait Analysis*
Hofflin Publishing Ltd.

Cunliffe, J. (1991) *Show training for your dog*
Popular Dogs.

De La Rie, A. (1974) *The Saint Bernard Classic*
Briarcliff Publishing Ltd.

Fleischli, J.H. (1954) *The Saint Bernard*
Judy Publishing Company.

Fogle, B. (1990) *The Dog's Mind*
Pelham Books.

Grossman, L. (1993) *The dog's tail*
BBC Books.

Harmar, H. (1968) *Dogs and how to breed them*
John Gifford Ltd.

Heim, Prof. A; *et al (1966) The New Complete Saint Bernard.*
(Howell Book House)

Kennel Club UK (1989) *The Kennel Club's Illustrated Breed Standard*
Cresset Press.

Lyons, M. (1978) *The Dog In Action*
Howell Book House.

Miller, W.C. & West, G.P. (1964) *Black's Medical Dictionary*
Adam and Charles Black.

Morsiani, A. (1985) *Il San Bernardo – Standard e Commenti*
Kynosverlag.

Muggleton, P., Wensley, A. & Wensley, M. (1992) *The Complete Saint Bernard*
Ringpress Books.

Page-Elliott, R. (1983) *The New Dog Steps*
Howell Book House.

Paschoud, J. M. (1994) *The Swiss Canine Breeds FCI Standards* Paul Haupt, Berne.

Portman-Graham, Capt. R. (1956) *The Practical Guide to Showing Dogs*
Popular Dogs.

Woodhouse, B. (1959) *The Book of Show Dogs*
Max Parish and Company.